African languages, development and the state

Multilingualism is a fact of African life; multilingualism a's lingua franca. Why then is African multilingualism so often seen as a handicap to development? The contributors to *African Languages, Development and the State* argue that multilingualism needs to be developed as a strength, not castigated as a failure.

The contributors – Africans and Europeans, language planners and anthropologists – examine the rhetoric of language policy and also present detailed case studies of local outcomes. They believe that African language planning must be based on the researched facts of African life and not on preconceived ideas of the relations that should hold between entities called language, development and the state. Since most of Africa has now gained over thirty years of post-colonial experience in language planning, it is possible to assess the legacy of these years and to compare the best and worst practices. Particular attention is paid to the Nigerian experience which, as the most populous of the African states with many years' experience in the formulation of language policy, furnishes an invaluable intra-African example for policy makers in other parts of Africa, particularly in South Africa, where crucial decisions on language policy are currently under discussion.

The essays in this volume clearly show that multiculturalism, pluralism and multilingualism as facts of African life have to be seen positively as resources upon which development must build and not as impediments to national unity and development. The contributors' cross-disciplinary approach demonstrates the basic fact that all facets of social life, from the farm and the factory to the home or the debating chamber, are embedded in language. This volume will therefore appeal to a wide readership of all those concerned with development policy in Africa – economists, political scientists, language planners and anthropologists.

Richard Fardon is Reader in West African Anthropology, and **Graham Furniss** is Senior Lecturer in Hausa, both at the School of Oriental and African Studies, London.

EIDOS (European Inter-University Development Opportunities Study-Group) was founded in 1985 and brought together British, Dutch and German anthropologists actively engaged in the study of development. The broad purpose of EIDOS workshops has been to assess critically the dissemination and specialization of anthropological and sociological knowledge in different European centres and to further the understanding of the ways in which that knowledge has directly influenced development.

Editorial Board

David Parkin (School of Oriental and African Studies, University of London)
Hans-Dieter Evers (University of Bielefeld)
Philip Quarles van Ufford (Free University, Amsterdam)

Editorial Committee

Franz von Benda-Beckmann (Wageningen Agricultural University)
Elisabeth Croll (School of Oriental and African Studies, London)
Mark Hobart (School of Oriental and African Studies, London)
Rüdiger Korff (University of Bielefeld)
Norman Long (Wageningen Agricultural University)
Günther Schlee (University of Bielefeld)

African languages, development and the state

Edited by
Richard Fardon and Graham Furniss

LONDON AND NEW YORK

First published 1994 by Routledge

2 Park Square, Milton Park, Abingdon, Oxon OX14 4RN
605 Third Avenue, New York, NY 10017

Routledge is an imprint of the Taylor & Francis Group, an informa business

First issued in paperback 2022

Copyright © 1994 Richard Fardon and Graham Furniss, the collection as a whole; individual chapters with the contributors

Typeset in Times by Michael Mepham, Frome, Somerset

All rights reserved. No part of this book may be reprinted or reproduced or utilised in any form or by any electronic, mechanical, or other means, now known or hereafter invented, including photocopying and recording, or in any information storage or retrieval system, without permission in writing from the publishers.

Notice:
Product or corporate names may be trademarks or registered trademarks, and are used only for identification and explanation without intent to infringe.

Publisher's Note
The publisher has gone to great lengths to ensure the quality of this reprint but points out that some imperfections in the original copies may be apparent

British Library Cataloguing in Publication Data
A catalogue record for this book is available from the British Library.

Library of Congress Cataloging in Publication Data
African languages, development and the state/edited
  by Richard Fardon and Graham Furniss.
  p. cm.
  Includes bibliographical references and index.
  1. African languages–Political aspects. 2. Language and languages–Political aspects. 3. Language policy–Africa.
  4. Language planning–Africa I. Fardon, Richard. II. Furniss, Graham
P119.32.A3A38   1993
306.4'49'096–dc20   93–17208 CIP

ISBN 978-0-415-09476-4 (hbk)
ISBN 978-1-03-234042-5 (pbk)
DOI: 10.4324/9780203422571

Contents

Notes on contributors   vii
Preface   ix

1 Introduction: Frontiers and boundaries – African languages as political environment
  Richard Fardon and Graham Furniss   1

Part I West Africa

2 Pride and prejudice in multilingualism and development
  Ayo Bamgbose   33

3 Official and unofficial attitudes and policy towards Krio as the main lingua franca in Sierra Leone
  C. Magbaily Fyle   44

4 The politics of language in Bénin
  Mamoud Akanni Igué and Raphael Windali N'Ouéni   55

5 Minority language development in Nigeria: a situation report on Rivers and Bendel States
  Ben Ohi Elugbe   62

6 Using existing structures: three phases of mother tongue literacy among Chumburung speakers in Ghana
  Gillian F. Hansford   76

Part II Central and Southern Africa

7 The language situation and language use in Mozambique
  J. M. M. Katupha   89

vi *African languages, development and the state*

8 Language and the struggle for racial equality in the development of a non-racial Southern African nation
Jean Benjamin — 9

9 Dismantling the Tower of Babel: in search of a new language policy for a post-Apartheid South Africa
Nhlanhla P. Maake — 11

10 Healthy production and reproduction: agricultural, medical and linguistic pluralism in a Bwisha community, Eastern Zaïre
James Fairhead — 12:

11 Minority language, ethnicity and the state in two African situations: the Nkoya of Zambia and the Kalanga of Botswana
Wim van Binsbergen — 14:

Part III East Africa

12 Loanwords in Oromo and Rendille as a mirror of past inter-ethnic relations
Günther Schlee — 191

13 The metaphors of development and modernization in Tanzanian language policy and research
Jan Blommaert — 213

14 Language, government and the play on purity and impurity: Arabic, Swahili and the vernaculars in Kenya
David Parkin — 227

Name index — 246
Subject index — 249

Contributors

Ayo Bamgbose: Professor of Linguistics, University of Ibadan, Department of Linguistics and African Languages, Ibadan, Nigeria.

Jean Benjamin: Lecturer, University of the Western Cape, Department of Psychology, South Africa.

Wim van Binsbergen: Fellow at the African Studies Centre, Leiden, and Professor of Ethnicity, Ideology and Development at the Free University, Amsterdam, Netherlands.

Jan Blommaert: Research Director, International Pragmatics Association (IPrA) Research Centre; and Lecturer in Intercultural and International Communication, University of Antwerp, Belgium.

Ben Ohi Elugbe: Professor of Linguistics, University of Ibadan, Department of Linguistics and African Languages, Ibadan, Nigeria.

James Fairhead: Associate Member of the Centre of African Studies, University of London, United Kingdom; currently Senior Research Officer at the Natwal Resources Institute, Social Sciences Group.

Richard Fardon: Reader in West African Anthropology in the University of London, School of Oriental and African Studies, Department of Anthropology and Sociology, United Kingdom.

Graham Furniss: Senior Lecturer in Hausa at the School of Oriental and African Studies, Department of African Languages and Cultures; and Chairman of the Centre of African Studies of the University of London, United Kingdom.

C. Magbaily Fyle: Professor of History, Fourah Bay College, Institute of African Studies, Freetown, Sierra Leone.

Gillian F. Hansford: Summer Institute of Linguistics, High Wycombe, United Kingdom.

viii *African languages, development and the state*

Mamoud Akanni Igué: Directeur du Centre National de Linguistique Appliqué, Cotonou, République du Bénin.

J. M. M. Katupha: Minister of Culture, Youth and Sport; Eduardo Mondlane University, Mozambique.

Nhlanhla P. Maake: Lecturer in Zulu at the School of Oriental and African Studies, Department of African Languages and Cultures, University of London, United Kingdom.

Raphael Windali N'Ouéni: Visiting Scholar, Institut für Ethnologie, Free University, Berlin, Germany; Département de Linguistique et de Traditions Orales, Université National du Bénin, République du Bénin.

David Parkin: Professor of African Anthropology in the University of London, School of Oriental and African Studies, Department of Anthropology and Sociology, United Kingdom.

Günther Schlee: Professor of Social Anthropology, Faculty of Sociology, University of Bielefeld, Germany.

Preface

The chapters in this collection record a workshop held at the School of Oriental and African Studies, in April 1991, under the joint auspices of the Centre of African Studies of the University of London (CAS) and EIDOS (European Inter-University Development Opportunities Study-Group; a network of European anthropologists concerned with theoretical issues in development policy). CAS undertook the invitation of African language policy planners to the meeting, while Mark Hobart on behalf of EIDOS kindly assumed responsibility for organizing EIDOS participation. As a result of drawing on these two networks, the workshop was an occasion for a dialogue between the theoretical and policy orientations of European and African commentators. This outcome was by design contrary to a common pattern for 'inside' and 'outside' views to be segregated from one another which is unfortunate on several grounds, not least because it produces the impression that major divisions of opinion exist between European or American and African commentators. The London meeting revealed just how far from the truth this impression is: language policy within Africa is not monolithic, neither do European anthropologists share a single perspective on it. The patterns of agreement and disagreement which emerged from the meeting (more of the former than the latter) cannot be simplified into a mold of African versus European or policy versus practice.

Language policy in Africa has been dominated by nineteenth century European ideals of the coincidence of a singular people, nation and state united by culture and language. There is a growing feeling in many African countries that this ideal is not only unattainable as a goal in Africa but even undesirable. This awareness coincides with developments in Europe which may serve to undermine the monolingual ideal there also.

The key to the change in language policy has involved a reassessment of what 'language' should be assumed to be for the purposes of planning. Critical examination of the discourse of earlier language planning is, therefore, a vital element in the practical task of improving future language planning. To what extent do the purported divisiveness and impracticality of multilingualism derive – not from the fact of people who are competent in diverse language practices – but from the way in which language has been objectified and portrayed as the historical vehicle of attitudes and consequences?

This collection begins from the premise that African language planning must be based on the researched facts of African life and not on preconceived ideas of the relations that should hold between entities called language, development and the state. Multiculturalism, pluralism and multilingualism as facts of African life have to seen positively as resources upon which development must build and not just as impediments to national unity and development. Policy needs to be geared to popular realities and populist demands; the state has neither the capacity nor the resources to bring to fruition schemes that attempt to counter trends in language use that stem from the (only apparently) opposite poles of grassroots practice and global processes.

Within this very general prognosis, finer points of national language policy are likely to admit varied statal responses. Particular attention is paid in this volume to the Nigerian experience. As the most populous of the African states with thirty years', post-colonial experience in the formulation of policy, Nigeria should furnish a crucial, intra-African example for policy makers in Lusophone Africa and South Africa, where crucial decisions on language policy are presently under discussion. Many of the assumptions on which Nigerian policy is now based have become commonplace among specialists on African language development; but questions about the translation of these objectives into practice remain to be answered.

In general, the contributors to this collection argue that planners should be concerned not with language so much as with discursive patterns. Government policy, wherever feasible, should be directed to enabling people to acquire, and where necessary become literate in, workable portfolios of language competence. Distinctions between languages and dialects in Africa are highly conventionalized and often owe as much to associations with ethnicity, class and religion as to narrowly linguistic criteria. All languages remain vital by incorporating ideas, terms and constructions from other languages in their vicinity. The fetishization of language diversity, instead of attention to discursive variety, is an impediment to any realistic appreciation of the limitations to language planning. To a large extent language practice develops irrespective of government policy. Historically and unhappily, government capacity to engineer perverse effects through policy, for instance through fostering division, has been more remarkable than its capacity to intervene constructively. This is partly because the national horizon is not the only goal to which language policy needs to be directed; there is need for trans-national cooperation in the choice and development of African lingua francas (including pidgins) as well as for recognition that European and Arabic auxiliary languages of wider use will remain vital in external relations.

Finally, although policy statements on language, especially the Nigerian case to which we have drawn attention, have become highly sophisticated in their recognition of the multilingual character of African societies and individuals, policy and practice diverge. The state might recognize and support local initiatives that occur outside state sponsorship to produce orthographies and literatures in hitherto unwritten languages to a greater degree than it currently does. On this matter, the international funding agencies with their tendency to conceive development in narrowly technical terms need education in the extent to which all development occurs in and through language.

Among those who contributed as paper givers or discussants, but whose names do not otherwise appear in this collection, we gratefully acknowledge: Clinton Robinson, Joseph Sheppherd, Gbenga Fagborun, Frances Harding, Salem Mezhoud, Akin Oyetade, Michael Mann, Ogi Igwara, David Crozier, Martin Orwin, Bruce Connell, Linda Hunter, Bertrand Masquelier, Murray Last, Sister M. A. Uwalaka. A special note of thanks goes to Jean Benjamin for her contribution of a paper that was not presented to our original workshop but complements the range of discussion in Part II.

The editors also wish to thank the British Council, the British Academy, and the Research and Publications Committee of the School of Oriental and African Studies for support which made the workshop possible. Without the help of Jackie Collis and Sally Simmonds of the Centre of African Studies and Sharon Lewis of the Department of Anthropology and Sociology neither the meeting nor the proceedings could have been organized as efficiently as they have been.

Richard Fardon and Graham Furniss
London, January 1993

1 Introduction
Frontiers and boundaries – African languages as political environment

Richard Fardon and Graham Furniss

MAKING LANGUAGE PROBLEMS APPEAR

That parts of Africa[1] have a food problem seems indisputable when people are starving. That there is an environmental problem seems equally clear from the evidence of once fertile land that can no longer support cultivation. But no such, apparently hard, evidence exists to underline the immediacy of the 'language problem' believed also to be Africa's lot.[2] When people have organized empires and trading diasporas over several millennia, adapted older languages and adopted new ones, contributed with distinction to world poetry, novels, drama, films, music and numerous academic disciplines, and continue to develop popular cultures with astonishing multilingual competence, it could not be more apparent that Africans are starved neither of words nor of the capacity to use them with skill and purpose. A language problem, to labour the obvious, has to be made to appear historically in relation to some deficit – specifically the deficit between what language (under some definition) should be 'doing' and what it is felt actually to be 'doing'. A language problem's solution is called forth by the desire to make good this deficit. This is not to suggest that problems of food supply or environmental degradation are simple, either in terms of their causation or solution, but in their starkest forms both are imagined as conditions of dearth. By contrast, Africa's language problem, like its problem of 'tribalism', is imagined at the extreme as a condition of plenty. When Africa is not thought to suffer from undersupply, its fate is to suffer from oversupply; in short, Africa seems to be marked by dearth or glut, but never a just or appropriate measure, and both dearth and glut produce a 'problem'. Africa is claimed to have too many languages (plenty), but none of them 'do' what they ought (dearth). But who has the right to make such judgements, relative to what, and what is to be done about it? What makes a 'language problem' appear? Perhaps the most pernicious aspect

2 *African languages, development and the state*

of the assumption of a, singular, language problem is the implication that it has a, singular, final solution. Instead, we are going to suggest that the complexities of language use in Africa should elicit, at most, shifting, labile and pragmatic accommodations on the part of state authorities to situations which in themselves are also shifting, labile and largely pragmatic.

The paper of which this Introduction is a revised version was originally written as an opening presentation for a two-day workshop held at the School of Oriental and African Studies in 1991. Our intention in holding the workshop was to bring together (insofar as resources permitted) a roughly equivalent number of African academics and language planners, and European anthropologists or anthropologically inclined language specialists working on Africa in order to promote dialogue between them on the relationships between African languages, the state and development. A notably high degree of agreement on issues emerged from the meeting; so, if we adopt as a starting point a distinction between the discursive and strategic problems facing African nationals and European investigators who address issues surrounding African languages, this is simply a heuristic device and not evidence for differently entrenched 'mind sets' relating to the issues we discussed. As specialists in Northern Nigeria and Northern Cameroon, who also share an anthropological approach to problems of language, our joint paper brings further, ethnographic and theoretical biases to the topic. This Introduction retains, therefore, the spirit of our original position paper rather than attempting a synopsis of this volume's contents, which we supply briefly in prefatory notes to its three, regionally organized, sections.[3]

Concern with language is common both to academics and to policy planners in African states and to social and cultural anthropologists writing about African societies. These people may, of course, be one and the same: academics in African universities, drawing upon insights from anthropological studies and also concerned with the formulation of language policy. But initially we shall write as if they were not the same people, and that their efforts were to be located in distinct discursive fields: which is to say, fields of writing and practice structured by different assumptions and, correlatively, by differing apprehensions of what constitute pressing problems of language requiring urgent address. Having pushed the simplifying assumptions as far as seems useful heuristically, they will have to be abandoned. But the point of making them is to contrast perspectives predominantly associated with Africans planning language policy in the context of their own national politics with those associated with European and American outsiders approaching the issues of language from the context of academic agendas established in

Introduction: frontiers and boundaries 3

their professional and university disciplines. This further exaggerates our initial and tendentious assumption, but does allow us to address issues in ideal terms that are far more nuanced in reality. Of these issues, the most fundamental concerns the ways that a 'language problem' is made to appear from anthropological or policy perspectives.

An anthropological perspective could mean as many different things as there are types of anthropology; here we wish to emphasize two aspects of recent anthropological scholarship: 1) a critical deconstruction of the terms of current debate to discover their presuppositions, and 2) a preference for local level perspectives with an emphasis on practice.[4] These translate into two immediate aims: to question the way that the term 'language' has featured in considerations of African languages, development and the state, and to shift attention from African languages to specific linguistic practices in contemporary Africa, in particular 'the politics of discursive practice' (Grillo 1989: 17) as these emerge in situations of multilingualism. One guiding thread to our remarks derives from the contrast between boundaries (connoting exclusive and distinct phenomena) and frontiers (suggesting the interpenetration of phenomena). The distinction is deployed differently according to context, but we use it to point out the consequences that follow from treating language either from a top-down perspective (starting from the assumption of diverse languages) or from a bottom-up perspective (starting from the assumption that language is most importantly instantiated in its practical diversity). The top-down perspective is dominant in those language planning discourses that address problems posed in terms of national, international, continental or intercontinental relations; the bottom-up perspective dominates anthropological discourses that address problems arising from local researches. The two are not mutually exclusive, but each is certainly ill at ease with the other's agenda. Detailed anthropological descriptions of language practice risk seeming impractical, or worse irrelevant, to language planners to the same degree that policy documents may seem insensitive, or worse coercive, to ethnographers. This happens not because either party fails to appreciate what the other is trying to do, but because in starting from differing presuppositions about the object they call language, language planners and anthropologists create accounts for different purposes which are not fully commensurable.[5] This might matter less if that conceptual cluster of terms which includes language, but also culture, tribe, ethnicity, people and so forth, were politically compounded in less complex ways than it is.[6]

A variety of circumstances combine to explain the crucial importance of the politics of language in Africa. Many of these circumstances are not

4 *African languages, development and the state*

unique to Africa, but their African combination has been particularly closeknit and visible. Because of this, particular care has to be exercised when choosing examples from elsewhere (e.g. India or Melanesia) to compare with African cases. Among these circumstances writers looking at the problem top-down from the perspective of the state normally include the extremely large number of African languages, the enormous range in the numbers of their speakers (from a mere handful to many millions), the poor correlation between the frontiers of speech communities and the boundaries of African nation states, and the important roles of European languages, pidgins and of Arabic in particular functional or sectoral usages. Much needs to be said about each of these, but we want immediately to add another, bottom-up factor: the very high degree of multilingualism common in most of sub-Saharan Africa. To put the matter at its boldest, multilingualism is the African lingua franca.[7] Any African national or ethnographer of Africa will testify to a transcontinental genius for facilitating communication by drawing upon language competences however partially these may be held in common. The African lingua franca might best be envisaged not as a single language but as a multilayered and partially connected language chain, that offers a choice of varieties and registers in the speaker's immediate environment, and a steadily diminishing set of options to be employed in more distant interactions, albeit a set that is always liable to be reconnected more densely to a new environment by rapid secondary language learning, or by the development of new languages.

Whereas this capacity might be lauded elsewhere, it has been a commonplace to stress the negative side of the linguistic complexity of contemporary Africa.[8] Ayo Bamgbose refers to this trait as an obsession with the idea of 'one' in African discourses on the nation state in all its aspects. Practically, a complex pattern of language use does challenge the ingenuity of representatives of the state responsible for the organization of government (both legislative and executive), the imposition of law (both through the judiciary and police), the provision of education and health services, and a variety of interventions in the economic life of the citizens (agriculture, livestock, forestry, etc.). In short, African multilingualism poses problems of national governmentality in both the enabling and restrictive senses of this term. In the post-colonial state, these problems are compounded by questions of national autonomy, identity and authenticity that spill over into the fields of verbal creativity and philosophy. If the ideologically unconcerned among the citizenry may nonetheless be coping, to borrow a convenient term from recent development literature (e.g. Croll and Parkin 1992: 15), those involved in government, politics or the verbal expression of artistic or philosophical realities may find a 'language problem' of pressing concern. Whatever the grounds for them making it everyone else's concern, faced with the burgeoning literature on the topic, no one can doubt that there is governmental and academic unease with multilingualism in Africa. As members of a, generally speaking, monoglot (British) culture, we are equally receptive to another strand of writing about language which stresses the richness of the individual African's language competence. Although African language planning discourse has an undeniable concern with 'oneness', there is a countervailing theme of pride in the sheer numbers of African languages, and the linguistic skill implied by the fact that so many Africans operate in so many of them. If this richness is sometimes undervalued, if it appears in policy statements only to be countermanded by dictates of national integration and efficiency, this move stems at least in part from the continuing hegemonic influence in the world of European, nineteenth century, romantic as well as realpolitik, notions of the nation state as the embodiment of a unitary people, culture and language (Schlee). Given the inadequacy of this ideal in contemporary Europe, it is worth at least asking what Europeans might learn from African experience. Ekeh (1990) has recently suggested, in the context of tribalism, that concepts discarded in Euro-American metropolitan centres of opinion are prematurely superseded in African studies because Africanists too readily follow intellectual fashions. While this is a proper note of caution, the unwillingness to reject inappropriate European precedents may be just as unhelpful. On the evidence of a recent book by distinguished Nigerian authors (Emenanjo ed. 1990), the problematic relation between the state and language remains a major focus of current discussion, and this discussion is canalized around the ideal of a single, national language.[9] In Europe and America, on the other hand, recent writers have emphasized the diminishing pertinence of the national state as an encompassing framework for sociological research (as it was for most of the classical sociological writers). Instead, attention has shifted to the emergence of regional and global frameworks for analysis. The implications of this change in perspective may be crucial to the ways that the differing discourses on African languages can be made to speak to one another. What has been described as creolization in African settings is in some respects similar to the condition that Europeans and Americans experience as postmodernism or postpluralism (Parkin). Language as an object of concern finds itself subjected to, usually incompatible, desires for purity, authenticity, modernity, Africanness, national usage, equality and statal identity. Meanwhile, language as practice develops as if it had a life of its own under the influences of the pursuit of wealth or political influence, or more neutrally communication and sociality, to which ends it is only a means (Parkin, Blommaert). Africans have, at least since the opening of the Saharan and Atlantic trades, been coping with issues of multilingualism which Europeans in the Age of Nationalism managed, for a rather brief period it may transpire, largely to circumvent practically even as they were inflating the importance of the conceptual cluster around the terms language and political identity which has now been globalized.

LANGUAGE AS POLITICAL OBJECT[10]

In the preceding argument, we exaggerated the distinction between language as it appeared to ethnographers and to language planners in Africa. From the perspective of anthropological theory, or more precisely recent reflection on anthropological theory, we might as plausibly have begun by noting a series of similarities. Because African states are not monoglot, the politics of language necessarily involves relations between languages. Of course, relations between languages have also been central to the anthropological enterprise; although recognition of this fact has been more or less explicit at different times and to different schools of anthropology. We might alternatively compare policy and anthropological approaches to language at the point of relations between languages, rather than in terms of the contrast between distinct languages and the fact of the embeddedness of all cultural life in language (contexts too broad and distinct to be usable here). The analysis of relations between languages offers a pertinent point of comparison between anthropology and language policy, because degrees of objectification of language are required of both sets of discourses (putting neither, as it were, under an epistemological handicap).

The implications of one of Talal Asad's critical essays offer a convenient point of entry to one strand in recent anthropological discussion. In this essay, Asad (1986) sought to bring the notion of relations between weak and strong languages to bear upon the idea of cultural translation in anthropology. In contrast to ethnographically based analyses, Asad's macro-level approach objectifies language in ways similar to the policy discourses. Let us outline a few points of his argument briefly.

Asad begins by noting how cultural translation became accepted as a definition of anthropology by a generation of anthropologists many – although not all – of whom had, at one time or another, been associated with the Institute of Anthropology at Oxford (Evans-Pritchard, Godfrey Lienhardt, David Pocock, Max Gluckman and others). He takes issue not directly with this definition, but rather with one of its commentators, Ernest Gellner, who had published a critical article twenty-five years earlier (Gellner 1961) pointing to a problem that context posed for all theories of translation. Gellner had protested that given sufficient latitude in determining relevant context, anthropologists could never conclude that an assertion was either absurd or contradictory. Interpretive charity would always encourage them to discover a context in which the assertion or belief made sense. Asad must have felt this argument to be momentous to be persuaded to return to it so long after its original publication. The conundrum of translation is not unique to anthropologists, albeit they have a particularly vested professional interest in it. In various ways, translation is a condition of all comprehension, but it is particularly obvious when more than a single language is involved. The question 'what happens in translation?' is posed urgently in multilingual states.

The argument of Asad's paper becomes complex, and only a few of its points need concern us. One source of complexity is that, on some matters at least, he and Gellner share more than divides them. Albeit in different ways, neither of them restricts the question of translation to narrow linguistic criteria, both stress social contexts within which translation occurs. But they reach radically differing conclusions. Asad is able to dispatch Gellner's own examples of charitable interpretation with aplomb. Gellner's textual idea of translation – basically matching written sentences in the language from which he is translating with sentences in English – ignores what, for Asad, is the primary consideration that 'society is the cultural condition in which speakers act and are acted upon' (Asad 1986: 155). Anthropologists can apprehend the relevant contexts only by learning the coherence of discourses and of the practices in which they participate (1986: 153). The issue of context turns out to be resolvable only through practical competence. This is where Gellner and Asad converge, but they interpret the consequences of their convergence differently. For Gellner, social context masks the logical incoherence of ideology; for Asad, coherence is a quality to be sought only in social context. Gellner privileges the logic of abstract argument which he finds mystified by practice; Asad privileges the situational logic of discourse and practice which he claims is misrepresented by Gellner's translation into propositional logic.

At this point Asad breaks off his argument with Gellner and introduces the relational idea of weak and strong languages. In practice, languages are not equal. Anthropologists typically translate into strong languages from weaker languages. What makes one language stronger than another? Asad's explanation is suggestive but not fully developed. We recognize strong languages by a number of criteria. Strong languages are spoken by the strong: English (and other globally distributed Euro-

8 African languages, development and the state

pean languages) are associated with western countries that enjoy unequal political and economic relations with the rest of the world. These relations are, in the final analysis, underpinned by the historical forms of industrial capital. Strong languages more easily express knowledge desired by the strong from the privileged vantage assured by their modes of life. Weak languages cannot easily deploy the same knowledge except by being modified themselves (as he suggests has occurred in modern Arabic) or by undergoing modification during translation. In this sense, the evolution of weak languages and translation are examples of the same process acting at different rates. Borrowing Gramsci's terminology to make Asad's point, there is a hegemonic relation between strong and weak languages by virtue of the positions of their speakers. As David Parkin has noted, 'all discourse embodies hegemonic aspects, in the combined sense of shaping and dominating others' wills' (1984: 360). Asad goes further by arguing that speakers of stronger languages feel impelled to master the implicit in the discourse of the weak: this implicit is construed as something to which the strong have privileged access but which remains in principle occluded from the weak. In Parkin's terms, the will of the powerful is shaped by the power they feel their discourse to bear in relation to that of the weak.

These ideas broach a number of facets of the debate about African languages and the state: the plurality of languages, language as an index of Apartheid, contextual determination of the sense of what is said, the relations of power – including assumptions about privileged comprehension – between the agents of different languages. Asad's position is indebted to Foucault, and particularly to the way that Foucault's ideas were used by Edward Said in his works on academic and popular orientalism (Said 1978, and subsequently). But as stated, Asad's account poses as many problems as it illuminates. Asad's initial concern with context becomes marginalized in the course of his argument with Gellner until all that remains is a single enveloping context: between weak and strong languages. But does translation ever involve a *single* significant context on which all parties can agree? Asad's argument concludes with a monolithic, ineluctable and titanic struggle between languages. Strong and weak languages are reinforced in their initial relation by virtue of translation; translation is preeminently a vehicle of power (Asad 1986: 163). While this position has much to recommend it as a cautionary critique of the creation of metropolitan anthropologists' knowledge of peoples who are thereby peripheralized, can it be applied to relations between African languages in contemporary states? The argument bears the imprint of its origin in the polarized debate between the 'occident' and the 'orient'. The relation between Africa and Europe, let alone

Introduction: frontiers and boundaries 9

within African states, is less amenable to simple polarization. In the predominantly multilingual environment of Africa, languages are strong *and* weak according to context. Both translation *and* the refusal to translate can be vehicles of power. The 'same' language may be strong, when its members control the discourse of others by translation, but weak in contexts where its speakers are relatively powerless. Translation may facilitate control, but so may the withholding of translation either as a matter of deliberate policy or (in the long run, perhaps the same thing) because the powerful are hardly conscious of particular, minority language practices within the nation.

Asad's analysis tends to reduce the complexities of discursive practices to the effects of objectified language, thus rendering it difficult to distinguish any differences between instances of discourse in languages assumed consistently to be weak or strong. He thus falls foul of his own injunction to ground language practice in the social. But the idea that the relation between discursive practices is power-laden is too valuable to abandon because of shortcomings in his own use of it. Is it possible to retain Asad's notion of the indissociable relation between discourses in particular languages and power, but to apply this concept in a more nuanced way to the politics of discursive practice, rather than to language, in African cases?

We begin by noting that language does not always appear to be an object. In fact, the objectification of language is a property of particular types of discourse about language. Language appears as something different depending how we look at it. Objectification of language – as a thing – makes particular problems appear to demand urgent rectification. But how far is the problem 'language' or the way we are thinking about languages? Even if we accept the necessary objectification of language in relation to both policy and anthropological discourses, the terms in which the languages are contrasted to one another are extremely diverse. To look at African instances: languages (and variants of the 'same' language) may be contrasted as modernized or traditional (as in debates about the expansion of the lexicons of lingua francas to include terms appropriate to modern technology and scientific discourse, Blommaert); or as pure and impure (as in debates over the Arabization of lingua francas in Muslim communities, Parkin); purity and modernity may have to be reconciled (as in arguments about the appropriateness of borrowing terms for new objects, or borrowing only the concepts which ought to be rendered using new compounds of existing terms – instead of fridge, 'thing for keeping cold things'). Alternatively, discussion of language may hinge on authenticity or Africanness (as in the case of attitudes to Krio, Magbaily Fyle), or upon scale (Hansford, Elugbe).

10 *African languages, development and the state*

Clearly, relations between languages, and ideas about what happens in translation that cohere with these relations, involve more specific features than a simple contrast between weakness and strength, which risks becoming tautologous (when strong languages are considered the prerogative of those strong on quite independent criteria, and vice versa). This is not to deny that perceptions of relative strength do not provide one important context in which people situate a reflexive concern with language, but in common with the other contexts we have enumerated (religious, scientific, aesthetic, political, economic) these have to be understood as debates that are outside language in a narrow sense but inside language in a broader sense (because they involve discourses instantiated in language).

LANGUAGE AS THE SUBJECT OF DISCOURSE

In official statements, the political nature of language planning is often a submerged theme precisely because it is a dominant consideration. Policy discussions of language need to attain an appearance of objectivity, and the globally available rhetorics to achieve this include the discourses of human rights, economic utility and governmental efficiency, as well as aesthetic expression and the authenticity of personal and collective identities. In the creation of published programmes, African states find themselves playing not just to an internal audience but also to an external audience which governs some of the terms of discussion by virtue of holding the purse strings of aid and debt scheduling. Given that nation states in Africa have derived from colonial territorial units, to which other criteria of statehood and nation have had to be added, the ways in which language has been put, both literally and figuratively, on the map, have been politically and epistemologically crucial moves. The major devices through which policy makers have represented language diversity to themselves in print have been the map and the list.

Putting language on the map and into the list

Language is commonly viewed as an object – scientific object, political object, cultural object, etc. This usage is the most appropriate for many purposes, but it is, nonetheless, a specific type of usage, and its different instances tend to add credence to one another. Languages as objects need to be attributed such properties as (greater or lesser in each case): systematicity, distinctiveness, closure, and independence. The map is one master trope of this type of discourse: both as a physical object and as an image informing other discursive practices about language.[11] This is particularly clear in the African case. Four varieties of map[12] of Africa show a poor fit when superimposed upon one another, and unease about this fit problematizes 'language'. Further unease invests practices that take place, as it were, off the map.

The first map is the one we come across most often: the map of African states. Many of the lines on this map were drawn first with the infamous blue pencils of imperial delegates to late nineteenth century conferences. About a third of the lines are geometric. If the other two thirds have rationales owing less to ruler and compass, they often reflect only spheres of influence and trade carved out by the precursors of European colonialism. The linguistic correlates of this map of contemporary states owe much to an older terrain shaded in the colours of the occupying colonial powers. The slightly redefined nation states inherited the European language geography of their imperial overlords (Treffgarne 1975). To these have been added, in some cases, African national and/or official languages. In a few cases, European languages have lost the privilege of sponsorship by the state. These two maps (the colonial and the national) are the least contested (in the sense that the boundaries are generally known) but highly contentious all the same. The former is fixed thanks to having been historically superseded, the latter owes its permanence to the general agreement of the Organization of African Unity to live with its inherited national boundaries.

The third map is the linguists' creation. Each revision of this map tends to add to the number of named languages located in the virtual space of the diagram. Notoriously, this map fits ill with either the colonial or national maps. Some languages, often associated with past African imperial formations or with trading diasporas, are quite widely distributed on the map, others are so restricted that the map hardly allows space to inscribe their names. A higher level generalization of the language map groups languages into families. On this map we might note that in Central and Eastern and Southern Africa, many of the languages are close cognates sharing a high proportion of lexical items and grammatical structures. In West Africa the distribution is far more fractured. Related to the language map, but not entirely coincident with it, is the ethnographic map of the peoples of Africa. This divides the terrain by allotting it unambiguously to named peoples. These two maps, the linguistic and the ethnographic, are taken as signs of the process interrupted by colonialism as well as the evidence on which accounts of more distant history have largely to rely. Because they can be seen as compositions created on the ground prior to the inscription of colonialism on the map, the linguistic and ethnographic maps can easily be captured by rhetorics of 'authenticity'. But the linguistic and ethnographic maps are, even in their own terms, subject to dispute. The grounds of dispute are familiar: the relatively recent crystallization of singular, fixed ethnic identities; the inappropriateness of two-dimensional maps to represent any area in terms of more than a single salient language or ethnic identity; the interaction of ethnic and linguistic considerations that go into determining quite what constitutes an instance of language rather than dialect, and so forth. All the maps are possible because they rely on conventions; none is an unmediated reality, though each is treated as such in some discourses.

Each of the four maps could be thought of as a discursive register. The colonial map, which explains the distribution of European official languages in Africa, also refers to other aspects of imperial history; the map of nation states refers beyond itself to a global condition of nation states and a discourse of human rights embodied in organizations such as the United Nations; language and ethnic maps speak beyond themselves to processes that antedate colonialism but were nonetheless affected by it. Yet the maps can be envisaged to have succeeded one another over a period of not much more than a century. A discourse located in one of the maps, and its correlative register, can either disregard or explain its relation to the other maps. Single-mindedly sticking to a single map (in the fashion of a nationalist or ethnic irredentist rhetoric, for instance) renders the other registers 'off the map'. Not only do the four maps offer different registers, all four ignore much that is definitively off the map because it cannot fit into the two-dimensional imagination of this kind of map-making: the linguistic complexity of the burgeoning urban centres, or the multilingualism of most African communities, or the fact that all but global maps can always be encompassed by bigger maps.

The map of African languages already begs a process of naming and bounding which represents discursive realities in terms of objectified entities. This process of objectification is normally furthered through listing, which comes in two main varieties: lists organized according to the genetic and familial resemblances among languages, and lists ranked ordinally in terms of the numbers of mother tongue speakers of a language or the numbers competent in the language more generally. The latter list may be subdivided, to rank groups of languages as majority and minority, or according to more exact criteria of scale if required.

To repeat, we are not claiming that there is anything intrinsically wrong with map-making or listing, only that making languages appear according to these conventions also makes language 'problems' appear in a restricted range of forms. It is revealing to look at policy-oriented writings from this perspective. Typically, the horizon of policy-oriented writings is defined in terms of the governmental responsibilities of one or several nation states. These responsibilities hinge upon the polarity of unity versus diversity. Politically, economically, educationally, culturally... policy makers see themselves confronted by choices which have to be solved in terms of trade-offs between these two over-arching terms. The era of bold solutions, by the choice of single African languages in order to pursue only the goal of national unity, has generally been abandoned as impractical or self-defeating in its own terms. Policy-oriented writings conventionally begin from the idea of language diversity which is represented by references to maps of distribution, diverging trees of language relationship based on linguistic researches, and lists of languages showing the numbers of speakers ranked ordinally. Indeed, given the goals of policy-oriented writings, there may be no other place to start. But consequences are set in train: certain deductions become predictable while others are ruled out from the beginning. For instance, a writer appealing to the branching genealogy of language relatedness may feel it appropriate to note that, say, 70 per cent of languages in a state share membership of a single broad language family. But if these languages are not inter-comprehensible, it is unclear what practical consequence then follows – albeit the rhetorical gesture towards unity is palpably important. More generally, appeal to any of the maps, or to their correlative lists, necessarily triggers the broader, divisive, conceptual clusters we have noted: setting in train such objectified associations as language, culture, and tribe, or, European language, colonial geography, post-colonial identity, and so forth. Although languages are made to seem strong or weak, the reasoning which leads to this conclusion actually proceeds from extra-linguistic associations (in the narrow sense of objectified language) towards conclusions that are then seen to prevail at the level of discourse. Discursive practices are certainly marked by relations of unequal power, but not in so simple, or univocal, a fashion as that implied in analyses which proceed from a top-down approach to the distribution of languages.

Language and sectoral usage

Language may be objectified spatially, or pseudo-spatially, in terms of genealogies and lists, but it may also be objectified functionally by allotting different languages sectoral uses. The allocation may be formally installed, where particular African and European languages are current in contemporary states as official or national languages to be used for definite purposes (economic, legal, political, educational, bureaucratic and so forth), or it may be based informally in common recognition that particular language practices are required for the 'language of commerce', 'language of the hearth', 'language of religion', etc. The idea of sectoral use is often combined with the notion that certain languages are either appropriate or current in particular 'levels' of society. In this objectification of language, the functional 'location' of language tends also to imply correlated social emplacement. In common with the spatialization of language on the map, the notion of sectoral specialization presents a divisive objectification of language, and this is so whether the specialized languages are European or African. European languages potentially divide people along lines of educational background, rural/urban separation, class, religion and familial socialization, gender and so forth. African languages potentially divide people according to these criteria and according to the ethnic map.

Stronger languages empower speakers and therefore represent advantages for those who carry them in their language portfolio. This is not simply a matter of communicational competence. Following Bourdieu we could see linguistic proficiency (like education and culture more generally, see Bourdieu 1979) as a form of personal capital with social, symbolic and economic aspects. The perspective from functional and sectoral specialization in language involves extra-linguistic questions that take the form 'what does speaking such and such language imply in practical and/or symbolic terms?'.

Objectifying discourse

A third form of objectification, more typical of anthropological writings oriented from the bottom-up perspective, changes the view considerably. Instead of objectifying language we focus on individuals who are engaged in language as they go about their business. They read, listen to the media, are addressed, respond and discuss. These interactions may involve numerous languages in which the individuals feel more or less at home. Following the sectoral model, they may feel more at home in some languages for certain purposes only. We may find that conversations drift into and out of particular languages as the subject and register seem to require. Perhaps, it may be difficult to tell quite what 'language' some parts of some conversations are in. An approach that looks at the way people behave linguistically may arrive at conclusions radically at variance with the two types of objectification of language that we have sketched. We do not mean to suggest that close analytic attention to discursive patterning can escape being a form of objectification, but crucially it is not a form of objectification that readily corresponds to the other elements of the conceptual clusters we have suggested are inevitably evoked by the objectification of languages. Analyses may typically distinguish circumstances in which a mother tongue is used from situations in which varying types of multilingualism or polyglossia prevail. But extended situations conducted only in the mother tongue may be diminishing as a proportion of all language events in a country like, say, Nigeria. Moreover, mother tongues are not unchanging, and close investigation of the linguistic parameters of socialization may rapidly dispell the notion of uncontaminated 'authenticity' that the phrase 'mother tongue' tends to connote. Patterns of discourse cannot be fitted on to a language map and may complicate accounts of sectoral usage into no more than statistical probabilities. Although it is the most challenging of the objectifications to describe, and the most labile between situations and over time, it is this objectification which brings us to a concern with local-level practices and the power relations they entail. However, the particularity of the discourse model tends to make it seem interesting but impractical to the policy-oriented writer. The discursive model (involving discourse about discourse) seems to offer little in the way of (what seem to be) practical solutions to the pressing problems of economic integration, ethnic stabilization, or educational policy. While useful as an explanation of why policies have come to grief after the event, its potential for generating new policy seems limited. Its message appears to be that most kinds of intervention are impossible or else perverse in their outcomes. This is hardly sweet music to the ears of problem solvers; nor is it an account conducive to the attraction of project-tied foreign or international aid.

So we seem to be left with a hiatus between views – one, moreover, that is comprehensible and apparently even necessary given the situations of those who work from them. Dialogue is clearly feasible – our meeting demonstrated that policy-oriented and anthropological perspectives are entirely mutually comprehensible; and after all, neither is a complex position in principle. But can dialogue have any worthwhile outcome in practice?

REFASHIONING THE LANGUAGE MAP

In a recent attempt to summarize the fractured state of globalization in our shrinking world, Arjun Appadurai found it useful to separate heuristically a number of relatively independent descriptions of the global landscape. He itemizes ethnoscapes, mediascapes, technoscapes, finanscapes, and ideoscapes (Appadurai 1990). Technology has become unevenly distributed as high-tech industries are found cheek by jowl with

16 *African languages, development and the state*

peasant agriculture. Electronic media (TV, film, radio, audiocassettes and videocassettes, newspapers, etc.) reach further and faster than before (Mytton 1983). Ideologies (capitalist, socialist, religious) circulate globally. People (as migrants, as tourists, as students, as workers, as refugees) move in large numbers. The movement of financial capital has assumed a high degree of independence from manufacturing. And all of these globalizing tendencies have linguistic correlates. The mutual constitution of notions of global and local can be envisaged to occur within a variety of global landscapes that are not of necessity mutually consistent. African writers, academics, musicians, artists, politicians, financiers and so forth spend parts of their professional lives as inhabitants of globalized landscapes (whether or not they physically move). As consumers, the majority of people, especially urban people, are subject to inducements and imperatives to purchase that emanate from the advertising media of capitalist industries. Nor are the political goods on offer exclusively local, albeit they are locally appropriated (viz the advent of [national] Republicans and [social] Democrats in Nigeria). While the nation state remains an important political reality, to treat it as the only relevant unit so far as language policy is concerned is to rule out consideration of either the regional or global considerations that are steadily growing in significance.

Our first two objectifications of languages (by reference to various maps and lists, and by reference to function) suggested central roles for the state, our subsequent stresses on language use and on the global circumstances of national states introduce greater complexity into prognostications of the role that the state might like to, or even be capable of, playing in relation to language use. The objectification of language is itself subjected to different discursive strategies, and all of them are politically charged. While Asad is correct to stress that the relations between languages are marked by unequal power, such relations of hegemony are difficult to fix unequivocally outside the context of particular speech acts (and even in such contexts may be ambiguous). Part of the problem lies in envisaging the relation of hegemony to exist between languages rather than between social agents who are empowered or disempowered under specific conditions of language. 'Language' is objectified in the politics of discourse, but it may be the *imposition* on others of discourses and practices to do with language that constitutes the hegemonic relation – and not the language as an agency in itself. This perspective is occluded when rights are seen to attach to languages rather than to speakers. A recent publication of the Minority Rights Group, entitled *Language, Literacy and Minorities* (incidentally winner of the UNA Media Peace Prize) is significantly ambiguous in its account of the 'attachment' of rights to people or to languages. The author of this report argues from the linguists' demonstration that languages are cognitively equal, to the proposition that they (i.e. the languages) ought to have equal political rights, and from that proposition to the idea that the domination of one language by another (note again that language is made agentive) reflects an ideology of linguicism that is closely akin to racism (Skutnabb-Kangas 1990: 7-8). While the liberal intention of the chain of reasoning is obvious, the practical outcome of pursuing this logical sequence would be antithetical even to the most nuanced version of policy-oriented African language discourse which recognizes the contradictory ways in which unity and diversity impinge on any language programme.

HEGEMONY AND THE STATE

Reference to hegemony usually implies another classical Gramscian distinction: that between state and civil society. The difference between the two is highly contestable, and indeed impossible to maintain in the same form across contexts. Explicitly drawing attention to the shifting analytic status of the state is something (contrary to some critics) which is a potential strength of the Gramscian antinomies. Practically the extent of the state is unpredictable: our media (African or European) constantly astonish us with tales of the surveillance the state can exert over our lives and, contrariwise, with the seemingly simple tasks that state apparatuses prove incapable of discharging. That the state is both weak and strong is a familiar paradox. In relation to our preoccupations here, two aspects of the sponsorship of language need to be separated: let's call them programmatic sponsorship and pragmatic sponsorship. The two frequently conflict. By programmatic language sponsorship we mean to understand the official policy of the state expressed in its regulations about recruitment, education, the judicial process, the media and so forth (e.g. UNESCO 1981). By pragmatic sponsorship, we mean those effects in and through language that the policy of the state brings about.

Sponsorship of language by the state (both programmatically and pragmatically) is always crucial, but may be especially so when the state, like the African state, is often the major player in employment and the distribution of wealth, and when language has become as politically charged as we have suggested it is in Africa. Authorities involved in nation-building are rightly advised to avoid contentious separatism in their language policy, and many African countries have moved increasingly towards a pluralist stance in their official programmes. In part, we suggested earlier, this has required recognition of the inappropriateness of the European, romantic notion of the state as the culmination and embodiment of a unitary people, culture and language. The short term attempt to subordinate regional linguistic practices has transpired to be a sure recipe for longer term discord. The state may sponsor a vision of language use, within limits it can bring it about (especially through education and through making a certain portfolio of competence the condition of empowerment), but it cannot legislate a desired situation into being nor can it determine how people will interpret the changes it sponsors. The state may programmatically sponsor a workable language portfolio, one that promises to be feasible within the various definitions of language use. But, in addition to this, state authorities need to be sensitive to the pragmatic outcomes of their activities. All too often a species of linguistic bad faith finds state authorities programmatically sponsoring one set of initiatives while pragmatically reinforcing another, whether by intention or not. Unfortunately, the effects of ill-considered interventions to impose discursive practices can be much more startling than a gradualist approach.[13] The penalties for getting things wrong (at least in the short term) are greater than the rewards for getting them right.

David Laitin's recent summation of the different interests in play in the processes of language rationalization and state-building in Africa sets out to show how game theory might aid African politicians avoid some of the pitfalls that await them (Laitin 1992). Formulaically, he suggests that the outcome of language rationalization in African states is liable to converge in most countries on a 3±1 formula, which is to say that individual language repertoires will be required to include competence in between two and four languages. The three most commonly occurring languages will be 1) a language of wider communication for official and international purposes, which will commonly be a European language, 2) an African lingua franca (standardized from an indigenous language, pidgin or creole), 3) a regional vernacular. Where individuals are socialized in one of the larger languages that is nevertheless not the regional vernacular, they will need to acquire four languages; however, an individual who is socialized in an African lingua franca, which is also a local vernacular, will need to learn only two languages. More generally, the number of languages in which individuals require proficiency will be affected by the range of mobility to which they aspire.

Laitin's 3±1 formula comes close to stating the status quo in much of post-colonial Africa; the originality of his interpretation lies in demonstrating that radical departure from this pattern is highly unlikely. On the one hand, there are macro forces that require international and national communication, on the other hand, there is a micro dynamics of language use which is reflected in the individual's language repertoire (akin to what we are calling language portfolio) and in the fluidity of contemporary linguistic interactions, which may switch between languages and registers. Mediating the macro and micro level factors, there is a pattern of diverse political claims articulated by the representatives of interests wedded to international, national and regional language interests. If none of these interests is entirely to be overridden, then the policy makers would be well advised to offer each of them some endorsement in both policy and practice.

As the most sustained attempt to reconcile top-down and bottom-up perspectives on Africa's language problem, Laitin's argument deserves the attention of all policy makers who wish to ease the pain of transition to an outcome he feels is inevitable. Whether the games theoretic, equilibrium outcome will eventuate is more difficult to predict. Nigerian policy (see notes 13 and 15) clearly tends in this direction, at least programmatically. But it is not obvious that the state will be able to afford to implement its policy, or indeed have the political means or will to do so. As van Binsbergen emphasizes, state apparatuses function at numerous levels (from the national to the local), and the political aspects of language and ethnicity are not necessarily consistent between these situations. More generally, Laitin assumes that decisions concerning language will be made through legitimate state apparatuses and that this will occur as part of a process of state-building. One can only hope he is correct in this, but alternative scenarios of the disintegration of the state, control of its remaining powers by factional interests, and a general decline in statal ability to sponsor developments of national scope are all too readily to hand. The formulation of state policy on language may transpire to be a symbolic political contest with only tangential effects upon the development of discursive practices adopted by most people, most of the time.

LANGUAGE AND DEVELOPMENT

To complete the triad of terms of our original workshop title, we turn to what we might want to understand by development and what role the state can play both in relation to the necessary embeddedness of all development in language and with specific regard to language policy. Tables of Gross Domestic Product may appear to transcend language and aspire to a realm of pure statistics; but the components of the gross product were made under particular conditions of language (the language of farm or factory or financial institution). This point has been emphasized in studies of rural development and agricultural extension work where the rhetorics of development, the attempted imposition of expertise, and the corresponding attribution of ignorance to local farmers have been analysed (e. g. Richards 1985; Pottier 1989; Parkin 1975; Hobart ed. 1993). If development is a process of empowerment then it must be differentiated according to whom it seeks to empower, and in what terms: cultural, technical, educational, economic, political. Unfortunately different criteria of development do not necessarily point towards the same policy. However, if this maligned term has one virtue, it is that it points to its own base line: development must be development of some existing situation.

Arguments specifically concerned with language often share many of the suppositions of broader discourses about cultural development. Language features in different developmental discourses depending on whether it is conceived 'pragmatically', as a functional device for communication and technical education, or 'expressively', as a vehicle and manifestation of culture. Looked at in the latter way, language debates belong to arguments over the uses of African and European languages waged among African writers and critics (Ngũgĩ 1986; Chinweizu et al. 1985; Soyinka 1976; Okpewho 1988), over the differing natures of African and European philosophy (Hountondji 1977; Mudimbe 1988), about the nature of an African as opposed to European socialism (in the writings of Nkrumah, Nyerere and others), and, within the broad context of the *négritude* movement (July 1987). The arguments differ, but each is grounded in some appeal to African authenticity (Blommaert).

To privilege some part of the existing field, other variant practices must be declared 'inauthentic', and thus not worthy of further development. The tensions involved here are also those implicated in the different discourses on language, development and the state. In order to take a stance on the question of 'language', critics must objectify language and ignore discursive practices. Thus for Chinweizu and his associates, only 'works done by Africans and in African languages, whether these works are oral or written, constitute the historically indisputable core of the canon of African literature' (1985: 13). Other, less clearcut, works must be vetted in terms of 'some decision procedure' (1985: 12). These decision procedures cannot help but be contentious since they do not start from existing discursive practices in African societies but from an 'indisputable' history. The character both of language and history is begged. But can African writing be divorced from the current nature of African societies, which are marked by complex language practices? Who decides that some of these practices are more authentically 'African' than others, given that all are done by Africans? This question refers us to broader issues: how far can premeditated change in linguistic practice be sponsored? And, anyway, does 'authenticity' constitute a ground for sponsoring change when the rhetoric of authenticity is so peculiarly malleable to factional interests?[14]

The state, we have argued, is severely constrained in its programmatic sponsorship of language change. These constraints issue from the post-pluralist nature of the civil society to be changed, the degree to which civil society has captured the state, the linkages between national issues and a variety of regional and global projects over which slight influence can be exercised, and the degree that state policies pragmatically encourage outcomes contrary to their programmes.

A classic example of mismatch between Government edict and popular practice can be seen in the case of written Hausa. In 1917, Hans Vischer, then Director of Education for the north of Nigeria, set out rules for Hausa spelling which he published and communicated to a few of his colonial colleagues at a time before Hausa had been written in Roman script to a great extent. This orthography was adopted throughout northern Nigeria. In 1917, linguists and administrators had the opportunity to establish norms. Contrast the situation in 1966 when a group of linguists meeting at a UNESCO conference on the orthography of African languages in Bamako proposed a new orthography for Hausa to bring its conventions into line with those used for other African languages. When the proposals were put into effect in Niger, a situation resulted in which Hausa was written in one way in Niger and in another in Nigeria. Fifty years of experience in Nigeria had been ignored. The situation persisted until the authorities in Niger decided to adopt the Nigerian orthography. As a result of the intervention of prescriptive linguists, and the state's sponsorship of their plans, the difficulties facing people wishing to teach, learn, read and write in Hausa had been multiplied. The linguists and administrators simply failed to recognize the historical inappropriateness of their suggestions and their inability to impose them on Hausa-speaking peoples.

HAUSA AS MOTHER TONGUE AND AS LINGUA FRANCA

Proponents of the need for language policy argue that the key question is 'what happens in schools?'. This question is closely related to assessments of the balance between the number of speakers using a language as mother tongue and those using it as lingua franca. Mother tongue and lingua franca are often portrayed as poles around which certain features necessarily agglomerate. But such agglomerations are not self-evident from the perspectives of discursive practice and the attitudes taken towards languages, registers and styles of speech in particular communities. Neither mother tongue nor lingua franca are the objectively bounded entities these usages suggest. An approach from the 'bottom up', which emphasizes features of discursive context, demonstrates further difficulties that state authorities face in imposing policy. In Nigeria, it has generally been argued that it would be impossible immediately to declare Hausa, Yoruba or Igbo the national language because to do so would upset the delicate political balance between these three ethnic blocks. Instead, the preference has been for social engineering to promote a variety of languages in different degrees in order to maintain or create political balances of various kinds.[15] By these strategies of deliberate underdevelopment of certain languages and development of others, it has been assumed that the state can promote its integration through 'nation-building'. The distinction between mother tongue and lingua franca has been crucial to this proposal. The mother tongue is assumed to be that used within homogenous language groups, and the lingua francas are envisaged as means of communication between members of different ethnic and cultural groupings. While the emphasis on multilingualism is welcome, the presuppositions justifying the programme may be oversimplified. How many extended language situations in Nigeria involve only groups of homogenous, mother tongue speakers? Not many. Even in the heartland of the Hausa-speaking communities of Katsina, Daura or Kano conversations may switch into and out of English, and there are frequent occasions for members of the Hausa community to converse with Yoruba, or Igbo, or Tuareg, or Kanuri speaking peoples. Yet these circumstances are straightforward compared to those in Taraba, Adamawa, or Borno states, where people sometimes use Kanuri or Fulfulde, sometimes Hausa or English, and on other occasions one or more of the less widely spoken languages of the region.[16]

The significance attached to language choice is highly variable in these different circumstances. A mother tongue Hausa speaker using Hausa in Kano might also subscribe to ideas of Hausa culture, Hausa centrality in the north, and Hausa nationalism that are widely shared in his or her community; but for a speaker using Hausa in Adamawa, Taraba or Borno, the language might be an expedient to allow communication between Shuwa and Kanuri, or Kanuri and Fulani, or it might signify personal allegiance to a particular group within Maiduguri or the wider north. The variety of perceptions of significance in language choice, especially in multilingual settings, invites misunderstandings: a language use that is pragmatic from one perspective might be interpreted ideologically from another. The campaigning carried out by the Sardauna during the 1950s promoted the use of Hausa as an element of his attempt to create a greater Northern Nigeria. From his perspective, speakers of Tiv, Gwari or other larger, minority languages, could not make independent contributions to a 'greater northern good'. But it would be a mistake on this account to believe that the transformation of Numan, where forty years ago most people transacted their daily business in Bachama, into a town where a majority of the population speaks Hausa, is any indication of the incorporation of Numan, or the Bachama, into a collective northern Hausa identity. While changing patterns of multilingualism have political implications, these cannot be read off directly.

The contrast between Northern Nigeria and Northern Cameroon is illuminating. The spread of Hausa and Hausa-ization in Nigeria is mirrored in the spread of Fulfulde and Fulbe-ization in Cameroon (Burnham 1991). Chamba in Cameroon have been among the peoples who have tended to resist Fulbe-ization; many other non-Fulbe peoples have shown a tendency to Fulbe-ize in town. The preference, especially of Christian Cameroonian Chamba, is for French as a lingua franca and, although no data exist to clinch the point, many express a preference to migrate entirely outside the area of Fulbe hegemony if they choose to leave their homelands. For Chamba in Nigeria, the use of Hausa as lingua franca finesses the implications of speaking Fulfulde. Again relying on impressionistic evidence, it seems that use of Fulfulde as a second language has been in decline historically in Adamawa and Taraba States. The fact of the existence of the Fulfulde-speaking Adamawa Emirate in the nineteenth century has had different outcomes in Nigeria and Cameroon, but it has significantly invested attitudes to Fulfulde in both countries. The encouragement (so far mostly on paper) of Chamba as a medium of instruction in primary schools in Ganye Local Government Area (where Chamba are a local majority), apart from raising practical problems about orthography and written materials, will reproduce a smaller scale version of the political challenges. Which of many dialects is to be adopted as the standard written form? What are to be the hegemonic implications of the fillip given to the growing Ñnakenyaré Chamba lingua franca spoken around the local Government headquarters at Ganye – both in relation to Chamba dialects which will become subordinated and to the languages spoken by local minorities (Koma, Vomni, and – in this context of reversal – even Fulfulde)?

CONCLUSION

The current Nigerian policy of encouraging knowledge of at least one and often two of the three major lingua francas at school level aims both to encourage language versatility and to reduce the links between language, ethnicity and political affiliation. These aims are highly laudable in principle, and that of changing present patterns of multilingualism may be feasible not least because it moves in the direction that events already tend – especially with respect to Hausa for Yoruba and Igbo speakers. However, the link between a particular pattern of multilingualism and nation-building is complex. Because ethnic identities (and thus the significance of language practices) are being reshaped continuously, because language use never ceases to undergo change, and because the past is always a present concern – in short because history will not stop to allow legislators respite – the objectification of language at the expense of discursive practice is a dangerous impediment to the success of state-sponsored development. Experience suggests that the state can sponsor dramatic language reform only under exceptional circumstances (as in the revival of Hebrew in Israel), but that its capacity to engineer perverse effects is always remarkable.

Pragmatic language sponsorship suggests a modest and constantly revised understanding of the changing patterns of language use combined with a willingness to seize opportunities that arise at levels between the state and the immediate locality. Such a pragmatic and populist policy might support initiatives made by local organizations, regional government and non-statal associations, but equally importantly it would involve the removal or lessening of constraints upon local initiatives, whether in the form of language lobbies or specific restrictions on future language development. Such pragmatic policy might run counter to programmatic policies adopted centrally by the state in the short run. But in the longer run it could act as a balance both to modify the excesses of programmatic implementation, and to ensure that the changing nature of current language use and the limitations of prescription remain clearly in focus.

Monolingualism has never been the norm in Africa that it is in much of Europe. The state may best serve its own interests by enabling people to develop the personal language portfolios they will anyway continue to acquire so long as there are incentives to speak to neighbours, acquire religious, scientific and technical knowledge, and pursue careers in local, national, regional and international forums. But this will only become possible when multilingualism (in African languages of differing importance, in Arabic and in European languages) is developed as a strength rather than compensated as a national problem. Our conclusion, therefore, is that dialogue between the different discourses on language can be productive to the extent that each can identify with the aims of the

Introduction: frontiers and boundaries 25

others in favour of a broadly conceived programme to empower language users.

NOTES

1 Throughout this volume, Africa is used with the sense of sub-Saharan Africa unless otherwise specified. Internal references to papers in this collection are given by author name without further specification.
2 For further discussion of the so-called 'problem' of Africa's languages, see Bamgbose (1991: 2–9).
3 One of us (Furniss) works on a majority language, Hausa; the other (Fardon) has researched on a minority language, Chamba Daka. In this respect, at least, our personal biases may cancel out one another.
4 Our introduction is indebted to two recent reviews of anthropology, politics and language (Parkin 1984; Grillo 1989). Very full references to recent debates in anthropology can be found in the bibliographies to these articles. For recent discussions of African language policy we have profited especially from two collections: Ngalasso and Ricard 1986; Emenanjo 1990. We regret being unable to cite many of the contributions to the Nigerian debate itemized in the bibliography to the latter collection, but the most recent of these are not available to us in London.
5 David Laitin's recent, wide-ranging synthesis of writings on language policy in Africa, has attempted to deal evenhandedly with what he dubs micro dynamics and macro forces affecting language use. Despite the best endeavours of this exemplary work, he finds it impossible to retain a nuanced appreciation of the diversity of language practices when he comes to discuss language policy. The very act of naming languages (Swahili, Hausa, English, French . . .) tells against the plurality of language in use. The problem is akin to the virtual impossibility of discussing ethnicity other than in terms of labels that are 'tribal'. The resources of available terms in language fail to match the conceptual complexity that would be required.
6 As Fairhead argues, understanding patterns of discursive practice involves understanding also their insertion into local technological and political debates.
7 This striking formulation is Paul Richards', to whom a special note of gratitude is owed more generally for his invitation to present this paper for discussion at a seminar of the Department of Anthropology, University College London, from which we derived much intellectual stimulation and clarification.
8 This tendency has been notably resisted by Elugbe (1990: 13–14); but he shares the aspiration to a national language although he envisages this occurring over a period measured in centuries (1990: 17).
9 The contributors to the Emenanjo volume (1990) differ widely in their preferences, from Sofunke who proposes Igala (an idea not endorsed by the editor's introduction) to Rotimi Badejo who favours the early introduction of English to schools' curricula as a counterweight to the advantage that otherwise accrues to Nigerians who speak English as a first language. However, none of the contributors explicitly rejects the logic of the case for a single national language at some time in the future.

10 The sub-title is borrowed from Grillo (1989: 8).
11 Following Foucault's example in *The Order of Things* we might have begun by examining the idea of the 'list' which often accompanies the language map but may appear separately. The map orders languages in two-dimensional space, so that extension seems crucial; the list is necessarily ordinal, so that assessment of the numbers of speakers becomes the crucial organizing principle. The list is particularly important in discussions of the relative numbers of people speaking a major language as a 'mother tongue' and as a 'lingua franca'. However, we are reminded by the Derives that frequency of usage is as significant as numbers of speakers in assessing the range of lingua francas (Derive and Derive 1986: 45). Lists of languages have been particularly important in the discussion of the, roughly, 400 languages spoken within Nigeria (discussed below).
12 As Wim van Binsbergen remarked at our meeting, our discussion of cartography as a trope refers to the conventional, two-dimensional maps in common circulation and might be complicated by consideration of three-dimensional maps capable of encoding greater complexity and co-territoriality. We restrict our attention to conventional, two-dimensional maps on the grounds that more complex maps have not so far featured sufficiently commonly to be generalized as a rhetorical, and conceptual, trope.
13 The history of Sudan is cautionary in this respect (see Miller 1986); the imposition of Arabic caused English to become a political cause for southerners. The example warns us to be cautious of assuming that political claims will always be articulated around the right to use African languages in public affairs. The political importance of English in the anglophone Cameroon is another case in point. The expansion of Sango in Zaïre (at least according to Diki-Kidiri's account, 1986) seems to show the value of the state recognizing and encouraging changes already under way. The national language of the Central African Republic emerged independently of specific sponsorship.
For all the practical problems it faces, at least if it is given the necessary resources and time to settle down, the Nigerian 6-3-3-4 programme (the numbers refer to years of primary, junior secondary, senior secondary and tertiary education), with an explicit commitment to pluralism, may represent a Government sponsored recognition of multilingualism that avoids the worst aspects of over-hasty engineering (see the National Policy on Education of 1977 and 1981, and such supporting literature as the 'Guidelines' and 'Newsletter' of the 6-3-3-4 committee). However, the very explicitness of the way that relations between languages are specified in the Nigerian case necessarily invites some contention. In addition to Bamgbose and Elugbe, see Akinnaso (1989; 1991) for the Nigerian language situation and policy.
14 Ngalasso suggests that intellectuals' and politicians' accounts of 'authenticity' may be unconvincing to rural people who feel that the proponents of such a view are not only living in comparatively splendid (if 'unauthentic') style but also appropriating the signs of authenticity from the villages they have left (Ngalasso 1986: 25-6).
15 Apart from the three major lingua francas (four when Pidgin is included), and English, it has been calculated (from estimated 1986 population figures) that twelve or thirteen other Nigerian languages have over a million speakers, while a further twenty-four languages have more than a hundred thousand speakers (Jibril 1990). This leaves roughly 360 languages with fewer than a

hundred thousand speakers. The National Policy on Education sees a role for instruction in some of the minor languages (at least those dominant in local Government areas) at the levels of primary and junior secondary school. Nigerian children are to learn at least one national language (one of the *Wazobia* languages: Hausa, Igbo, Yoruba) other than their mother tongue. For the sixty-four million mother tongue speakers of a national language, this means acquiring two national languages.

16 See Okwudishu (1990) for a survey of the language situation in Gongola State (now divided into Adamawa and Taraba States).

REFERENCES

Akinnaso, F. N. (1989) 'One nation, four hundred languages: unity and diversity in Nigeria's language policy', *Language Problems and Language Planning*, 13(2): 133–46.
—— (1991) 'On the mother tongue education policy in Nigeria', *Educational Review*, 43(1): 89–106.
Appadurai, A. (1990) 'Disjuncture and difference in the cultural global economy', *Theory, Culture and Society* 7(2–3): 295–310.
Asad, T. (1986) 'The concept of cultural translation in British social anthropology', in J. Clifford and G. E. Marcus (eds.) *Writing Culture: the Poetics and Politics of Ethnography*, Berkeley: University of California Press.
Bamgbose, A. (1991) *Language and the Nation: the Language Question in Sub-Saharan Africa*, Edinburgh: Edinburgh University Press for the International African Institute.
Bourdieu, P. (1986) (originally 1979) *Distinction: a Social Critique of the Judgement of Taste*, trans. R. Nice, London: Routledge.
Burnham, P. (1991) 'L'ethnie, la religion et l'État: le rôle des Peules dans la vie politique et sociale du Nord-Cameroun', *Journal des africanistes*, 61: 73–102.
Chinweizu, Onwuchekwa, J. and Ihecheckwu M. (1985) *Toward the Decolonization of African Literature: African Fiction and Poetry and their Critics*, London: Kegan Paul International. (First published in Nigeria in 1980 by Fourth Dimension Publishers.)
Chumbow, B. S. (1990) 'The place of the mother tongue in the national policy of education', in E. N. Emenanjo (ed.) *Multilingualism, Minority Languages and Language Policy in Nigeria*, Agbor: Central Books Ltd. in collaboration with the Linguistic Association of Nigeria.
Croll, E. and Parkin, D. (1992) 'Cultural understandings and the environment', in E. Croll and D. Parkin (eds.) *Bush Base: Forest Farm. Culture, Environment and Development*, London: Routledge.
Derive, J. and M. J. (1986) 'Francophonie et pratique linguistique en Côte d'Ivoire', in N. M. Ngalasso and A. Ricard (eds.) *Des langues et des états, Politique Africaine* 23, Paris: Karthala.
Diki-Kidiri, M. (1986) 'Le sango dans la formation de la nation centrafricaine', in N. M. Ngalasso and A. Ricard (eds.) *Des langues et des états, Politique Africaine* 23, Paris: Karthala.
Ekeh, P. B. (1990) 'Social anthropology and two contrasting uses of tribalism in Africa', *Comparative Studies in Society and History* 32(4): 660–700.
Elugbe, B. (1990) 'National language and national development', in E. N.

Emenanjo (ed.) *Multilingualism, Minority Languages and Language Policy in Nigeria*, Agbor: Central Books Ltd. in collaboration with the Linguistic Association of Nigeria.

Emenanjo, E. N. (ed.) (1990) *Multilingualism, Minority Languages and Language Policy in Nigeria*, Agbor: Central Books Ltd. in collaboration with the Linguistic Association of Nigeria.

Federal Republic of Nigeria (1977) *National Policy on Education* (revised 1981), Yola: Educational Resource Centre.

Foucault, M. (1970) (originally 1966) *The Order of Things: an Archaeology of the Human Sciences*, trans. Alan Sheridan, London: Tavistock.

Gellner, E. (1970) (originally 1961) 'Concepts and society', reprinted in B. R. Wilson (ed.) *Rationality*, Oxford: Blackwell.

Grillo, R. (ed.) (1989a) *Social Anthropology and the Politics of Language*, Sociological Review Monograph 36, London: Routledge.

—— (1989b) 'Anthropology, language and politics', in R. Grillo (ed.) *Social Anthropology and the Politics of Language*, Sociological Review Monograph 36, London: Routledge.

Hobart, M. (ed.) (1993) *An Anthropological Critique of Development: the Growth of Ignorance*, London: Routledge.

Hountondji, P. (1977) *Sur la 'philosophie africaine': critique de l'ethnophilosophie*, Paris: François Maspero, trans. 1983 as *African Philosophy: Myth and Reality* by H. Evans and J. Rée, London: Hutchinson University Library for Africa.

Implementation Committee for the National Policy on Education (1988) *Guidelines for the Implementation of the 6–3–3–4 Education System*, Lagos: Federal Ministry of Education.

—— (1988) *Newsletter* 1(1), Lagos: Implementation Committee.

Jibril, M. (1990) 'Minority languages and lingua francas in Nigerian education', in E. N. Emenanjo (ed.) *Multilingualism, Minority Languages and Language Policy in Nigeria*, Agbor: Central Books Ltd. in collaboration with the Linguistic Association of Nigeria.

July, R. W. (1987) *An African Voice: the Role of the Humanities in African Independence*, Durham: Duke University Press.

Laitin, D. D. (1992) *Language Repertoires and State Construction in Africa*, Cambridge: Cambridge University Press (Cambridge studies in comparative politics).

Miller, C. (1986) 'Langues et intégration nationale au Soudan', in N. M. Ngalasso and A. Ricard (eds.), *Des langues et des états, Politique Africaine* 23, Paris: Karthala.

Mudimbe, V. Y. (1988) *The Invention of Africa: Gnosis, Philosophy, and the Order of Knowledge*, Bloomington: Indiana University Press.

Mytton, G. (1983) *Mass Communication in Africa*, London: Edward Arnold.

Ngalasso, M. M. and Ricard A. (eds.) (1986) *Des langues et des états, Politique Africaine* 23, Paris: Karthala.

Ngalasso, M. M. (1986) 'État des langues et langues de l'État au Zaïre', in N. M. Ngalasso and A. Ricard (eds.) *Des langues et des états, Politique Africaine* 23, Paris: Karthala.

Ngũgĩ wa Thiong'o (1986) *Decolonising the Mind: the Politics of Language in African Literature*, London: James Currey.

Okpewho, I. (1988) 'African poetry: the modern writer and the oral tradition',

in E. D. Jones, E. Palmer and M. Jones (eds.) *Oral and Written Poetry, African Literature Today* 16, London: James Currey.
Okwudishu, A. U. (1990) 'Plurilingualism in Gongola State: a preliminary report', in E. N. Emenanjo (ed.) *Multilingualism, Minority Languages and Language Policy in Nigeria*, Agbor: Central Books Ltd. in collaboration with the Linguistic Association of Nigeria.
Parkin, D. (1975) 'The rhetoric of responsibility: bureaucratic communications in a Kenya farming area', in M. Bloch (ed.) *Political Language and Oratory in Traditional Society*, London: Academic Press.
—— (1984) 'Political language', *Annual Review of Anthropology* 13: 345–65.
Pottier, J. (1989) '"Three's a crowd": knowledge, ignorance and power in the context of urban agriculture in Rwanda', *Africa* 59(4): 461–77.
Richards, P. (1985) *Indigenous Agricultural Revolution: Ecology and Food Production in West Africa*, London: Hutchinson.
Rotimi, B. P. (1990) 'Asymmetrical bilingualism and national language policy', in E. N. Emenanjo (ed.) *Multilingualism, Minority Languages and Language Policy in Nigeria*, Agbor: Central Books Ltd. in collaboration with the Linguistic Association of Nigeria.
Said, E. (1978) *Orientalism*, London: Routledge and Kegan Paul.
Sofunke, B. (1990) 'National language policy for democratic Nigeria', in E. N. Emenanjo (ed.) *Multilingualism, Minority Languages and Language Policy in Nigeria*, Agbor: Central Books Ltd. in collaboration with the Linguistic Association of Nigeria.
Soyinka, W. (1976) *Myth, Literature and the African World*, Cambridge: Cambridge University Press.
Treffgarne, C. (1975) *The Role of English and French as Languages of Communication between Anglophone and Francophone West African States*, Africa Educational Trust research project January 1973–June 1974, London: Africa Educational Trust.
UNESCO (1981) *La définition d'une stratégie relative à la promotion des langues africaines: documents de la réunion d'experts qui a lieu à Conakry (Guinée) 21–25 septembre 1981*, UNESCO.

Part I
West Africa

Bamgbose's opening paper discusses the broad issues of national language policy in pluralist states. Moving from this wide-ranging perspective, the subsequent papers focus on increasingly more local contexts in West Africa – Fyle on an aspect of language policy in Sierra Leone, Igué and N'Ouéni on national policy and practice in the Republic of Bénin, Elugbe on experience of initiatives at the level of constituent states within the Federal Republic of Nigeria, and Hansford on NGO and church activity in a part of Ghana.

Bamgbose's paper criticizes current thinking about language policy on two fronts: widespread myths about multilingualism, and present definitions of development. He notes that the overwhelming majority of contemporary nation states are multilingual and that the tyranny of 'one' – one nation, one language, one people – has influenced the policy aspirations of states whose national reality has been quite different. It is an inescapable fact that national development must take place in the context of linguistic and ethnic heterogeneity. Multilingualism is, as Bamgbose indicates, not necessarily divisive, nor is it necessarily disadvantageous to the citizen. He makes the point, made also by other contributors, that participation in development entails language competence. Lingua francas and local languages are essential components of any sustainable development effort. Bamgbose goes further to criticize the prevailing narrow definition of 'development'. In his view, material and technical development must be linked to social and cultural development, and in that context he places particular emphasis on self-reliance, 'intellectual aid as a surer basis of development in preference to material aid', the domestication of technology, and popular participation.

The paper by Fyle on Sierra Leone discusses the way in which Krio, a widely used lingua franca, impinges minimally on the formulation of state language policy which is predicated on national representation for the major population groups – Mende and Temne. Fyle's paper points to the importance of understanding actual patterns of language use rather than the geo-political balances that go to make up the state. The short paper by Igué and N'Ouéni provides, for Francophone Africa in the shape of the Republic of Bénin, an illustration of the way in which, with the coming to power of Kerekou in 1972, a new rhetoric of self-reliance and revaluation of indigenous culture promised great things for the languages of Bénin. New institutions were to be founded and new prescriptions put forward which would promote Béninois languages until they equalled French. After twenty years, according to N'Ouéni, little seems to have changed. French remains paramount, and the majority of the population, lacking French, remain largely excluded from participation in national life and economic development.

Elugbe and Hansford (Nigeria and Ghana respectively) present papers which trace in detail initiatives to develop minority languages that have foundered on the rocks of educational practice. Local initiatives work in fits and starts, local enthusiasms have difficulty in engendering a self-sustaining momentum without long term insertion into the school systems, and both authors appeal for either positive support or, at the very least, the removal of hindrances put, by the state, in the way of local initiatives.

2 Pride and prejudice in multilingualism and development

Ayo Bamgbose

The title of Jane Austen's novel *Pride and Prejudice* is perhaps not inappropriate as a caption for a discussion of the myths that surround multilingualism and its role in national integration and development. There is a simple equation such that prejudice in multilingualism corresponds to pride in monolingualism and vice versa.

The role of language as a means of communication and social interaction, a medium of education, and a vehicle for cultural expression is fairly well-known. In any nation state, language is also often regarded as a symbol of nationality. This, in turn, is based on the equally well-known function of language as a solidarity marker. A speech community has its 'in-group' language that marks it off from other speech communities. This same speech community may have an 'out-group' language that it shares with a wider group. Alternatively, the solidarity function of a language may be restricted to special purposes, such as religion. In all these cases, language marks a person as belonging to a group which may vary from a village community or a religious sect, to an ethnic group or the entire nation.

MYTHS ABOUT LANGUAGE AND NATIONAL INTEGRATION

The perceived solidarity function of language has led to the development of two complementary myths: the first is that having several languages in a country (multilingualism) always divides: the other is that having only one language (monolingualism) always unites, hence, national integration is believed to be possible only through one national or official language.

Since most African countries are multilingual, the myth of linguistic divisiveness is often associated with African languages. Hence, it has been suggested that 'differences between indigenous languages keep the people apart, perpetuate ethnic hostilities, weaken national loyalties and increase the danger of separatist sentiment' (Schwarz 1965: 39). African languages are, therefore, mainly seen as sources of potential instability and, consequently, a threat to the well-being of the nation state.

Contrary to the above assertion, multilingualism is not necessarily a barrier to national unity and integration. In fact, in the African situation, it is questionable who is the better integrated citizen, 'he who speaks only one language, preferably the official language, or he who is able to manipulate several languages which are used for communication in the country' (Kashoki 1982: 24). It is also not the case that ethnic division can always be equated with linguistic division. In Nigeria, for example, Hausa is spoken by several ethnic groups, while the Edo ethnic group speaks several languages belonging to the Edoid language family.

Conflicts between groups of people within a country rarely have anything to do with linguistic differences. As Le Page (1964: 16) has rightly observed, 'Language is like skin colour in that it is an easily identifiable badge for those who wish to form a gang or fight against another gang; the reasons for the gang warfare lie deeper than either language or colour'. Fishman (1968a: 45) too has made the important observation that language differences need not be divisive, since both divisiveness and unification are ideologized positions: minor differences can be magnified, just as major ones can be minimized.

An example of differences being played down can be seen in the way some lingua francas are emerging in Africa. Because of the utility of such languages as Akan in Ghana, Wolof in Senegal, Hausa in Northern Nigeria, Lingala in Zaire, not to talk of the more widely-spoken Swahili in Eastern Africa, speakers of different languages are embracing them as second languages. Another example is the way differences in dialects which have been magnified in the past almost to the point of language status are now played down considerably (e.g. Twi and Fante which are now seen simply as dialects of Akan; these two speech forms were listed as separate languages in the list of nine languages approved for education in post-Independence Ghana). The converse of this is that differences between closely-related languages which have largely been ignored in the past may suddenly assume a major dimension. For example, the Efik-Ibibio dialect cluster in Nigeria has for years been accepted as practically one language with Efik as the literary form of the language. This position is now being reversed and Ibibio is more and more being emphasized as a separate language with its own orthography. This trend is likely to be intensified with the creation of a new state, Akwa-Ibom, in 1987 in which the Ibibio form the dominant group.

Some of the real causes of divisiveness in African countries have nothing to do with language. They include exploitation of ethnicity by the élite in order to gain political or economic advantage, the problem of sharing scarce resources with the inevitable competition (e.g. for jobs, positions, facilities, etc.), uneven development, and sometimes external instigation based on nationalistic, ideological or religious motives. In Nigeria, for instance, the causes of our conflicts have to do with power-sharing, particularly among the élite, and access to and control of the national wealth and the economy. Dissatisfaction with political, economic, educational, or social conditions is often expressed in ethnic terms, particularly by the self-appointed leaders of the group. It is then that one hears that such and such an ethnic group is being discriminated against in terms of jobs, amenities, educational facilities, etc. In my view, a more pernicious kind of discrimination is 'statism' which effectively disenfranchises persons that 'belong' to another state. As is well-known, such Nigerians are often subjected to double taxation, differential tuition fees, and discrimination in employment and admission to schools.

The second myth espouses and exaggerates the importance of a common language in that it assumes that national unity is not possible unless a country has a single common language. This position is often forcefully stated in such statements as 'Language is a nation's most obvious and most important attribute. There is no such thing as a nation without a common linguistic basis' (Isayev 1977: 192). 'A people without a language of its own is only half a nation. A nation should guard its language more than its territories – 'tis a surer barrier, a more important frontier than fortress or river' (attributed to Thomas Davies and quoted in Fishman (1973: 49)).

The underlying assumption in the above position is that nationhood also involves linguistic unity. Experience, however, shows that there are viable nations which are multilingual and yet get on very well while operating in two or more languages, with none of them common to the entire populace. Canada operates with English and French, Switzerland operates with French, German and Italian. Hence, it is true that a common language 'is not a necessary condition for a unified state and that one or more major language groups can coexist in a system with minimal conflict between them' (Kelman 1971: 34). Even in many countries that have a so-called common language, there are minority groups that speak other languages and have to become bilingual, or else make use of the services of those who are bilingual in the official language and their own language. This situation cannot be better put than Le Page does as follows:

> It might be thought self-evident that for effective government and administration of law the rulers, the judges and the ruled should form

one homogeneous linguistic community. From a vantage point in Western Europe or North America it might appear as if democracy could not possibly work unless these conditions were satisfied; with an elected government passing laws in a language which the people can understand, so that they can discuss them; with newspapers reporting discussion, and politicians addressing the people directly in their own language either face to face or through the medium of broadcasting and television; with the judges and lawyers discussing the law in the same language in which the plaintiff and defendant instruct their counsel. But if these are the conditions for democracy to flourish, then it must be admitted that democracy has very rarely had a chance to flourish because these conditions have rarely existed in history and exist in very few parts of the world today. Even in a comparatively small country like Britain, the Welsh-speaking Welsh and the Gaelic-speaking Scots . . . need bilingual intermediaries between themselves and the government and for dealings in the law.

(Le Page 1964: 15)

In Africa, it seems that we are obsessed with the number 'one'. Not only must we have *one* national language, we must also have a *one*-party system. The mistaken belief is that in such oneness of language or party we would achieve socio-cultural cohesion and political unity in our multi-ethnic, multilingual, and multicultural societies (Kashoki 1982: 21). Some will even go further to advocate a supra-national language instead of the assumed explosive alternative of evolving a national language; and the favourite candidate for this role, it has been suggested, should be Swahili (Soyinka 1977). In their preoccupation with one language, others often advocate the development of a composite language comprising elements of the country's languages. Suffice it to say that only those who are ignorant of the characteristics of language and the science of language will support such a proposal. Experts in language know very well that such a hybrid language is virtually impossible to evolve, and, if formed, cannot cope with the complex demands made on natural languages. For an example of such an artificial language proposed for Nigeria, see Bamgbose (1985: 100–1).

While it must be conceded that a common language is a potentially unifying force, the point must be made that other factors conducive to unity must be present before a common language can unify. Political, economic, educational and social arrangements must be such that the different groups in the polity feel a sense of belonging and a conviction that their needs and aspirations are being met; see Duggal (1981: 48).

MYTHS ABOUT LANGUAGE AND NATIONAL DEVELOPMENT

National development is usually described in terms of economic growth, attainment of economic targets, growth rate, increase in Gross National Product (GNP) or Gross Domestic Product (GDP), rise in *per capita* income, etc. It is, of course, possible to make a detailed breakdown of such indicators of national development as Allardt (1973: 268–71) has done in terms of societal allocations, embracing allocations to different sectors of the economy (industry, defence, education, technology, administration, communication, etc.); societal goals, embracing economic prosperity and growth as expressed in *per capita* and employment rates, political efficiency, political participation and modernization efforts; and individual goals, embracing level of welfare as expressed in private consumption and housing, life expectancy, freedom to choose jobs or belong to organizations. Whichever way this concept of national development is amplified, it is to be considered a narrow one in the sense that it equates national development with socio-economic development.

Even assuming the narrow conception of national development, the question arises about the role of language in socio-economic development. The assumption is that language does have a role to play, but the nature of that role is hardly spelt out. One major problem, however, to which attention has been drawn is the relationship between linguistic heterogeneity and development. Linguistically heterogeneous states are said to be characterized by low or very low *per capita* GNP and are usually economically underdeveloped, while linguistically homogeneous states have a high or medium *per capita* GNP and are relatively economically well-developed (Banks and Textor 1963). Fishman (1968b), making use of the Banks and Textor cross-polity files, has shown that there is no necessary correlation between linguistic heterogeneity and low economic status and vice versa. Of the 114 countries examined, fifty-two are linguistically homogeneous, while sixty-two are heterogeneous. Of the fifty-two homogeneous countries, twenty-five (or about 50 per cent) have low or very low *per capita* GNP, while forty-seven of the sixty-two heterogeneous countries (about 75 per cent) have low or very low *per capita* GNP. All the countries in Africa, with the exception of South Africa, belong to the category of low or very low *per capita* GNP; and these include not only the linguistically homogeneous Arab countries of North Africa, but also homogeneous black countries such as Burundi, Rwanda, Somalia and Madagascar. Clearly this evidence suggests that there must be other variables at work. Whatever may be responsible for the economic plight of the poorer countries, the crucial variable cannot possibly be language.

In spite of the above, heterogeneity continues to be viewed as a deficiency or disadvantage. As Pool (1972: 214) has put it, 'it is said that language diversity slows down economic development, by, for example, breaking occupational mobility, reducing the number of people available for mobilization into the modern sector of the economy, decreasing efficiency and preventing the diffusion of innovative techniques'. While rejecting a correlation between linguistic heterogeneity and underdevelopment, even Fishman (1968b: 63) concluded that sectionalism and the presence of politically unassimilated minorities are two distinguishing characteristics of linguistic heterogeneity, and obviously, these would be seen as impediments to national integration and national development.

Homogeneity of modern states, whether linguistic or ethnic, is a myth. In a survey of 132 states, Connor (1972: 320) found only twelve (9.1 per cent) that can be described as ethnically homogeneous. An additional twenty-five states (18.9 per cent) contain an ethnic group which accounts for 90 per cent of the state's population, and in a further twenty-five states, the largest element constitutes between 75 per cent and 89 per cent of the total population, and in thirty-nine states (29.5 per cent), the largest group does not even account for half the population of the state. Taking a cut-off point of 90 per cent to determine homogeneity, the situation is that, by stretching the meaning of homogeneity, not more than 28 per cent of all the states can be said to be homogeneous. The norm, therefore, for contemporary states is heterogeneity which becomes more striking still when ethnic diversity within states is taken into consideration. For instance, Connor found that the number of distinct ethnic groups in some states runs into hundreds and that in as many as fifty-three states (40 per cent of the total number of states), there are at least five different units into which the population can be divided. National development, even when narrowly defined as socio-economic development, therefore has to take place largely in the context of linguistic and ethnic heterogeneity.

THE ROLE OF LANGUAGE IN DEVELOPMENT

There are at least two areas in which language is crucial to national development, even in its restricted definition as socio-economic development: literacy and communication. There is an obvious link between literacy and development. For instance, the world's poorest countries are also the countries with the highest rates of illiteracy. Since literacy liberates untapped human potential and leads to increased productivity and better living conditions, it is not surprising that countries with the highest rates of literacy are also the most economically advanced. Similarly, mass communication with its emphasis on flow of information can provide a suitable climate for national development.

It is mistaken, however, to equate national development with socio-economic development. A wider and more satisfactory conception of national development is that which sees it as total human development. In this model of development, the emphasis is on a full realization of the human potential and a maximum utilization of the nation's resources for the benefit of all.

The primacy of man as the source of all economic development is a point which Schumacher (1973) has effectively made. It is man, he says, who provides the primary resources and 'the key factor of all economic development comes out of the mind of man'. However, a crucial factor in this creativity is education whose essence is the transmission of values. Although poverty may be traced to material factors such as lack of natural wealth, capital or infrastructure, those factors are entirely secondary. The primary causes of poverty are really deficiencies in education, organization and discipline. It is these, rather than material goods that can stimulate development, as can be shown by the economic miracles achieved by countries without material resources but with the crucial factors of education, organization and discipline intact. Hence, development cannot be created, bought, ordered, or transferred. The crucial factors have to become a property of not just a few, but of the whole society.

The conclusion by Schumacher which is most relevant for our purpose is that looking at development in quantitative terms such as GNP, investment and savings is not really useful for developing countries:

> Economic development is something much wider and deeper than economics, let alone econometrics. Its roots lie outside the economic sphere, in education, organization, discipline, and beyond that, in political independence and a national consciousness of self-reliance .... It can succeed only if it is carried forward as a broad, popular 'movement of reconstruction' with primary emphasis on the full utilization of the drive, enthusiasm, intelligence, and labour power of everyone.
>
> (Schumacher 1973: 190–1)

To do otherwise is to follow a course that must lead to failure.

The man-centredness and human face of development are now increasingly accepted as the correct path to development. In the words of former President Julius Nyerere of Tanzania:

> In the Third World we talk a great deal about economic development,

about expanding the number of goods and services, and the capacity to produce them. But the goods are needed to serve men; services are required to make the lives of men more easeful as well as more fruitful. Political, social, and economic organization is needed to enlarge the freedom and dignity of men. Always we come back to Man – to Liberated Man – as the purpose of activity, the purpose of development. So development is for man, by Man and of Man.

(Excerpt from a talk given at the International Conference on Adult Education, Dar-es-Salaam, 21 June 1976, and reproduced as a preface in Bataille (1976))

The Declaration of Persepolis which emerged from the International Symposium for Literacy held at Persepolis, Iran from 3–8 September 1975 also came out strongly in favour of man-based development in declaring that literacy is not merely acquiring the skills of reading, writing and arithmetic 'but a contribution to the liberation of man and his full development' (Bataille 1976: 273–4). It should stimulate initiative, encourage participation with a view to achieving 'authentic human development' (ibid.).

Inspired by Schumacher, Ansre (1976) has proposed four elements relevant to an overall national development: economic development, politico-judicial development, socio-cultural development and intellectual and educational development. In all this, he claims that the role of language is crucial since in wealth-getting and wealth-sharing, a minority official language cannot produce the best results. At best, it will only produce a wealthy few. On the other hand, a language shared by many should ensure greater productivity and fairer distribution. Similarly, law is only just and meaningful if the language in which it is couched is accessible to all. Socio-cultural development obviously points to indigenous languages, while even intellectual and educational development needs to have its roots in the language of the community.

A summary of the elements that should go into national development as defined in a broader sense include:

1 Integrated development in which economic development is linked to social and cultural development, and the combination of all three is designed to improve the condition of man in society.
2 Self-reliance as the basis of all development instead of mass importation of expertise.
3 Intellectual aid as a surer basis of development in preference to material aid.
4 Technology whenever transferred to be domesticated and in-

digenized to conform with the socio-cultural norms and conditions of the country.
5 Mass participation and grassroots involvement in order to ensure widespread and genuine development.

In the light of an examination of national development in its narrow and broad senses, we are now in a position to consider the role of language. As usual, two models present themselves: the model of use of official languages, usually Languages of Wider Communication (LWCs) and the model of use of indigenous languages.

Given that the development effort aims to reach the masses, it is obvious that the language to be used in literacy and communication, for example, must be one that is capable of reaching a large proportion of the population. In literacy education, the pride of place has usually belonged to indigenous languages. Earlier attempts to use foreign official languages, such as French in Mali (Dumont 1973) or English for tobacco growers in Western Nigeria, ended in dismal failure. Among the African countries that have a vigorous programme of literacy in African languages are Mali, Togo, Somalia, Tanzania, Nigeria, Guinea, Niger, Burundi and Zambia. The advantages of such media are that cultural forms and knowledge of cultural values are better learnt and transmitted, the positive attitude to language encourages greater motivation to learn, the course of instruction is psychologically more adequate as the concepts are already familiar, and the choice of language is in consonance with cultural and political attitudes (UNESCO 1976: 23–4).

Similarly, in the area of mass communication the undoubted advantages that can be achieved through a greater flow of information necessarily call for an intensification of the use of African languages in the media. Unfortunately, communication specialists tend to play down the role of such languages. For example Schramm (1964: 101–2) sees Africa as 'a veritable crazy quilt of languages' the use of which inevitably makes for small audiences. In contrast, he suggests that the use of Spanish in Latin America and Portuguese in Brazil may have facilitated the growth of the press, while in India the use of regional and tribal languages increases the problems of national broadcasting and exchange of information. Similarly, Weiner (1967: 192) sees multiplicity of languages as a barrier to communication, and particularly the development of Indian tribal languages as divisive, since literacy leads to a deepening of divisions in terms of reading materials. The familiar bogey of linguistic heterogeneity and its alleged disadvantages are seen at work here again. The point which is often ignored is that the logic of mass participation points to not less, but increased, use of the many languages available in a country in order to reach the widest possible segment of the community. The conclusion which seems inevitable in the situation of most developing countries is that a multilingual policy is the only viable avenue for development. African languages will have well-defined roles in education, culture and mass communication without prejudice to the complementary role of LWCs. But what this means is that monolingualism is not sufficient. Even Fishman who had earlier associated a LWC with efficiency now seems to see the drawback of a position that equates efficiency with monolingualism; for not only does he debunk the ludicrous idea that 'English improves the crops, raises the gross national product, avoids drought and earthquakes, and improves television' (Fishman 1978: 45), he now affirms that 'In a multilingual world it is obviously more efficient and rational to be multilingual than not' (1978: 47).

Foreign ideas, concepts and technology will undoubtedly be imported in a foreign language, but such concepts must be transmitted to the masses in a language that they can understand. The economic miracle achieved by countries such as Japan is not based on a widespread dissemination of English, rather it is a result of the domestication of foreign technology in Japanese, and the translation of the productive processes into terms that the ordinary factory hand can understand.

REFERENCES

Allardt, E. (1973) 'Individual needs, social structures and indicators of national development', in S.N. Eisenstadt and S. Rokkan (eds.) *Building States and Nations*, vol. 1, Beverly Hills: Sage Publications.
Ansre, G. (1976) 'National development and language', paper given at the Twelfth West African Languages Congress, mimeo.
Bamgbose, A. (1985) 'Language and nation-building', *Review of English and Literary Studies* 2, 2: 95–108.
Banks, A. and Textor, R.B. (1963) *A Cross-Polity Survey*, Cambridge Mass: M.I.T. Press.
Bataille, L. (ed.) (1976) *A Turning Point for Literacy*, Oxford: Pergamon Press.
Connor, W. (1972) 'Nation building or nation destroying?' *World Politics* 24: 319–50.
Duggal, N.K. (ed.) (1981) *Toward a Language Policy for Namibia*, Lusaka: United Nations Institute for Namibia.
Dumont, B. (1973) *Functional Literacy in Mali: Training for Development*, Paris: UNESCO Press.
Fishman J. (1968a) 'Nationality-nationalism and nation-nationalism', in J. Fishman, C. Ferguson and J. DasGupta (eds.) *Language Problems of Developing Nations*, New York: John Wiley and Sons.
—— (1968b) 'Some contrasts between linguistically homogeneous and

linguistically heterogeneous states', in J. Fishman, C. Ferguson and J. DasGupta (eds.) *Language Problems of Developing Nations*, New York: John Wiley and Sons.

—— (1973) *Language and Nationalism*, Rowley Mass: Newbury House Publishers.

—— (1978) 'Positive bilingualism: some overlooked rationales and forefathers', in J.E. Alatis (ed.) *Georgetown University Round Table on Language and Linguistics 1978*, Washington D. C. : Georgetown University Press.

Isayev, M. I. (1977) *National Languages in the USSR: Problems and Solutions*, Moscow: Progress Publications.

Kashoki, M. (1982) 'Language policies and practices in independent black Africa: trends and prospects', in A. Olabimtan (ed.) *African Universities and the Development and Wider Use of African Languages*, Lagos: UNESCO.

Kelman, H. (1971) 'Language as an aid and a barrier to involvement in the national system', in J. Rubin and B. Jernudd (eds.) *Can Language Be Planned?*, Honolulu: University Press of Hawaii.

Le Page, R.B. (1964) *The National Language Question*, London: Oxford University Press.

Pool, J. (1972) 'National development and language diversity', in J. Fishman (ed.) *Advances in the Sociology of Language*, vol. 2, The Hague: Mouton.

Schramm, W. (1964) *Mass Media and National Development*, Stanford: Stanford University Press and Paris: UNESCO.

Schumacher, E. F. (1973) *Small is Beautiful*, London: Blond and Briggs.

Schwarz Jr., F. A. O. (1965) *Nigeria: The Tribes, the Nation or the Race – the Politics of Independence*, Cambridge, Mass: M.I.T. Press.

Soyinka, W. (1977) 'The scholar in African society', in A.V. Iwara and E. Mveng (eds.) *Second World Black and African Festival of Arts and Culture: Colloquium in Black Civilisation and Education*, vol. 1, Lagos: Federal Military Government of Nigeria.

UNESCO (1976) 'Literacy in the world since the 1965 Teheran Conference: shortcomings, achievement, tendencies', in L. Bataille (ed.) *A Turning Point for Literacy*, Oxford: Pergamon Press.

Weiner, Myron (1967) 'A note on communication and development in India', in D. Lerner and W. Schramm (eds.) *Communication and Change in the Developing Countries*, Honolulu: East West Center Press.

3 Official and unofficial attitudes and policy towards Krio as the main lingua franca in Sierra Leone

C. Magbaily Fyle

Sierra Leone, a small country on the west coast of West Africa with a population of some four million people, has some eighteen indigenous ethnic groups within its borders. The largest of these groups, the Temne and Mende, together comprise some 50 per cent of the total population. One of the smaller groups, the Krio, making up less than 2 per cent of the population, has historically and linguistically developed an importance out of all proportion to its numbers. The Krio language grew to become the main lingua franca in Sierra Leone. This essay proposes to explore the background to this development as a way of demonstrating the nature of official and unofficial attitudes and policy, both of the people and the government, to this language.

THE EMERGENCE OF KRIO SOCIETY AND LANGUAGE

Krio society developed out of a colonial situation where groups of captured slaves had been landed in the colony of Sierra Leone since the late eighteenth century. This involved, roughly speaking, two segments. The first is usually referred to in Sierra Leone historiography as the Settlers. There were three components of this segment. Firstly, the black poor, freed domestic slaves from England following the decision of Chief Justice Mansfield in England in 1772 that slavery was unknown to English law. The second component, the Nova Scotians, were former black American slaves who had obtained their freedom by fighting on the side of the British during the American War of Independence. Finally the Maroons were former slaves in Jamaica who had fought for their freedom and had consequently been sent packing through Nova Scotia to Sierra Leone (Fyfe 1962; Fyle and Fyle 1981). These Settlers had all become largely unfamiliar with African culture. They, particularly the black poor and Nova Scotians, had, like their parents and often grandparents before them, been born and bred in the western world and had imbibed western culture, albeit diluted with survivals from their African background. They had also come to absorb the prejudices of western society towards Africa, thus producing in them dismissive attitudes towards African culture generally.

The other segment is usually referred to in the literature as the Liberated Africans or recaptives. These were people who had been captured at various places in West Africa and sold as slaves, but were recaptured by the British navy trying to give effect to British anti-slave trade laws on the West African coast. They were all landed in Sierra Leone, conveniently chosen for the purpose of liberating these ex-slaves, as a British 'colony' already existed there, taken over by the British Crown in 1808. The recaptives came from a variety of African sub-cultures (Koelle, a German missionary working in the colony at the time, recorded some 200 of them).

There arose a need to communicate among this motley group. The communication pattern which emerged developed under the 'supervision' of the English authorities who insisted on their own values and language, which also quickly became the criteria for advancement. For those who could readily communicate with the colonial establishment, there was an increased chance of obtaining contracts and jobs as carpenters, masons, washer women, domestic servants and so on. These were the 'plum' jobs of the time in the early colony, carrying with them a consequent social prestige and status. For this reason therefore, English, and variants of it, which perforce developed among the Settlers and recaptives, became an 'official' means of contact. But most of the Settlers and recaptives had at best only a smattering of English, used when necessary. The Nova Scotians had elements of what became Black American English as spoken in the southern United States, mostly in the rural areas where the blacks were largely found. But the Nova Scotians were few to start with, as many of them died in an unfamiliar climate and environment. The individual languages of the recaptives, who comprised the vast majority, persisted but did not provide a means of inter-group communication. Against this background developed a language system using mostly English derived words, but having a syntax based almost entirely on the African languages from which it drew support (Fyle and Jones 1980).

As the language developed, most of the English derived words, and phrases coined from them, altered their meaning, some losing their original meanings and others adding new ones. This resulted often from the need to express concepts relating to the local environment and situation through words drawn from a language coming from a radically different culture and environment. For example, 'sweet' comes to mean 'tasty'; the word 'brook' in Krio means 'to launder', taken from the fact that laundry was done, in earlier times, almost entirely at the brook. The word 'line', apart from its usual meanings in English, developed an added sense as 'road'. This constituted a revision of the traditional local concept of a road. In pre-colonial times there were winding tracks in a forest environment, meant to protect the location of settlements from outsiders; with the new colonial system, roads tended to be constructed along straight lines, and so the new meaning. To use metaphorically the Krio phrase *i de na layn* means literally 'he is on the road', more properly 'in the forefront' or 'prominent'.

After English the next largest block of vocabulary in Krio came from Yoruba, as apparently the largest group of recaptives came from that ethnic group. Their enslavement was as a result of the Yoruba civil war following the collapse of the Oyo empire about the end of the eighteenth century. Many Yoruba who would have been transported across the Atlantic into slavery in the Americas, were thus recaptured and landed in Freetown. Names of a number of food items – *agidi* 'corn meal', *ɔbiata* 'a vegetable dish', *ɛba gari* 'meal made from grated cassava'; of cultural institutions – *awujɔ* 'a feast of charity', *kɔmɔjade* 'a naming ceremony', *ɔjeh* 'a cult association', are all from Yoruba. Thus while Krio has been regarded as one of the Creole languages and has hitherto been so called by the Krio themselves, recent research has shown that the name Krio used by people when speaking about the language, is the real name of the people, deriving from the Yoruba word *akiriyo*, 'a people who walk about from place to place', as the Krio were wont to do (Fyle 1992).

As this research has become known to leading Krio elements they have hotly contested this issue, insisting that the people are Creole and the language is Krio. Objecting to names which are thought to be demeaning and unattractive is not new among the Krio. Debates of this nature emerged early in this century when the appellation 'Creole' was becoming more commonly applied to these people. The most vocal of them resented the term 'Creole' stating that they were not Creole but Ibo, Popo, etc. Summarizing this debate, Wyse writes:

> In a 1927 discussion of Colonial Under-Secretary Ormsby-Gore's report of his visit to West Africa, in which he used the term Creole, there ensued what was almost a public debate. A. E. Tuboku-Metzger, elected Rural Area representative in the Legislative Council, and vice president of the local branch of the National Congress of British West Africa angrily retorted 'I am not a Creole. I dislike the expression

which is being misused in the colony when the word Sierra Leonean could be appropriately used...'

(1980: 12)

CURRENT SITUATION OF THE KRIO LANGUAGE

The need to communicate between a large number of ethnic groups led to the emergence of the Krio language and to Krio becoming the main lingua franca in Sierra Leone. To some extent, Mende in the south and Temne in the north of Sierra Leone can be said to operate as lingua francas among a few ethnic groups (Sesay 1984: 33). But this is very limited. Even in the north and south of Sierra Leone, Krio became the language connecting most people of different ethnic groups. Even in the remotest villages in rural Sierra Leone, it is not difficult to find people who speak Krio. Even where a local villager does not feel comfortable in the language, he will often understand statements in Krio.

Thus the Krio language has come to assume unofficial recognition as the main vehicle of communication in Sierra Leone, the language of the market place. It is used very widely by politicians when campaigning for elections outside their own mother tongue areas or where they do not speak the local language. Heads of State in Sierra Leone regularly make policy statements during tours to open public shows, health centres, bridges or other such facilities. Ninety per cent of such speeches are made in Krio which is perhaps seen as having less regional bias than any other language. In many schools in the main towns in the Provinces, and also in Freetown, Krio is used to introduce pupils to English, the official language in Sierra Leone. Phrases are rendered in Krio with the English equivalent simultaneously presented for repetition by children beginning to learn English. Thus it is often seen as 'essential' to know Krio to get into the modern educational sector for schooling.

Indeed Krio in Sierra Leone has long taken the place of West African English, as shown in the observation by Grieve, in the early independence period, that Krio is 'the language of the market place in those centres where people from many tribes mix, above all the language of education almost from its beginning' (quoted in Sesay 1984: 36).

In fact one of the most popular forms of entertainment in Sierra Leone today is drama in Krio. Although they are presented usually in Freetown, such performances are often taken to provincial towns with huge success. In 1989, the Sierra Leone Broadcasting Service launched a drama series in Krio entitled 'The Professionals'. It was so successful that it was illegally recorded and played in public transportation. 'The Professionals' began performing in public entertainments on a regular basis, being hired to perform by a variety of organizations. Krio is used increasingly in advertisements, street signs and notices throughout the country.

KRIO ATTITUDES TOWARDS THE KRIO LANGUAGE

We have earlier mentioned the issue of Krio people themselves decrying the use of the term Krio to apply to their ethnic group. There has developed an ambivalent attitude among the Krio towards their language, at once recognizing the prevalence and importance of their language in Sierra Leone, while at the same time regarding the language as somewhat inferior, this time to English. Thus Krio people still tend to speak English in more 'élite' situations where the occasion was felt to be too classy for Krio to be spoken. Even the poorly educated Krio would in such circumstances endeavour to speak English, no matter how badly, rather than talk Krio. In other circumstances, Krio people would place markedly English words and phrases very deliberately into the Krio they speak – saying 'bucket' for 'bokit', 'window' for 'winda', 'water' for 'wata'. In fact in some leading secondary schools, particularly in Freetown up to the present day, it is forbidden for the pupils to speak Krio during school hours, with specified punishment being meted out for such an 'offence', and this in schools headed by Krio principals. They are, however, equally discouraged from speaking Mende or Temne. But the opposition to speaking Krio is based partly on the conviction that Krio is a bastardized form of the English language, a 'patois' or, as some older Krio called it, 'broken English', which will present a worrying distortion of the English being learnt in school. It is never realized that learning English as a second language in the milieu of other indigenous languages will inevitably mean that influence from the indigenous languages will affect the English. The same is clearly true for learning any second language within an environment where the original indigenous language predominates (Robin 1970: 513–30; Mackey 1970: 554–84).

But equally contributory to this attitude to the Krio language among the Krio themselves was the inheritance from earlier colonial attitudes. Within the colonial situation, Africans were taught to believe that their culture, including language, was demeaning and backward; conversely, everything western, in this case English, was progressive and worthwhile. Thus to speak Krio, to pronounce English derived words with an African slant and intonation, was believed to be retrograde. Where the pronunciation of a few English words was known, near illiterate Krio speakers would jump at the chance to show that they too were 'with it'.

This attitude has therefore increased the rate at which new English words have entered the language.

NON-KRIO SIERRA LEONEANS AND THE KRIO LANGUAGE

People of other ethnic groups have acquired and related to the Krio language, and understanding their position will help us to appreciate the way in which the language has spread over the whole country. It will also help to clarify the issue of variants of the Krio language spoken in Sierra Leone.

Other ethnic groups began to acquire the Krio language through migrants moving into Freetown to seek job opportunities more readily available, within the colonial system, in the capital. This pattern of concentration of facilities in the capital, inherited from colonial rule, has continued into the post-colonial era. The best jobs, bright lights, and other social amenities, were mostly found in Freetown. In consequence the population of Freetown, at about half a million, is far above that of the second largest town, Bo, which has only about half that number. Since Krio was the language of Freetown, staying in Freetown became synonymous with speaking Krio. Thus, as people returned home to the Provinces, temporarily or permanently, they took this acquired language with them.

Associated with this migratory trend was the wardship system which served as a means whereby people from the Provinces were able to get their children to acquire western education in the Colony, where the best schools were situated. Such children were placed in Krio homes where they acquired Krio culture, the language being an integral part of this acquisition process. In fact some of them had their names changed to English/Krio names since the Krio believed, like their colonial overlords, that only such names were truly 'Christian' names. Thus the wardship system served as a means for people from the Provinces to come to Freetown and acquire from Krio homes that advancement – western values – which colonial rule had taught was necessary.

Over time there emerged two versions of the Krio language. Native speakers of Krio generally distinguish between 'Freetown Krio' and 'Up-line' Krio (the term 'up-line' being derived from the colonial expression 'up-country', the Provinces, along the railway line which was at that time the chief means of transportation for getting to parts of Sierra Leone outside Freetown). Native speakers use Freetown Krio, the variant of the heartland area, while 'up-line' Krio would be spoken by second language speakers, usually from the Provinces. But Freetown Krio is also spoken by non-native speakers who have lived for a long time in Freetown and by those who grew up in Krio homes.

On account of their colonial position, Krio people began to believe that they had acquired western values as a group and were superior to other, non-Krio, ethnic groups, who had not done so. This view mirrored and extended the way the English had thought about them.

By the 1950s, the political situation in Sierra Leone was changing. The departing colonial authorities decided to devolve political power in Sierra Leone on the majority, meaning the people from the Provinces. This went against what they had led the Krio to believe would be the post-colonial dispensation since the Krio, having acquired the desired western values, were better placed to take the best jobs, the prime social positions and consequently to inherit political power in Sierra Leone. Acting on that belief, the Krio leadership hotly contested the handing over of political power to non-Krio, meaning, in their view, people who had not yet acquired western values and therefore were unfit to inherit western style political roles.

Nobody at the time seemed quite to understand the background to this complex struggle, or to explain it fully. All that was clear was that the majority, meaning non-Krio people, would inherit political office and the colonial rulers were leaving. But the Krio opposition to political rule by people from the Provinces came to be seen by others as a general uppishness on the part of the Krio, arising from their view that the western aspects of their culture made them superior. Non-Krio peoples consequently reacted to this, and this reaction rubbed off on their attitude to the Krio language as well. There developed a marked desire on the part of non-Krio to speak their own local languages as opposed to Krio, even in situations of mixed ethnic company. The anti-Krio 'people and language' feeling was linked to a resurgence of ethnic identity associated with newly assumed political power.

But within a decade, as political competition came less and less to be seen along ethnic lines, this anti-Krio sentiment largely subsided. Slowly, the Krio language began to regain the position it had begun to hold before independence.

Prejudices among the Krio people also relate to Freetown Krio versus up-line Krio. Some of the phrases and expressions from up-line Krio which are entering the Freetown variant have become a source of worry to first language speakers. For example, where in Freetown Krio one would say *wetin yu bring fɔmi*, in up-line Krio the same expression is rendered *wetin yu sɛn fɔmi* 'what have you brought for me'. For the expression in Freetown Krio, *dɛn de mek am*, someone speaking up-line Krio would say *dɛn de pan mek am* 'it is being done/made'. Children of native Krio speakers have begun to acquire these expressions from up-line Krio through association with second language Krio speakers from the Provinces, largely in the Freetown schools where the latter are numerically predominant. The concern expressed by native Krio speakers on this issue relates to their idea that theirs is the 'pure' language while the other is a bastardized form. There is also a lingering fear among them that their language might ultimately disappear. Language is, of course, a living phenomenon and therefore subject to considerable change over time, nevertheless it is not uncommon to hear Krio speakers express concerns similar to those expressed by Englishmen as Americanisms enter their 'own' version of the English language.

OFFICIAL ATTITUDE AND POLICY

The prevalence of Krio however cannot negate the significance of other Sierra Leonean languages, particularly the two largest, Mende and Temne, as well as Limba, the third largest. There was for some time no clearcut policy or official position as regards indigenous languages in Sierra Leone. Since the late 1960s, it had been policy to utilize Krio, along with Mende, Temne and Limba for the daily evening news. The news in English was usually read at a separate time from the news in local languages. Other local languages were served by a 'weekly newsletter', summarizing the major events in that week's news.

There has been an obvious hesitation about acknowledging the use of Krio for official purposes. This is partly due to prejudice against the 'status' of the language, explained earlier, in relation to the small size but former predominance of the Krio ethnic group. But hesitation also comes from what any such acknowledgement would be saying about Mende, Temne and Limba. Limba, the third largest ethnic group, has acquired a more prominent position than it would otherwise have had because two successive presidents of the Republic have been Limba. President Momoh, it is often said, paid much greater attention than his predecessor to the Limba as a group in terms of filling offices and leading positions. Thus it has gradually become fashionable for Limba to identify themselves as such and to develop a pride in speaking their language publicly.

By 1977, the Sierra Leone Government began to consider more seriously the issue of using indigenous languages in the formal education system. An Indigenous Languages Education Program (ILEP) was launched, and early in 1978, a training course in language teaching was organized by the Ministry of Education to familiarize potential teachers with the general approaches to language learning and teaching (Horton 1985: 93–6).

A decision was made to start teaching in indigenous languages in early primary education. No transition class appears to have been specified but an understanding grew that the first three years of primary schooling would be taught in indigenous languages. It was decided to start a pilot project using three languages – Mende, Temne and Limba – in thirty-six selected schools in areas where these languages are spoken as mother tongues. The criterion in choosing which languages was the number of *mother tongue* speakers, thus Krio was unable to feature in such a decision. After further workshops to standardize and harmonize orthographies, teaching in these languages started in the first year of primary education in September 1979. With a lot of enthusiastic support from local communities where the programmes were started, it was reported that at the end-of-year exams, pupils from the pilot schools did better than those in other schools in the area.

The Ministry of Education then appeared to become more enthusiastic. In October 1979, it set up a National Planning Committee to advise on advancing the programme, and producing a standard orthography. For two years, a number of big workshops resulted, largely under the influence of voluntary organizations like Canadian University Service Overseas (CUSO), the German Adult Education Organization (DVV), the United Methodist Church (UMC), the Provincial Literature Bureau, the Institute for Sierra Leonean Languages. Typically, areas of Sierra Leone Government activity not considered priority areas produced a lot of talk but no money, so that voluntary agencies tended to become more prominent in the committee. However, it did receive some government support and maintained a sense of direction at this point.

Even though the terms of reference of the Planning Committee did not include Krio, a decision was taken at these workshops to standardize orthography, and other matters, in Krio. This was a recognition of the prominent role Krio could play in literacy. But since that time, no one in officialdom has taken seriously the issue of introducing Krio in schools. No pilot schools were ever selected for teaching Krio, the argument appearing to be that it had few native speakers.

This programme has not received any official support in recent years. It has not gone beyond the pilot school stage for lack of finance to provide adequate supplies of the texts which had been produced for the first four classes of primary school. In terms of Krio, the importance of the language was recognized, but the question was should it be taught in schools with a population of only a few native speakers? No texts were produced for Krio in these workshops.

Clearly political considerations go a long way towards determining what official recognition will be given to any particular language within a multi-ethnic situation like Sierra Leone. The official line sometimes does not relate to the reality of the usage pattern of particular languages and one becoming more significant as a lingua franca than the others. In the Sierra Leone context a minority language like Krio (in terms of numbers of mother tongue speakers) has become important, but that importance is at one level almost ignored by native speakers themselves, and this fact does not argue for the increased recognition of the language officially (Wyse and Fyle 1979).

The Krio language will however persist, partly because of an overestimation of its link with English by the population in general, thus giving it an enhanced status as a prestige language in Sierra Leone. The persistence of its major function as a lingua franca throughout the country means it cannot be replaced by English, the official language, because learning English to that extent would involve massive infusions of capital. The country cannot afford and, for other additional reasons, will not consider this option.

The fact that Krio is seen as representing a tiny minority ethnic group, often seen by other Sierra Leoneans as uppish, will perhaps continue to militate against any move to use Krio officially at more than its current unofficially recognized levels. However, progress in the promotion of the Krio language can be seen more in the relative proliferation of writing in Krio and the development of a literary tradition. Plays in Krio performed in Freetown have earlier been referred to. These were not only written by native Krio speakers. One of the prominent playwrights in Krio in Sierra Leone by the 1980s was John Kargbo, a non-Krio. Regardless of official policy there appear to be grassroots developments in Krio which may well make a major contribution to literacy in Sierra Leone in the next few years.

REFERENCES

Fyfe, C. (1962) *History of Sierra Leone*, Oxford: Oxford University Press.
Fyle, C. N. (1992) 'Krio' *BBC Focus on Africa* 3, 3.
—— and Jones, E. D. (1980) *A Krio-English Dictionary*, Oxford: Oxford University Press and Sierra Leone University Press.
—— and Fyle, C. Magbaily (1981) *The History of Sierra Leone: a Concise Introduction*, London: Evans.
Horton, R. M. F. (1985) 'A study and analysis of mother tongue teaching during the primary years with implications for Sierra Leone', unpublished Ph.D. dissertation, University of Southern Illinois, Carbondale.

Mackey, W. F. (1970) 'The description of bilingualism', in J. A. Fishman (ed.) *Readings in the Sociology of Language*, The Hague: Mouton.

Robin, J. (1970) 'Bilingual usage in Paraguay', in J. A. Fishman (ed.) *Readings in the Sociology of Language*, The Hague: Mouton.

Sesay, K. (1984) 'The position of English in Sierra Leone in relation to the local languages', *Africana Research Bulletin* 13, 3: 32–61, Institute of African Studies, Fourah Bay College, Freetown.

Wyse, A. J. G. (1980) *Searchlight on the Krio of Sierra Leone* (Occasional Paper No. 3), Institute of African Studies, Fourah Bay College, Freetown.

—— and Fyle, C. Magbaily (1979) 'Kriodom: a maligned culture', *Journal of the Historical Society of Sierra Leone* 3, 1/2: 37–48.

4 The politics of language in Bénin

Mamoud Akanni Igué and Raphael Windali N'Ouéni

MAMOUD AKANNI IGUÉ WRITES

In the early years after the independence of Dahomey in 1960, the government set the economic development of the country as its priority and was then subject to a number of coups stemming from the fact that Dahomey had little by way of resources with which to effect such development. These difficulties were aggravated in the immediate post-Independence period as a result of the repatriation of many hundreds of Dahomeans from other francophone African countries when those countries became independent themselves. These returning expatriates joined forces with a locally-produced, newly-graduating élite in search of salaried employment. As a result of trade union and student strikes, the régime of the first president of the Dahomean Republic, Hubert Maga, fell in 1963. The army, having deposed Maga, ceded power first to Ahomadegbe and then Apithy. Two years later the army intervened again, and Colonel Soglo ruled with the assistance of civilians until 1967, when Lieutenant-Colonel Alphonse Alley became Head of State following another coup. In August 1968 the army named Dr Zinsou as Head of State following the annulment of presidential elections because of election irregularities. Then in 1969 Lieutenant-Colonel De Souza overthrew Dr Zinsou. On the 26th October 1972 a further military coup saw the rise to power of Lieutenant-Colonel Mathieu Kerekou.

In November 1972, the new régime under Kerekou set out a programme of reconstruction and national independence whose general thrust was a rejection of foreign models. For the first time the programme of the new 'revolutionary military' government addressed the issue of language policy for the new République Populaire du Bénin proclaimed in November 1975:

> until now teaching, education and culture have been at the service of foreign domination and exploitation. Equally this new policy of na-

tional independence breaks with the stifling collar around our national values placed there by traditional schooling. From this perspective it is imperative to establish a democratic and patriotic system of education which will allow the teaching of modern science and technology in the interests of the people. For this it will be necessary to:

- Establish an authentic reform of the education system in line with the requirements of the new policy. This reform will need to put in place structures and teaching objectives appropriate to the needs of independent national economic development.
- Recognise the importance of our national languages.
- Rehabilitate our cultures.
- Open our university to all forms of knowledge and all the contemporary currents of scientific thought. It must have a specifically African character while remaining universal and yet must retain a privileged place for the varied kinds of accumulated experience from sister universities....

It will be necessary to ensure the development of popular culture by the organisation of mass literacy in the national languages, a crucial factor in our development. It is necessary to create a linguistics institute which will be charged with removing all obstacles in the way of utilising national languages as vehicles of knowledge.

(Éducation et Formation in Discours Programme du 30 Novembre, 1972 [sic]: 10–11)

Prior to this resounding declaration there had been no government policy in relation to 'national languages'. During the colonial period, the leitmotiv of colonial policy was the assimilation of the colonized. The imposition of French language within the education and administrative system was a key means in the assimilationist process. Pierre Alexandre typified the spirit of the age in these terms:

Only one language is taught in the schools, recognized in law courts, and used in administration: French, as defined by the opinions of the Academy and the decrees of the minister of public education. All other languages belong to the realm of folklore, dancing around the maypole, and riding hobbyhorses and are signs of disintegration of the French Republic.

(1972: 77)

A policy of not only spreading the French language but also suppressing local languages naturally follows from such a position. It was a matter of making the young Béninois, facing the process of schooling, into a black Frenchman in heart and mind, devoted to the cause of his master and useful to his endeavours. In convincing him it was necessary to make him believe that he had no language, merely an 'idiom' with a restricted vocabulary, lacking abstract terms. His speech had rudimentary grammatical structures, little syntax, and made sense through the juxtaposition of monosyllables. His 'idiom' was inappropriate for rational argument, for intellectual rigour, and for science. The intention here is not to trace the details of how these views were promulgated and maintained but to indicate the degree of disdain for national languages that informed the context into which the 'modern state' was implanted. Those who took up the reins from the colonizers were precisely those in whom this disdain had been inculcated most strongly. Thus, in the years following Independence there were rhetorical ruptures with the colonial period involving debates around the issue of 'national pride', but the notion of national pride included contradictory references to *notre appartenance à une culture multi-séculaire*, on the one hand, and the promotion of French as a tool of 'national unity' in diversity, on the other. Before looking at the implications of multilingualism and the position of French in contemporary Bénin, the next section will follow the implementation of the post-1972 policy on national languages indicating what steps were taken at the level of state intervention and what the effects have been.

In the three years after the original articulation of a new language policy in 1972 a number of initiatives were taken. A National Linguistic Commission (later the National Centre of Applied Linguistics) was established to produce a sociolinguistic atlas (which listed fifty languages for Bénin), provide systematic descriptions of languages, and to collect oral and other texts. A mass literacy programme was instituted through a *Direction de l'Alphabétisation et de la Presse Rurale* along with a Ministry of Alphabetization and Popular Culture. A Department of Linguistics and Oral Traditions was established at the University which, since 1974, has produced over a hundred graduates in language studies. The targets set for the literacy campaigns in seventeen languages were originally planned to affect 1,113,500 people over the period from 1974 to 1990. That same period saw, in fact, 88,898 people involved in literacy programmes of which there were three kinds:

A – minimal initiation aimed at assisting incorporation into collective agricultural enterprises;
B – numeracy aimed at providing skills for the management of agricultural produce at the village level;

C – literacy programmes aimed at reading and writing skills appropriate to local public needs.

The lack of success of these programmes was due in part to the decline in the number of teachers from 5,000 in 1979 to a few hundred now. A further important factor was the lack of primers, readers and general reading materials for the use of those who had gained the rudimentary skills. A certain amount of reading material in the form of news-sheets and regional newspapers was part-financed by Swiss Government aid. These journals were printed in the languages of the literacy campaigns.

Because of the lack of resources to match the ambitions of the new language policy of Bénin, national languages were formally introduced nowhere other than the National Assembly and the Centres for the Encouragement of Youth (CESE). The 1972 declaration of intentions, alluded to above, constituted a rupture with perceived prior practice and yet the results obtained some twenty years later clearly indicate that the advance of French – as both the official language and the only language accepted in public life – has been little affected.

RAPHAEL N'OUÉNI WRITES

In spite of the élite position of French, multilingualism remains alive and is developing apace. At the current stage of our research it appears that there are a number of degrees of multilingualism in Bénin. A survey carried out in 1988 in the six *départements* of the country by one of the authors (N'Ouéni) indicated the following:

> Bilingualism – nearly every Béninois speaks at least two languages, a mother tongue and another national language as a second language. Ninety-eight per cent of Béninois were shown by the survey to be at least bilingual.
> Trilingualism – the proportion of Béninois who speak three national languages is about 70 per cent. This is particularly true of northerners living in the south of the country and vice versa.
> A substantial proportion of the people of Bénin speak more than three languages:
> - 50 per cent speak four languages
> - 30 per cent speak five languages
> - 20 per cent speak six languages
> - 10 per cent speak seven or eight languages.

The people who speak the most number of languages tend to be the traders and civil servants (teachers, health workers, police) who for professional reasons spend periods of time in various parts of the country. The multiplicity of languages, which is often considered to be a handicap to development, does not in fact constitute an insurmountable problem since nearly all Béninois have command of a number of languages. In the south of the country, in the regions of Atlantique, Mono, Ouémé and Zou, nine out of ten people speak Fon-mina, Fon-goun, Fon-aizo, Adja-mina, Yoruba-goun, Sahwè-mina, Sahwè-fon, Yoruba-fon, and six people out of ten speak Adja-fon. In the north of the country a similar situation is to be found where each person operates in two languages other than their mother tongue, in addition to Dendi, the lingua franca of the region. It would therefore be possible to choose two or three languages for the purposes of 'national' communication, and the state could concentrate its efforts on the promotion of perhaps three languages through their progressive introduction into the education and administrative system alongside French. However, far from having such a vision, the various régimes that have ruled over the country have simply followed the path of colonial policy, imposing the use of French on all citizens in all areas of development and administration. This option has had grave consequences for the ability and willingness of the various populations to participate in the processes of national, social, cultural and economic development.

In justifying the imposition of French in teaching and administration as the official language for all Béninois, the various Governments have deployed the same arguments summarized as follows:

- the French language is the language of nobody in particular, it is therefore able to act as the means to achieving national unity within such a young country,
- schooling will be easier to institute and to develop rapidly,
- communication with the outside world can be effected in French, an international language, and mastery of scientific and technological knowledge can be achieved more easily allowing the importation of the means necessary for the rapid development of the country.

However, contrary to the expectations of the intellectual élite the consequences of this option have been catastrophic for the prospects of economic growth. In effect, as in many parts of sub-Saharan Africa, it is possible to identify the following trends:

- a segregation between the minority who have mastery of the French language and the majority of the population who know and speak the languages of Bénin,
- access to knowledge, to money and to power is reserved exclusively

for those who are able to speak, read and write the language of 'superior social status'.

Even information to be transmitted to people in the spheres of agriculture, hygiene, and the health of mothers and children does not get through, precisely because it is transmitted in French through programmes financed by international organisations, NGOs, and countries whose stated intention is to assist the country in its economic development. In this way the majority of the people do not participate in the push towards development since they are not able to be integrated into the communication process that is fundamental to the economic, social, political and cultural structures of the modern state.

Schooling in French has undergone a great decline. A continuing increase in the cost of teaching French has been accompanied by a noticeable drop in the competence levels attained by school graduates. This non-mastery has a broad effect upon attainment in other areas since the language of instruction, the 'vehicle of knowledge' is French. The paths to modern knowledge are open to a small minority. The use of French to promote national unity has not diminished tribalism, a factor which remains a reality in the country. One has only to look at the recent legislative and presidential elections in March 1991, when inter-tribal clashes produced many injuries in Parakou, capital of the northern region; and Soglo was elected only with the support of the people of the South who make up more than 60 per cent of the total population. In reality the purported neutrality of the borrowed language, French, with its minority base reinforces each group in its own singularity. It acts as a screen which blocks the development of certain national languages such as Fongbé, Dendi and Mina which were already lingua francas before the colonial period.

CONCLUSION

It is clear that multilingualism has been a watchword often brandished by the state in Bénin which has served as an obfuscating mechanism to avoid the task of thinking through and putting into effect a language policy. The same argument has allowed the intellectuals to exclude the population from the management of public affairs. It is also evident that development can never occur when the great majority are marginalized by the use of a language which simply allows an élite to conduct a monologue with itself.

REFERENCE

Alexandre, P. (1972) *An Introduction to Languages and Language in Africa*, trans. F. A. Leary, London, Ibadan and Nairobi: Heinemann.

5 Minority language development in Nigeria
A situation report on Rivers and Bendel States

Ben Ohi Elugbe

Perhaps the best known fact about Nigeria is that it is a country of extreme linguistic diversity. Although its land mass is less than 7 per cent of the total area of the African continent, it is agreed by scholars that fully 20 per cent of Africa's 2,000 odd languages are spoken in Nigeria (Dalby 1980: 100). Hansford *et al.* (1976) listed 394 languages but the revised version of the publication (Crozier and Blench: in press) will show a figure above 400.

Nigeria falls squarely within the Fragmentation Belt, 'a zone of extreme linguistic complexity stretching from Senegal to Ethiopia' (Dalby 1977: 6). Of the four language phyla recognized by orthodox or mainstream scholarship in African language classification, three are widely represented in Nigeria: Niger-Congo, Nilo-Saharan, and Afroasiatic. Only the rather small Khoisan (or click) languages, almost all in south-western Africa, are not represented in Nigeria.

Although three of the languages of Nigeria – Hausa, Igbo, and Yoruba – are clearly dominant by virtue of the numerical strength of their speakers (both as first and second language) the vast majority are spoken by comparatively small groups. It is the practice in Nigeria to refer to Hausa, Igbo and Yoruba as the major languages. The three are also called Nigeria's national languages in a multilingual practice in which English remains the official language.

As might be expected, some of the states of Nigeria (there are now thirty of them) are more linguistically complex than others. In Nigeria, certainly in the south, the two linguistically most complex states are Rivers and Bendel. (Although Bendel was, in August 1990, split into Delta and Edo states in an exercise that raised the number of states in Nigeria from twenty-one to thirty, we shall work with 'Bendel' in this report because it concerns the old Bendel State. In addition, we shall feel free to use 'Bendel' without the tag 'state' – Bendel, it is now obvious, remains an enduring concept.)

In this report, we shall see how these two states have reacted to linguistic diversity. In each case, we should start by showing just how complex the state is in linguistic terms, followed by the response of the state to that complexity. Before doing so, I present a very brief summary of language policy in Nigeria.

LANGUAGE POLICY AND NATIONAL DEVELOPMENT IN NIGERIA

There are two main sources of modern pronouncements on language in Nigeria: the National Policy on Education (NPE) (1977, revised in 1981), and the 1979 Constitution. Two other sources are the report of the Political Bureau (MAMSER 1987: 184–6) and the 1989 Constitution of the Federal Republic of Nigeria, but they contain nothing new and are not yet recognized as policy statements. In the NPE, some of the pronouncements are actually made in a section broadly headed 'The Importance of Language'.

An examination of language policy in Nigeria, as seen in the two sources mentioned above, reveals that the language policy has addressed three issues which Government considers important to national development. These are education, unity and independence.

Education

The policy is aimed mainly at education. It makes pronouncements on the role of language in education. At the pre-primary level the policy states that 'the medium of instruction will be principally the mother tongue or the language of the immediate community' (1981: 10). It states that at the primary level 'the medium of instruction [will be] initially the mother tongue or language of the immediate community and, at a later stage, English' (1981: 13).

At the Junior Secondary School (JSS) level, the NPE proposed that the pupil should study two Nigerian languages, 'the language of their own area in addition to any of the three main Nigerian languages, Hausa, Ibo [= Igbo], and Yoruba, subject to availability of teachers' (1981: 17).

At the Senior Secondary School (SSS) level, any Nigerian language, whether major or not, is recommended as one of the core subjects to be offered. This policy extends to the tertiary level where different languages are studied – for example, Ẹdo at the University of Benin, Yoruba and Igbo at Ibadan, Ẹdo, Igbo, Yoruba at Lagos, etc.

The policy also takes into account those who are already too old to benefit from the formal school system. Government therefore plans to embark on a mass literacy campaign. It is not said in what language literacy is being sought but we may assume that it is literacy in the mother tongue or in the dominant language of the immediate community. The policy thus goes beyond education in the narrow sense. It will enable everybody to participate fully in the national process, thus ensuring national integration which is vital to the development of the state.

Unity

The Federal Government recognizes the need for national unity. It also recognizes the role of language in fostering national unity. Hence, in addition to education and culture:

> Government considers it to be in the interest of national unity that each child should be encouraged to learn one of the three major languages other than his mother tongue. In this connection, the Government considers the three major languages in Nigeria to be Hausa, Ibo and Yoruba.
>
> (1981, Section 1: 8)

There is no contradiction in Government's position: the best policy for education is a multilingual one based on the mother tongue principle to which the Government commits itself. Yet, it obviously still believes that a common language is useful, if not necessary, for the promotion of national unity. National unity will itself create the kind of peaceful atmosphere required for meaningful development of the state. Language in education is an urgent concern but the emergence of a unifying national language lies in the future.

Independence

Young nations with a colonial history often see a national language not only as a symbol of oneness, but also as evidence of the completeness of their independence and the achievement of nationhood. In the case of Nigeria, the Military Government of General Obasanjo actually inserted Hausa, Igbo and Yoruba into the 1979 Constitution as national languages. Amayo cites Ikara (1981) as pointing out that the Obasanjo administration's reason for this insertion was that 'it would have been embarrassing at this stage of our political development to continue to use English alone' (1983: 11). It is interesting to note that there is no attempt here to do away with English which remains the official language, allows Nigeria to communicate with the outside world and, above all, remains (along with Nigerian Pidgin) the only ethnically neutral language to which all Nigerians can relate. English is therefore also vital to national development in Nigeria. But English also suffers from a certain disability as the language of colonialism. (As for Nigerian Pidgin, it has no official status whatsoever and is seen as a debased version of English so that its possible role in national development is for now not appreciated.)

Thus the 1979 Constitution contains attempts to promote some Nigerian languages as co-official languages with English. At the national level, the 1979 Constitution recommends that 'the business of the National Assembly shall be conducted in English and in Hausa, Ibo and Yoruba, when adequate arrangements have been made therefor' (Section 51). And, at the state level, it recommends that 'the business of the House of Assembly shall be conducted in English but the House may in addition to English conduct the business in one or more languages spoken in the State as the House may by resolution approve' (Section 91). This, in addition to the assertion in the same Constitution that Nigeria's national languages are Hausa, Igbo, and Yoruba, underlines Nigeria's determination that our independence should be reflected in our national languages. We return now to the matter of minority language development in Rivers and Bendel States.

LINGUISTIC DIVERSITY IN RIVERS STATE

The languages of Rivers State are all Niger-Congo (ignoring Nigerian Pidgin (English) (NP) whose classification is probably Indo-European in view of its lexicon). In the latest classification (Williamson 1989), the languages of Rivers State fall into two major families: Ijoid and Benue-Congo. Within Benue-Congo, three branches are represented: Cross River, Igboid and Edoid.

Ijoid

Following the most recent classification of Ijoid (Jenewari 1989) this family is divided into Ijo and Defaka. According to Jenewari (1989: 107), 'Defaka [is] better known as Afakani by the Ịjọ'. He describes it as 'a tiny, fast receding language spoken in the Niger Delta'.

By contrast, the rest of Ijoid (i.e. Ịjọ or the Ịjọ dialects) is a fairly large group of over a million speakers. Ịjọ is spoken mainly in the Niger Delta and adjacent creeks in Rivers, Bendel and Ondo States (Jenewari 1989: 107). Drawing from Williamson (1980), Jenewari (1989) and Lee and Williamson (1990), the Ịjọ dialects of Rivers State may be listed as follows:

West Africa

A	Eastern	1 Kalab̩ari̩
		2 Okrika
		3 I̩bani̩
		4 Nkoro
B	Brass	1 Nembe
		2 Akassa
C	Izon	With many dialects
D	Inland	1 Biseni
		2 O̩ko̩di̩a

Ijoid languages are spoken mainly in the creek belt of the Rivers State.

Benue-Congo

Cross River

This branch of Benue-Congo has three of the groups within it represented in Rivers State. These groups all belong to the Delta Cross arm of Cross River. The Cross River languages are spoken in the central and eastern parts of the state. Within Delta Cross therefore the following are represented:

A Central Delta
1 Abua   5 Ogbronuagum
2 Od̩ual   6 Obulom (Abuloma)
3 Kugbo   7 Ogbogolo
4 O̩gbia   8 Mini

B Ogoni
1 Eleme   3 Kana (Khana)
2 Ogoi   4 Gokana

C Lower Cross
   Obolo (Andoni) (Obolo extends into Akwa Ibom State)

Igboid

This is the group formerly called Lower Niger. In Rivers State, the Igboid languages are:

1 Ekpeye   6 Ndoni
2 Ikwere   7 Ndoki/Asa
3 Ogbah   8 Opobo
4 Egbema   9 Igbo-Igbani
5 Echie

The Igboid languages are spoken in the northern, most inland parts of the state. Igbo is normally a second language acquired by the Igboid communities for wider communication.

Edoid

The Delta Edoid subgroup of Edoid exists wholly in Rivers State. The Delta Edoid languages exist alongside the Ijọ dialects in the western and central areas.

Delta Edoid 1 Dẹgẹma
 2 Engenni (Egene)
 3 Epie-Atịsa

Rivers State is relatively small with a large part of its area covered by rivers and creeks. There is no one language which effectively covers the state, whether in terms of geographic spread or in terms of use. Two languages which have a useful number of second language speakers are Igbo and Nigerian Pidgin (NP) which is English-based. Unfortunately, memories of the civil war of 1967–70 and the creation of states, which severed Rivers State from the Igbo area, have created an observable degree of resentment against Igbo. As for NP, it is still stigmatized as a bad form of English and thus denied a role in education. In news broadcasting, Igbo continues to be excluded totally while NP is used in radio news under the title 'News in Special English'. On television, Ikwere, Ịzọn, Kalaḅarị, and Kana were, for quite some time, the only ones used. Other languages have been added to the list since the early 1980s because its speakers were not covered by any other language. Williamson (1980: 87) points out that this situation gave rise to the Rivers Readers Project.

The Rivers Readers Project

Williamson (1977, 1980 and elsewhere) has written extensively on the Rivers Readers Project. As might be assumed, the project 'aims to produce readers and supporting materials for primary school use in as many as possible of the local languages of the Rivers State' (Williamson 1980: 87). This was to enable children to 'learn to read in their own speech-form before going on [to] English'. Although the Rivers Readers Project (RRP) 'is sponsored by the Rivers State Government through its Ministry of Education', it benefited initially from small grants from UNESCO and the Ford Foundation. The University of Ibadan also helped by housing the project initially, but it was later moved to the University of Port Harcourt.

The project operates through Language Committees; in fact, the first step towards the development of a target language is to set up a Language Committee made up of people from the whole dialect spectrum of the language. The members are people who are interested in the language and are acknowledged to be good speakers or users of it. Members may be invited individually or as representatives of organizations such as church denominations, progress organizations, etc. Experienced teachers are usually prime targets for inclusion in the Language Committee. According to Williamson:

> The function of the Language Committee is to represent the general feelings of the people about their language, to agree to an orthography, to go over in detail the drafts of the reader, to launch the final product in the community ... [and to guide] the often considerable enthusiasm of the speakers of the language into productive channels.
> (Williamson 1980: 87)

The production of a reader is followed by a launching (which is usually a festive occasion) and a workshop for teachers who will use the book. The two events are organized into one with the launching taking place on the first day and the teachers' workshops following on the second day.

The Rivers Readers Project produces more than readers. It also produces what Williamson refers to as support materials in the form of teachers' notes, orthography booklets, and occasional publications (Williamson 1980: 88). Professor Williamson, who is the main language expert on the Project, wrote in 1980 'We have not yet ... achieved the aim of the Project', and she gave a number of reasons to support her statement. These included the fact that in Rivers schools only English is taught even where a local language is mentioned on the time-table; the fact that teachers are not taught how to handle the different languages; and the fact that teachers need time to become familiar with the modern, often revised, orthographies in the readers.

In 1991, Professor Williamson (personal communication) remains largely unhappy about the effectiveness of the Project. The problem of teachers remains and distribution of readers and other materials is sadly discouraging. Beyond the ecstasy of the noisy launching, enthusiasm dies down quickly and those who have responsibility for distributing the readers and other materials are often found wanting. Even where materials have been distributed to pupils, there has been no matching enthusiasm to use them in the classroom. The Ministry of Education has not intervened in a way forceful enough to ensure use of the materials.

All this is traceable to the problem of teacher-training and negative attitudes which have persisted in spite of the new policies which are more favourable to Nigerian languages. There is also, at the national level, a policy of *oral* teaching and examining of the mother tongue which encourages teachers to ignore available materials. The 'oral' policy was in fact designed to encourage states without the necessary materials.

An important point to note about the Rivers Readers Project is that it was established long before the Federal Government had woken up to the need for a meaningful statement on the important issue of language in Nigeria.

LINGUISTIC DIVERSITY IN BENDEL STATE

My experience of the Bendel situation is a very practical one. Since 1974, I have been heavily involved in various attempts by the State Government as well as by Local Government and individuals to come to terms with linguistic diversity in the State.

It is often said that Bendel State is Nigeria in miniature. The reason for this is the observation that Bendel State is linguistically (and ethnically) as fractured (and fractious) as Nigeria itself. In some parts of Bendel, two communities, each with its own distinct language, may be found in the same town as, for example, at Otuo in Owan Local Government Area. The formerly separate Edoid and Ebiroid settlements of Enwa and Igarra in Akoko Edo LGA have now become geographically one, though inhabitants of the area know where Igarra ends and Enwa begins. Ẹtụnọ, the language of Igarra, is a dialect of Ebira (Igbirra) (see below).

Most of the languages of Bendel State belong to the (New) Benue-Congo family of the Niger-Congo phylum. The only non-Benue-Congo languages of Bendel State belong to the Ijoid family which is much less related to the others. In the Delta areas, Ijoid and Benue-Congo languages exist side by side (as in Rivers State). The best known of the Ijoid languages is Ịzọn, the variety of Ịjọ used on Radio Nigeria.

As pointed out above, the Edoid group is the dominant one in Bendel State. Edoid languages occupy virtually all of northern Bendel, most of the central areas, and almost all of the areas in the south (including the Delta). The most visibly non-Edoid part of Bendel is the eastern part of the central area of the State where Igboid languages such as Ụkwụanị (Kwale), Ịka, and Igbo (Aniọcha) are spoken.

The languages of Bendel State can be classified genetically under six groups: Edoid, Igboid, Yoruboid, Ebiroid (all New Benue-Congo), Ukaan (Kakumo), and Ijoid. The groups can be represented as follows:

Benue-Congo

Edoid

The group falls into four coordinate subgroups (Elugbe 1989). The southernmost subgroup, called Delta Edoid, is not represented in Bendel State. The others are South-western Edoid (SWE) (all in the western Delta), North-central Edoid (NCE) covering the central parts of the State and North-western Edoid (NWE) in the northern fringes of the State and into the Akoko area of Ondo State.

1 South-western Edoid
   Erųwa (Erohwa, Arohwa)
   Isoko
   Okpẹ
   Urhobo (Sobo)
   Uvwiẹ (Effurun, Evhron)
2 North-central Edoid
   Ẹdo (Bini)
   Esan (Ishan)
   Ora-Emai-Iuleha (including Ivbimion)
   Yẹkhee (Etsako, Afenmai, Kukuruku; including Ivbiadaobi)
   Ghotuọ (Otuọ, Otwa)
   Unẹmẹ
   Atẹ (Atte) -Okpela-North Ibie
   Ikpeshi
   Sasaru-Ẹnwa-Igwẹ
   Ọsọsọ
3 North-western Edoid
   Ọkpamheri (including Ọlọma)
   Ọkpẹ-Idesa
   Uhami-Iyayu
   Ukue (Ukpe) -Ehueun (Ekpenmi, Epenmi) in Ondo State

Igboid

I list below only the better known Igboid languages of Bendel State:

   Igbo/Ibo (Aniọcha)
   Ịka
   Ụkwụanị (Kwate, including Aboh)

Yoruboid

The main Yoruboid group in Bendel is:

Iṣẹkiri (Itsekiri, Shekiri, Jekri, etc.)

Other Yoruboid languages are the Igala dialects along the west bank of the River Niger from opposite Idah down to opposite Onitsha. The only Yoruba settlements in Bendel State are Olukumi in Aniọcha area and Imeri on the northern fringes of Bendel State, just north of Otuo and west of Somorika. By the latest state creation exercise, Imeri is now ceded to Ondo State. It was otherwise in the Akoko Edo Local Government Area of Bendel State.

Ebiroid

Etụnọ (spoken exclusively at Igarra, the Akoko Edo Local Government Headquarters) and Ebira are mutually intelligible dialects of Ebira. Etụnọ is the main Ebiroid language in Bendel State. However, there are many Ebira (Igbirra) farm settlements which have become permanent so that Ebira itself is now one of the languages of Bendel. Blench (1989) classifies Ebira as part of Nupoid but that classification is questionable and still subject to supporting evidence – hence Ebiroid is used here.

Ukaan

This is a small language spoken in Kakumo, possibly the northernmost settlement in Bendel State. It is, in spite of its small size, a group in its own right, coordinate with Edoid, Igboid, etc.

Ijoid

The main (possibly only) Ijoid language of Bendel State is Ịzọn (including Kolokuma, Mein, etc.). It is also spoken in Rivers State and is the variety of Ịjọ used by Radio Nigeria.

LANGUAGE DEVELOPMENT IN BENDEL

As with Rivers State, attempts to grapple with the language problem in Bendel State antedate those of the Federal Government. Following the publication of Ogieriaixi's *Edo Orthography* in 1972 and the circulation of Elugbe's 1972 criticism of the revised orthography proposed there, the then Mid-West State Government set up a Mid-West Language Committee to propose an acceptable writing system for Edo and, very importantly in my view, to determine the dominant languages of the State and propose alphabets for them. The Mid-West Language Committee submitted two documents to the Government: the report of a seminar it had organized at the University of Lagos on 'Edo orthography' (Ministry of Education 1974), and the overall report of the committee dealing with the language situation in Bendel (Ministry of Education 1975). The seminar proposed for Edo an orthography which has proved enduring. The Committee found that fourteen languages were dominant in the State and proposed an alphabet for each of them:

1 Esan	8 Ịzọn (Ijaw)
2 Edo	9 Ora-Emai-Iuleha
3 Ghotuọ	10 Ọkpamheri
4 Igbo (Aniọcha)	11 Unẹmẹ
5 Isoko	12 Urhobo
6 Iṣẹkiri	13 Ukwuani (Kwale)
7 Ika	14 Yẹhee (Etsako)

The Committee recommended that 'all of these ... languages should be developed for use in education at [the] primary level. Some [other] languages can also be considered for development if there is sufficient local interest and activity' (p. 9). The implication of this is that other languages not regarded as dominant can also be developed. The report, regrettably, says nothing about Nigerian Pidgin which is easily the most widely-spoken language in Bendel. In fairness to the Committee, it should be noted that NP was nowhere mentioned in the responses to the questionnaires sent out all over the State.

We see here that while the Rivers Readers Project was aimed at developing every language, the Bendel effort was directed at 'the dominant languages'. It is not clear why Government decided to limit itself to the dominant languages: one possibility is that Government wanted to limit the cost of developing the languages of the State. The point should be made, however, that Federal Government policy allows for the two approaches since the languages recommended for use in the primary school are the mother tongue or the language of the immediate community. Another difference between the RRP and the Bendel situation is that the RRP was established with long term goals whereas the Mid-West Language Committee was dissolved as soon as it satisfied its terms of reference.

Three factors of overriding importance in language development are interest, finance, and expertise. An abundance of interest and/or finance can be used to locate and employ expertise but the fact remains that these three factors are a basic requirement for language development. These factors become even more important in the case of minority languages. In Nigeria, for example, Hausa, Igbo and Yoruba have been labelled 'national languages'; they are also the three major languages of Nigeria with a numerical strength which in itself guarantees all the ingredients required for development. By contrast, a minority language (in this case any language other than Hausa, Igbo, or Yoruba) cannot always be guaranteed development. Of course, some of these small languages are major in a state or in a Local Government Area. Otherwise, the communities that speak them have to raise their own funds and sponsor the development of their own languages.

The relevance of interest to language development is amply demonstrated by the following. In May, 1975, as the Mid-West Language Committee prepared to wind up and submit its report, I asked the Chairman, Mr E. C. Halim, if we were going to see urgent action on our recommendations. He replied that he could not be sure as it took only a change of government and an attendant change of personnel for a recommendation to be swept under the carpet. Two months later, in July 1975, there was a military coup and thus a change of government. That report has never been referred to again.

In 1988, my colleague, Dr A. P. Omamor, and I, reacting to a circular from the Ministry of Education, Benin City, went to see the Director-General of the Ministry. The circular to which we were reacting had been to Local Government Councils telling them to start teaching the languages of their areas. We wanted to know what plans the Government had for developing these local (minority) languages. The Director-General informed us that they planned to teach the local languages *orally* and examine them *orally* (in each case without written materials). He and his assistants maintained this position even when we pointed out that the true test of literacy in the mother tongue is the ability to *read* and *write* it. I have since found that this is a Nigeria-wide policy. It is clearly dictated by a lack of materials caused by a lack of finance.

I have been personally involved in some cases in which non-governmental interest has led, or is leading, to the development of a minority language, for example:

1 Iṣẹkiri
    In 1975 development of this language was actively sponsored by the Isekiri Land Trust. The expert who did the initial work was Dr A. P. Omamor. I and other members of the Department of African Lan-

guages and Linguistics at Ibadan were involved in the workshops to train teachers to teach Iṣẹkiri.

2 Okpẹ
In 1988 development was sponsored by Chief B. T. Owumi of Sapele. The expert is Dr A. P. Omamor.

3 Ghotuọ
Since 1990 Otuo Union has been the driving force behind development, and I am the expert in this case.

CONCLUSION

We have seen above how two relatively small but linguistically complex states have reacted to that complexity in different ways. Rivers State set up a project with no specified lifespan. Bendel State, by contrast, set up a Language Committee with orders to submit a final report within a year. In each case, the states acted in advance of Federal Government pronouncements.

We have seen already a lot of materials development in the case of the Rivers Readers Project. According to Emenanjo 'some sixty-two publications are available in twenty-one local – all minority – languages under the Rivers Readers Project' (1990: 94). By contrast, Bendel State cannot boast of producing any material in any of the dominant languages. The materials available have been sponsored by individuals and local communities. In Rivers State, some of the materials are currently undergoing revision (Williamson, personal communication).

There is, in Rivers State, an abundance of materials whereas there is very little in Bendel State, leading the Bendel Government to talk of *oral* teaching and examining of the mother tongue. In these two states we see contrasting directions: in Rivers State resources and investment were provided predominantly by the state, NGOs and the university, in Bendel private initiative has driven what development there has been. The trick may well be to bring all these forces together.

REFERENCES

Amayo, A. (1983) 'The search for national integration and national identity in Nigeria since Independence – the linguistic aspect', paper presented at the National Conference on 'Nigeria since Independence', Ahmadu Bello University, Zaria, 28–31 March.

Blench, R. (1989) 'Nupoid', in J. Bendor-Samuel (ed.) *The Niger-Congo Languages*, New York: University Press of America.

Crozier, D. and Blench, R. (in press) *An Index of Nigerian Languages* (a revised

and updated version of Hansford *et al.* (1976)), Dallas: Summer Institute of Linguistics.
Dalby, D. (1977) *Language Map of Africa and the Adjacent Islands* (provisional edition), London: International African Institute.
—— (1980) 'National language policy in the context of Africa', in A. Bamgbose (ed.) *Language in Education in Nigeria: Proceedings of the Language Symposium, Kaduna, October 31 – November 4 1977* (2 vols), Lagos: National Language Centre.
Elugbe, B. O. (1972) 'Some comments on *Edo orthography* (comments on Ogieriaixi 1972)', mimeograph.
—— (1989) *Comparative Edoid: Phonology and Lexicon* (Delta Series 6), Port Harcourt: University of Port Harcourt Press.
Emenanjo, E. N. (1990) 'In the tradition of majors: lessons in language engineering for the minority languages', in E. N. Emenanjo (ed.) *Multilingualism, Minority Languages, and Language Policy in Nigeria*, Agbor: Central Books Limited in association with the Linguistic Association of Nigeria.
Federal Republic Nigeria (1977) *National Policy on Education* (revised 1981), Lagos: Federal Ministry of Education.
—— (1979) *The Constitution of the Federal Republic of Nigeria*, Lagos: Federal Ministry of Information.
—— (1989) *The Constitution of the Federal Republic of Nigeria*, Lagos: Federal Ministry of Information.
Hansford, K. J., Bendor Samuel, J. and Stanford, R. (1976) 'An index of Nigerian languages', *Studies in Nigerian Languages* 5: 1–204.
Ikara, B. (1981) 'Towards participatory democracy in Nigeria', in B. Ikara (ed.) *Nigerian Languages and Cultural Development*, Lagos: National Language Centre.
Jenewari, E. C. (1989) 'Ijoid', in J. Bendor-Samuel (ed.) *The Niger-Congo Languages*, New York: University Press of America.
Lee, J. D. and Williamson, K. (1990) 'A lexicostatistic classification of Ijo dialects', *Journal of African Languages and Linguistics* 1, 1: 1–10.
MAMSER (1987) *Report of the Political Bureau, March, 1987* (reproduced for mass distribution), Abuja: Directorate for Social Mobilization (MAMSER).
Ministry of Education (1974) *Edo Language and its Orthography: Report of the Seminar on Edo Orthography, 15–18 May, 1974*, Benin City: Ministry of Education.
—— (1975) *Report of the Mid-West Language Committee*, Benin City: Ministry of Education.
Ogieriaixi, E. (1972) *Edo Orthography*, mimeograph.
Williamson, K. (1977) 'The Rivers Readers Project', *The Nigerian Language Teacher* 6, 2: 16–24.
—— (1980) 'Small languages in education: the Rivers Readers Project as case history', in A. Bamgbose (ed.) *Language in Education in Nigeria: Proceedings of the Language Symposium, Kaduna, October 31 – November 4, 1977*, Lagos: National Language Centre.
—— (1989) 'Niger-Congo Overview', in J. Bendor-Samuel (ed.) *The Niger-Congo Languages*, New York: University Press of America.

6 Using existing structures
Three phases of mother tongue literacy among Chumburung speakers in Ghana

Gillian F. Hansford

DEVELOPMENT

Whilst development usually entails improving things like agricultural skills, or health care, it is noteworthy that at the conference that gave rise to the papers in this volume, participants focussed rather on the development of languages, as part of national development. Bamgbose, in this volume, states that emphasis should be on 'a full realization of the human potential and a maximum utilization of the nation's resources for the benefit of all'. He backs up his argument by quoting from Schumacher, Nyerere of Tanzania and a UNESCO report. Of his five excellent summary points, the last is 'mass participation and grassroots involvement in order to ensure widespread and genuine development'. Participation is actually increased by 'the use of the many languages available in the country'. Elugbe adds, 'The development of a society is the development of individuals within it.' However, he says not only is there, in the case of Nigeria, 'no single document directed solely at the language problem' but Nigerian governments 'see the cost but do not see the benefits. They look for immediate results.' It has been estimated that only 5 per cent of the population of Nigeria are able to use English. Igué and N'Ouéni describe a similar situation for French in Bénin: 'schooling in French has undergone a great decline'.

The widespread use of a language is seen by people for whom it is not their mother tongue as an imposition. This is true whether it be English, or an African language such as Hausa, Igbo or Yoruba, which are mother tongues of many people, or Krio which is the mother tongue of a minority. Whilst Asad's distinction (1986) between strong and weak languages, referred to by Fardon and Furniss, is useful, we should not necessarily deduce that the speakers of the strong language view the encouragement of the use of their own language as a strategy to acquire supremacy. For it might be merely expedient in order to communicate with the largest number of people. However, if a language is used over a wide area and for diverse purposes, but fluency is achieved only by a few, has its 'imposition' achieved the desired ends? Further, as Fardon and Furniss point out, almost certainly some languages will remain underdeveloped.

A CASE STUDY OF THE CHUMBURUNG LANGUAGE

Chumburung of Ghana, being a minority language, is one likely to be underdeveloped in any programme that encourages the use of Asante or English. Of sixty languages in Ghana more than fifty could be called 'minority languages' in terms of the number of speakers. Akwapim, Asante, Fante, Ga and Ewe were developed as vernaculars over the last hundred years by mission and government policy. Some of the rest have been partly developed within the last fifty years by non-governmental organizations (NGOs), mainly in the area of adult literacy.

In this study of a grassroots non-governmental organization's contribution to literacy for minority groups I discuss the literacy project sponsored by the Ghana Institute of Linguistics, Literacy and Bible Translation (or GILLBT) amongst the Chumburung. It underwent three phases: adult literacy within the village authority system, children learning to read and write Chumburung in the schools, and lately classes held by the churches. Each stage took off when the previous one went into decline. The phase within the village authority structure 'failed' because it did not generate sufficient interest to attract those previously uninterested. However, it did supply teachers with practical experience for the phase in the schools. This phase failed because some of the teachers were temporarily removed from the classrooms, and because there was no clear policy concerning the languages of the classroom. The third phase has been able to make progress both because Christians have a desire to read the Scriptures, and because the ability to read Chumburung had by that time become more of a community value.

This paper goes on to consider some of the outline plans for more than one language to be used in schools, as proposed by fellow contributors to this volume for Nigeria, and by Gbedemah back in 1975 for Ghana. A concluding suggestion is made that, as a separate issue from learning the language orally, consideration must be given to the child's learning to read and write each language that will be used during the widening of the child's horizons.

The Chumburung, numbering around 27,000, live around the lower Daka river area in the Northern and Volta Regions of Ghana, and are primarily yam farmers. There is a cultural mix of ethnic groups living within the traditional Chumburung area. A dominant group to one side of them claim suzerainty over them, but this is denied by the Chumburung. On another side is a group with whom they share the worship of a certain god, but to whom they say they owe no political allegiance. However, the seats of local government, and hence the education offices, are situated not within Chumburung territory, but in two towns, one in each of those other areas. The trade language, also used frequently in the churches, is Asante. While one cannot but be aware of the many languages spoken by many Africans (as instanced by Igué and N'Ouéni), once again we need to be aware that fluency may not be great in the second and subsequent languages.

The language of education throughout Ghana is however not Asante but English. About a quarter of adult Chumburung have attended school in the past, but only 4 per cent actually finished primary and middle school. Children at the moment show a much higher attendance rate, around 90 per cent being on the register. However, they mostly leave school with an English reading age of eleven years or less. Secondary schools and job opportunities are outside the area, and few who go off in search of them return to the area.

FIRST PHASE OF CHUMBURUNG LITERACY – USING THE VILLAGE AUTHORITY STRUCTURE

Primers were prepared in the late 1970s using a well-tested phonic method, building up syllables. In contrast to the functional literacy programme that Igué and N'Ouéni cite, the beginning of the course is learning to read and write, leaving for the post-primer stage the actual acquisition of fresh knowledge. All the stories for practice reading are grounded in normal village life, and were written by a local man. Even teachers' instructions were in Chumburung. The chief and elders of each town or village were asked to choose people who had completed primary and middle school, and hence were literate in English, and were patient and trusted in their community. These men and women were then trained in what must have been the shortest teacher training course on record. On the first day, they learnt how to read Chumburung, and on the second day how to teach their own people, including illiterates. Two days is all that a farmer can spare from his work. Adult literacy classes in Chumburung were then set up in various villages, throughout the dry season for about five months. To counteract the shortness of the training of the teachers, a supervisor visited each class in action once a month. Normally adult literacy is in Asante or English, and comes within the province of the Department of Social Welfare and Community Development. Because they also encourage vernacular literacy, certificates were awarded jointly with GILLBT, and the number of those who became literate in Chumburung was included in their statistics.

However, the poor economic situation at that time did not encourage students to buy books, and the supervisors found it difficult to visit classes, most of which are rural, with only a bicycle. Not only were there the usual drop-outs from those first classes, but the impetus was not carried over to others, that is others were not motivated to feel a need to learn to read Chumburung themselves. Thus, over a three-year period in eleven towns, less than a hundred people became literate in Chumburung.

SECOND PHASE OF CHUMBURUNG LITERACY – USING THE EDUCATION SYSTEM

It was established that there were twenty-one primary schools and ten middle schools in the Daka river area, and that roughly half the children in these schools were mother tongue Chumburung speakers. Also there was at least one teacher in each school who was a mother tongue Chumburung speaker. These school-teachers, together with the teachers of adults, pressed the education authorities to allow Chumburung reading to be taught in the curriculum slot marked as being for vernacular languages. Of the sixty languages in Ghana, eleven are approved by the Bureau of Ghana Languages as 'official languages', although this does not include Chumburung. The 'official language' designated for the Chumburung area was, in fact, not being taught for various reasons. In part of the area, this is mainly because the language designated as official is that of the ethnic group whose dominance is contested. However, there is also a desperate lack of textbooks in all parts of the area. Since the slot was being underused, the local education authorities proved willing to employ those who had had experience teaching Chumburung adult literacy classes to teach the subject using the same primers as in the adult classes, and paid them a salary. GILLBT was able to obtain external funding for printing primers and anthologies of stories in larger quantities than previously. A committee to oversee both adult and school literacy included education officers and the head of a teacher training college, as well as the supervisors of the adult classes.

Sadly, two factors have stopped the schools programme. Firstly, owing to an upgrading of the middle schools to become junior secondary schools, teachers who had not previously been to teacher training college were required to complete a four-year course. This effectively removed teachers of reading in Chumburung for that period. Secondly, among education authorities, there was disagreement as to which Ghanaian language could be taught legitimately, and a ban was placed on the teaching of Chumburung literacy in schools until such time as the current educational policy is clarified or reviewed. Nevertheless, fifteen of the thirty-one schools had participated, and 900 children over three years had had some exposure to reading Chumburung, although some of these may not themselves have been Chumburung speakers.

THIRD PHASE OF CHUMBURUNG LITERACY – USING THE CHURCH STRUCTURE

About 10 per cent of the adult Chumburung population attends one of the seventy-four congregations representing thirteen denominations. One hundred duplicated copies of the first draft of the Chumburung New Testament by two local men were circulated, and a Bible correspondence course started. Nearly 300 people completed questions on at least one book of the New Testament, and two completed the entire New Testament.

During this third phase of Chumburung literacy, ecumenical gatherings were held in each town. One or two people in each congregation learnt how to teach adult Sunday school lessons in Chumburung. Since Asante is widely used in churches, each language group meets before the main service for religious instruction in their own language, a pattern already employed by some of the very large multilingual churches in the capital. Following the dedication of the printed New Testament in 1989, some churches have taken the opportunity to start literacy classes, either for church attenders or within the wider community.

Thus we see that, when adult literacy declined for lack of motivation, the programme progressed temporarily within the education system, and then more recently the church has advanced the process of reading in the mother tongue. While official figures for those who have become literate in Chumburung are still low, there is now an undercurrent of positive feeling among people towards reading in their own language. Wherever one travels, someone will say, 'I can read Chumburung too. So-and-so taught me'. Furthermore, some newly literate people have taught themselves to read Asante as well, and many non-schooled adults are now pressing for books to help them learn English.

FUTURE POSSIBILITIES FOR MOTHER TONGUE EDUCATION

Looking at the educational systems across a number of countries, we find two significant phrases used repeatedly. In English, we speak of the language used in the classroom as the 'medium of instruction'. In French the phrase is the 'vehicle of knowledge'. Both highlight the fact that if the language employed by the teacher is not well understood by the pupils, they will not learn. Since they also learn from written textbooks, they need also to be fluent in reading that language. What language might be best as a medium of both instruction and learning?

Elugbe has given a synopsis of Nigeria's plan for a progression of three languages to be consecutively used in the schools: mother tongue, national language, and English. Whereas Nigeria is raising three regional languages to the status of national languages, there is not a corresponding policy establishing a raised status for Asante in Ghana. In fact, as Gbedemah (1975) says, there would be reactions against it. Therefore I will retain the phrase 'regional languages' for languages that are more widely spoken in an area, which may or may not be the mother tongues for the pupils in the schools.

Language development plans refer both to language learning and the use of language as a medium of instruction. In Gbedemah's ideal plan, in the first four years, the Ghanaian child would be exposed 75 per cent of the time to the first language or mother tongue (which according to present administrative arrangements in Ghana would be the major regional language) in elementary school. What is not realised, or maybe it is realised but is too difficult to handle, is that for many children their mother tongue is *not* the regional language. Furthermore, the plans of Nigeria, Ghana and Bénin do not clearly state when reading and writing in each language are to be taught. Is it to be at the same time as acquisition of the language?

GILLBT is not the only organization to believe that literacy in the mother tongue is much easier than in any other language, since the words being read, often with a good phonic orthography, are immediately comprehended. Transition to reading another language with which people are orally familiar is expedited. The world of the primary school in any country deals as subject matter with the immediate environment. What language better to employ than the mother tongue? At this stage basic arithmetic is more likely to be understood in the mother tongue. As children's interests develop, they may begin to acquire verbal facility in a regional language. Chumburung children acquire Asante orally and painlessly, even if not to a great depth at this stage. This regional language could be taught as a subject orally at first, and when the children are able to read their own mother tongue they could start reading in the regional language. However, the two processes, oral acquisition and reading, need to be consecutive not contemporaneous. By junior secondary school, that regional language could become the medium of instruction. At this stage the subject matter is likely to be national in scope, e.g. national geography and history. Initially English would be taught orally as a subject. English notoriously has a complicated spelling system, but the children would have already mastered the letters and other reading skills, and would cope better when they first started to learn to read English. Then English could be used as a medium of instruction in senior secondary schools, containing much of the language of science and technology. The regional language could, of course, continue to be studied as a subject in its own right.

Such a progression from the small world of the local environment to the global world with its emphasis on technology, would obviate the need to construct specialized vocabulary artificially in the mother tongue for concepts not used in everyday life. After all, as Gbedemah (1975) points out, languages 'exist in different cultural matrices'.

As an example, let us take the case of Krio of Sierra Leone, the plight of whose mother tongue speakers is so graphically portrayed by Fyle in this volume. The status of Krio is of mother tongue for a minority, and trade language for many. For mother tongue speakers, they would be taught to read it at primary school, but other groups would learn to read their own mother tongue before progressing to Krio and finally English.

Such programmes, whilst apparently very costly, would 'enable everybody to participate fully in the national process' (Elugbe in this volume), assuming education was compulsory. It would also ensure that provision is made for speakers of minority languages, since no minority group would wish to abandon a mother tongue.

Whilst applauding Elugbe's plans for Nigerian universities, it is important to stress that most teachers are trained not in universities, but in teacher training colleges. The Chumburung programme has shown that if teaching in primary schools involves the mother tongue, more people are drawn into the teaching profession, thus utilizing more of the nation's resources. In the Chumburung case, it is to the credit of the village elders, who chose the teachers in the first phase, that most of them are still actively involved in the programme either in schools or in adult classes, or have themselves gone on to teacher training. This contrasts with the high teacher drop-out rate that Igué and N'Ouéni speak of in Bénin. Chumburung speakers themselves are looking forward to a time when training in teaching Chumburung reading and writing is taught at the Ajumako School of Languages, for this is the major establishment that trains students to teach one of the approved vernaculars as a subject in schools.

However, even if education in schools were to be compulsory, and the 'three language' plan fulfil its potential, there still remain those who are currently at school or who never had the opportunity. I believe the role of NGOs and churches is sadly neglected by governments. Elugbe cites the 'shamefully low' figure of twenty Nigerian languages which 'already have standard (official) orthographies developed for them'. What of the 118 languages that he says have also been reduced to writing? Rather than expending effort in standardizing the orthographies of these languages, would it not be better to encourage the use of existing books and training teachers in those languages? Fardon and Furniss show in this volume how difficult it is in practice to impose a new and theoretically 'better' orthography on an existing one. There also remain in Nigeria more than 200 languages for which orthographies have yet to be established.

The Rivers Readers Project in Nigeria has shown (I. and A. Gardner: private communication) that if a book is on the school syllabus, adults are more motivated to read it also. The language in fact acquires a certain prestige which of itself motivates more people. Certainly amongst Chumburung speakers, some women are beginning to learn to read Chumburung because their children have learnt in school. Literate mothers are also not to be undervalued as helpers of their small children in their first attempts at reading, and as a growing pool of potential teachers in nursery and primary schools.

CONCLUSION

At first sight the 'three language' plan is so daunting in concept as to be overwhelming for any government. However, if the state is committed to a 'full realization of the human potential and a maximum utilization of the nation's resources for the benefit of all', as I earlier quoted from Bamgbose in this volume, then I believe that it needs to recognise and encourage NGOs and churches in all the contributions they can make. From the Chumburung experience, we can see that more than one approach is necessary. If the NGOs are allowed to contribute to the school situation, not only do those pupils involved learn something they would not otherwise learn, but their parents and the wider community become involved also. This in turn results in having more and better teachers, and more parental cooperation in the education of the next generation of children.

REFERENCES

Asad, T. (1986) 'The concept of cultural translation in British social anthropology', in J. Clifford and G. E. Marcus (eds.) *Writing Culture: the Poetics and Politics of Ethnography*, Berkeley: University of California Press.

Gbedemah, F. F. K. (1975) *Alternative Language Policies for Education in Ghana* New York: Vantage Press.

Part II
Central and Southern Africa

The political imperatives that lie behind three of the papers in this section relate to the recognition of diversity within state boundaries where the state has hitherto recognised and promoted only one or some of the languages, predominantly those of the élites or of the former colonial power. In this respect, these papers, by Katupha, Benjamin and Maake, echo the programmatic statements that have been the subject of debate since the 1960s in other parts of Africa. They address policy issues about recognition and the allocation of state resources, based upon a restatement of the multi-ethnic and multilingual social reality of the state and a belief that a 'new' state can emerge, more cohesive and less conflict-ridden, through the recognition of legitimate aspirations to deploy and value 'own' language and culture within a state which recognizes a variety of such languages and cultures.

For Mozambique, Katupha characterizes Portuguese, which was promoted as a tool of national unification in the face of troubling diversity, as contributing to defining élite membership. Certainly, not knowing Portuguese excluded individuals from the élite. At the same time, economic and technological development, if it is to involve the majority of the people, can be promoted only through the use of African languages. Katupha's solution is the long term promotion, through the education system, of 'functional bilingualism' such that, with resources allocated to the development of African languages, it will be possible for Mozambican citizens to function in a variety of sectors in their own languages, while having access to other spheres of communication through Portuguese. For South Africa, the subject of the papers by Benjamin and Maake, the situation is further complicated by the fact that the development of the use of African languages was part of the agenda of the Apartheid state. Opposition to Apartheid involved, to some extent, the insistence on English as the medium for resistance; to promote the use of African languages was tantamount to endorsing the so-called 'independent homelands'. In this context, therefore, in recognition of the fact that National Party Governments since 1948 had vigorously, and successfully, promoted Afrikaans against English, resistance involved deliberately using English (as was demonstrated by the 1976 school strikes against the imposition of Afrikaans as medium of instruction in black schools).

Both Benjamin and Maake make programmatic statements which appeal for the recognition of diversity through the official promotion of varieties of 'functional multilingualism' on a regional basis within South Africa such that, for example, Southern Sotho, Afrikaans and English would become the 'official' languages of the Orange Free State, whereas Xhosa, Afrikaans and English would be the 'official' languages of the Cape. The protection of a right to be educated, and generally express oneself, in the mother tongue is carefully balanced with equal access to the lingua franca(s) which allow access to other spheres of social life. Insofar as those other spheres are the world of the existing and emerging élites, those whose mother tongue is the lingua franca will remain at an advantage; Maake looks to redress the balance by prescribing the learning of two languages for all children starting school. It is perhaps not surprising that it is South Africa that engenders the strongest prescriptive response among the papers presented here.

In contrast the final two papers in this part represent pragmatic perspectives on language issues. Fairhead examines the relation between Kinyabwisha, Swahili and French in Eastern Zaïre. His discussion concentrates upon the way in which patterns of language use mesh with local political and technological debates in which concepts are being translated into and out of alternating cultures. Viewed from the perspective of Kinyabwisha-speakers, Swahili is as 'foreign' as French. Kinyabwisha, the language, is a medium of communication anyone can learn, but a linked concept, *ikinyabwisha*, 'the economy of heat', constitutes an explanatory system representing the Bwisha 'form of life'. Fairhead's paper draws attention to the significance of contextual debates for an understanding of patterns of language use. Van Binsbergen's meticulous comparison between ethnic minorities and their languages in Zambia and Botswana broaches the complexities of state policies as they impinge upon the formation of ethnicities and the politicizing of language issues. His analysis challenges any facile equation between ethnicity and divisiveness within the nation state by revealing the multiplicity of historical circumstances which influence how ethnicity will become politically salient, as well as the multiplicity of levels of government upon which ethnic agendas may impinge to divergent effect. The relations between ethnicity and its anchorage in language change rapidly, and he identifies post-colonial hegemonizing of the state by particular language interests, as well as the moment of standardization of minority languages in writing, as key episodes in continuing processes of the objectification of ethnicity and language. Similar language policies in Botswana and Zambia furnished part of the context for understanding the trajectories of Kalanga and Nkoya ethnicities and their associated languages, but language policy cannot itself explain what happened in these two cases. In his espousal of a 'graded model' of recognition of languages for different uses at levels of statal organization, van Binsbergen carefully distances himself from the view that a single blueprint can be applied to the historical particularities of African states that have developed distinct characters and political problems during the post-colonial period.

7 The language situation and language use in Mozambique

J. M. M. Katupha

The choice of language and the use to which it is put is central to a people's definition of themselves in relation to the entire universe. Hence language has always been at the heart of the two contending social forces in the Africa of the twentieth century.

(wa Thiong'o 1986: 4)

Thinking about policy behind the current language situation in Mozambique is no different from other countries in independent black Africa today. It vacillates between dismantling colonial relationships on the one hand, and on the other striving for nation-building, technical development as well as openness to the outside world. This has led such countries generally to adopt language policies in which the language of the former colonizing power is used for official communication, while social communication relies largely on African languages. Indeed, in the process of purging society of colonial values, the languages of the colonizing powers are considered untouchable. This may be compared with the resolution passed by the Organisation of African Unity, which, while vehemently condemning the evils of colonialism, urges every member state to accept as sacred the current territorial boundaries, a product of colonialism. The aim of this paper (which was first presented at the nineteenth Annual African Linguistics Conference, Boston University, April 1988) is to discuss language use and its specificities as well as inherent contradictions in Mozambique arising from the current language policy.

The paper characterizes the multilingual situation of the country. Then it discusses the social use of each group of languages. Functional bilingualism emerges as a possible language policy to be adopted by Government. The last part of the paper suggests that functional bilingualism is a provisional solution securing cultural preservation and modernization until African languages are able to fulfil the functions of European languages.

THE LANGUAGE SITUATION IN MOZAMBIQUE

Mozambique is a multilingual country. Apart from European languages (Portuguese, English and others) all African languages spoken by Mozambicans belong to the Bantu group. The extent of dialectal variation amongst the Bantu languages of Mozambique requires further investigation. A preliminary survey indicates, however, the existence of languages from four of Guthrie's zones representing eight distinct language groups:

1 *Zone G*
   Language Group G40: Swahili
   Languages: ki-Swahili, ki-Mwaani
2 *Zone P*
   Language Group P20: Yao
   Languages: chi-Yao, chi-Makonde (chi-Maviha)
   Language Group P30: Makua
   Languages: e-Makhuwa, e-Lomwe, e-Chuwabo, e-Ngulu, etc.
3 *Zone N*
   Language Group N30: Nyanja
   Languages: chi-Nyanja, chi-Chewa (chi-Manganja), etc.
   Language Group N40: Nsenga-Sena
   Languages: chi-Nsenga, chi-Nyungwe, etc., chi-Sena (chi-Ruwe, chi-Podzo)
4 *Zone S*
   Language Group S10: Shona
   Languages: chi-Manyika, chi-Tewe, chi-Ndau
   Languages Group S50: Tsonga
   Languages: shi-Tswa, shi-Changana, shi-Ronga
   Language Group S60: Chopi
   Languages: chi-Chopi, gi-Tonga

There is a certain degree of inter-intelligibility amongst members of the same language group, to such an extent that they may be considered dialectal variants. This is the case within all language groups, with the exception of the Yao group of languages (P20: chi-Yao, chi-Makonde), the inter-intelligibility of which needs to be investigated. The Chopi group of languages (S60) occupies a restricted area within the zone of influence of the Tsonga group. It is often the case, therefore, that the native speakers of the former group can speak one of the language variants of the latter. Four most widely-spoken languages can be distinguished from within this language network:

1   e-Makhuwa 41 per cent

2 shi-Tsonga 19 per cent
3 chi-Nyanja 10 per cent
4 chi-Shona 8 per cent.

Other languages or groups of languages are spoken within the sphere of influence of the above four.

LANGUAGE POLICY AND LANGUAGE USE

Mozambique is no exception in the decisions made concerning the language of the former colonizing power within independent Africa. Portuguese was adopted during the armed struggle for independence waged by FRELIMO (Mozambican Liberation Front). In those days Portuguese was retained as a bridge in the face of inter-regional barriers to communication. Its adoption may be considered part of FRELIMO's ideological transformation from nationalistic to revolutionary ideas in which the identification of Mozambique as a nation to be (re)built was FRELIMO's main aim. Whereas under conditions of colonialism the possession of Portuguese was associated with an élite, during the armed struggle a functional Portuguese emerged within the army as well as in the liberated areas, having many of the characteristics of what Heine (1977) calls 'a horizontal medium of communication'. It was at that time proclaimed that exploitation could not be defined in terms of colour or language. One could be of any colour or race, speak a native language that people could understand, and yet be an exploiter. The use of Portuguese was therefore justified not only as overcoming regional problems of communication but also was considered the 'enemy's weapon' in the hands of FRELIMO. Portuguese was also used in the ideological development of the new administration in the liberated zones. In the meantime African languages remained a major emotional expression of nationalism, expressed in nationalist dances and songs. Since independence, Portuguese, accordingly, has been seen as playing the following roles:

1 a unifying language
2 a language of official communication
3 a language of formal learning including literacy campaigns.

These roles assigned to Portuguese are in contrast with its historical role under Portuguese colonialism which, pursuing an assimilationist philosophy, paid no attention to African languages. They were pejoratively treated as 'dialects'. Portuguese was the language everyone ought to know and speak. The colonial Portuguese administration, however, developed no school network across the country. Missionary schools were the places where, in the countryside, people could learn some Portuguese either through religious teaching or in the process of learning how to serve the colonial administration.

In the urban areas the so-called official schools were designed only for children of the colonizers. Some children of the few *assimilados* could go and study in such schools. Only in exceptional cases could such children go beyond secondary education. Both in the missionary and the official schools, speaking one's native language was strictly forbidden and when one was caught speaking it, the punishment could be either ridicule or severe physical beating. Being able to speak Portuguese meant, therefore, having in one way or another, experienced the humiliation of one's own native language. The resistance to this, especially amongst the peasants in the countryside, meant that the majority of Mozambicans could neither read nor speak in Portuguese. This has continued to be the case, despite all the efforts of the Government in expanding the school network across the country and in promoting literacy campaigns. Portuguese remains the language of the minority, mostly concentrated in the urban areas. On the other hand, culturally, the Bantu languages constitute the basis of Mozambican cultural identity. Mutual inter-comprehensibility derived from genetic relatedness and geographical closeness makes it easier to overcome the blocking of communication between or within ethnic groups. This reality, however, has been pragmatically ignored or strategically overshadowed in the language policy inherited from colonial history. In the adoption of Portuguese as the language of official communication, it appears that cultural development has been dissociated from technical development and the role of the Bantu languages passed over in silence.

Language in Mozambique shows two patterns of bilingual behaviour, that I have characterized as horizontal and vertical bilingualism. This opposition was used by Heine (1977) to distinguish informally acquired and socially neutral languages from languages usually formally acquired that create social distance. I had used this terminological distinction before I came across Heine's article (Katupha 1984a), with different implications. By horizontal bilingualism I mean the use of two genetically cognate languages as opposed to vertical bilingualism – the use of two genetically unrelated languages. The former is practised amongst speakers of Bantu languages and the latter amongst those speakers of both Portuguese and one (or usually more) Bantu languages. The 1980 census (Moçambique 1980) characterizes Mozambican vertical bilingualism in the following figures: Portuguese is spoken by 24.4 per cent of the population comprising 1.2 per cent who speak it as their mother tongue and a further 23.2 per cent who are bilingual, the remaining 75.6 per cent of the population speaking no Portuguese at all.

Although horizontal bilingualism has not been directly measured, it is likely to be far greater than the vertical bilingualism revealed by these figures. In communicative as well as developmental terms, the Bantu languages still play a great role internally, especially in the countryside. Indeed, this is recognized by the Government and in spite of the lack of a clear definition of their role, there has been concern that something should be done. The Minister of Information said recently, 'a challenge which must be rapidly confronted in broadcasting is to produce programmes in Mozambican languages and not limit ourselves to translating such programmes into them. The language issue is a fundamental question of culture and policy that should not be ignored through passivity, inertia and laissez-faire' (*Noticias*, 8 January 1988). This conspicuous manifestation of anxiety by a member of the Government, thirteen years after independence, is indicative of how difficult it has been to spell out an appropriate language policy in tune with the recognized political and cultural status that the African languages enjoy. Adopting measures for the economic and technological development of the country without at the same time developing the African languages would appear to ignore the fundamental question of the relationship between policy and culture. In other words, economic and technological development would be impaired if there were no clear definition of the role of Bantu languages in the country.

In general terms, although there are four languages relatively widely spoken in the country, no language is more important than any other. They enjoy equal status and social prestige within the current political framework of a developing language policy. Apart from in private social life they are officially used in the radio broadcasting network, but only at a regional level. Portuguese and English are used in nationwide and external broadcasting programmes. An attempt to use African languages in local 'walljournals' has proved ineffective, partly for lack of systematized and standardized alphabetic scripts on the one hand, and the high level of illiteracy on the other. Indeed, the lack of standard alphabetic scripts increases the number of illiterate people in as much as few of those who can write and read in Portuguese can do so in their own mother tongues. The different Christian sects constitute a sizeable sector making extensive use of African languages in worship, Bible and liturgical translation and religious instruction. Although no sociolinguistic survey has been carried out it is possible to signal three major categories of people according to the language they use in their social interaction:

1 those who can speak Portuguese
2 those who only speak local languages
3 those who can speak both local and foreign languages.

In the capital city of Maputo the following language valuations may be observed: Portuguese is generally regarded as a language of success, power and social prestige amongst those who speak only the local languages. Amongst those who can speak Portuguese, the great majority defend the view that the African languages ought to be used in all aspects of life as much as Portuguese. However, when it comes to comparing Portuguese and other European languages, most of those who can speak it regard English as the language for further opportunity, especially among the younger generation.

Despite kiSwahili being spoken within Mozambique (on the northern border with Tanzania) it is regarded as a foreign language and usually identified as the language of FRELIMO soldiers trained in Tanzania. Indeed, whenever there is a gathering of such people it is normal to hear them speaking some kiSwahili of a kind.

The influx and movement of people of differing language groups in the capital of the country, Maputo, divides the speakers of African languages into two major groups: those who can speak one of the variants of the Tsonga group and those who can not. Usually the latter are known as *swi-ngondo* (sing, *xi-ngondo*, from *Ku-gondagonda*, 'to utter meaningless or unfamiliar sounds', A. Sitoe, 1988, personal communication), a term apparently coined during the colonial era to mean 'barbarian', or 'those who cannot speak my language', and used to discriminate against any person coming from any part of the country beyond the Save river. The term appears to have been fostered and spread, during the struggle for independence, by the colonial forces in order psychologically to subdue those captured by the Portuguese soldiers in the northern part of the country and brought to the then Lourenço Marques, the 'land of civilized people'. Nowadays, though still with discriminatory and pejorative overtones, it has become accepted amongst residents of the capital.

FUNCTIONAL BILINGUALISM AND EDUCATION

The linguistic picture presented above indicates that Mozambique is, indeed, no exception in the move towards the use of African languages. The uncertain and rather sluggish move towards their use in public employment, administration, as well as the private sector, shows how the European model of modernization is entrenched in independent Africa. In an attempt to address the question of African languages, in 1978, the then Minister of Education declared that they should be developed in such a way as to bring them in line with the development of Portuguese (1978, Workshop on Methods of Portuguese Teaching, Maputo). This was to be done, apparently, not so much for reasons of cultural preservation but as part of a psychological strategy directed at the education of children in primary schools as well as people in the adult education sector. This education strategy, centring on the child's pre-school experience, as well as the world around it, is meant sharply to contrast with and replace the colonial educational strategy which gave no importance to the social environment of those who had access to education. The fact that in the new system of education, the pre-school experience as well as the world surrounding the students is constantly taken as an input for learning strategies brings the notion of functional bilingualism into play. Functional bilingualism is regarded as an underlying educational strategy which will allow the student's perception of the surrounding world, including his or her mother tongue, to contribute to the process of learning Portuguese. Learning the latter in this way means the oblivion of the former is avoided. However, economic and technical problems have so far prevented the implementation of such a strategy as far as language teaching is concerned. Whether functional bilingualism is to remain merely a curricular concept or whether it will become part of an overt official language policy in which the use of Portuguese and of African languages would become equal in all spheres of communication, is not yet clear.

My own view is that for economically ailing independent Africa, functional bilingualism is a realistic compromise between the preservation of cultural traditions and modernization. It is a step forward which deserves to be given a chance to prove itself right or wrong. Its full implementation should start in education for it reduces the imbalance in the take-up of learning opportunities between those who enter school already having some knowledge of the language of learning and those who do not. Indeed, whatever language policy is adopted African languages must have a well-defined place if the widening gap between cities and countryside is to be closed or, at least, minimized.

REFERENCES

Heine, B. (1977) 'Vertical and horizontal communication in Africa', *Afrika Spectrum* 12: 231–8.

Katupha, J. M. M. (1984a) 'Bilinguismo na Educaçao Formal e Nao Formal, comunicaçao apresentada no seminario sobre Comunicaçao Social em Apoio aos Programas de Desenvolvimento'. Paper given at a UNESCO/FUNUAP conference, Maputo, 12 November – 7 December.

—— (1984b) 'Alguna Dados sobre a Situaçao Linguistica na R. P. M. e as suas Implicaçoes para o Desenvolvimento Rural', unpublished manuscript, Maputo: Universidade Eduardo Mondlane.

Moçambique. (1980) *Recenseamento Geral da Populaçao, IV: Populaçao e Escolarizaçao*. Maputo: Direcçao Geral de Estatisticas.

wa Thiong'o, N. (1986) *Decolonizing the Mind: the Politics of Language in African Literature*, London: James Currey.

8 Language and the struggle for racial equality in the development of a non-racial Southern African nation

Jean Benjamin

Language is a tool for communication. It is the medium through which thoughts, values, attitudes, are transmitted within and between cultural groups. It is also an index of group and class categorization and identification, a tool for group mobilization, a medium for expressing and assessing knowledge and a tool for gaining access to class mobility. In South Africa the communicative function of language has been obscured by the tendency of those in power to use language as means to maintain relations of dominance of Whites over Blacks. In what follows, 'Black' is used as a collective term for all those who are not White South Africans. Where necessary, for instance when discussing the effects of Apartheid, reference will be made to 'Coloureds', 'Indians' and 'Africans'.

Apartheid language policy and planning functioned to exclude African languages from official status within South Africa. Language played a major role in the division of the society into racial and tribal groupings. Further, the low status afforded African languages and the unavailability of these as school subjects in White, Coloured and Indian schools severely affected the motivation of these groups to learn African languages. Mother tongue education ensured that English- and Afrikaans-speaking Whites would be equipped to participate in the national system; it served the opposite purpose for Africans. Whites benefited directly from this Anglo-European national culture, while it supplemented Apartheid legislation to prevent the integration of the Black population into the South African nation. The Afrikaner nationalists further appropriated Afrikaans and used it to promote their own nationalist identity; thus Afrikaans became stigmatized as the language of the oppressor amongst Africans. Resources were allocated for the development of Afrikaans to enable it to compete effectively with English on a technical level. The development of African languages was limited to the promotion of traditional ethnic identities subject to the control of Afrikaner officials who sat on language boards. Initially, the Apartheid government denied Africans access to English for fear of creating 'White Collar aspirations' amongst them. After the Soweto rebellion however, an English medium of instruction followed initial mother tongue instruction. However, lack of adequate allocation of educational resources and the subsequent crises in Bantu Education ensured that inadequate proficiency in English would remain a stumbling block to Black advancement.

This essay focusses on the role language has played in entrenching Apartheid inter-group relations. I argue that language should be recognized as a terrain of struggle for the attainment of racial equality in a South Africa within which all cultural groups are recognised. I attempt to spell out an alternative language dispensation for the development of a non-racial South African nation.

IMPORTANCE OF OFFICIAL STATUS

Apartheid language policies entrenched inequalities and divisions between groups by granting official status to English and Afrikaans to the exclusion of indigenous Black South African languages. The disadvantages of not having official recognition for one's language are most often quoted by Afrikaans linguists concerned that Afrikaans may lose its official status in a new dispensation in which only English has official recognition. These disadvantages include the considerations that:

1 knowledge of the official language becomes a prerequisite for appointment and promotion in state institutions (thus non-speakers are excluded from state jobs);
2 in the case of a powerful official language, such as English, the language can become irresistible even in non-state institutions such as the church;
3 psychological pressure leads to parents preferring the official language as sole medium of education, sometimes leading to it becoming the home language of non-speakers (for the sake of the children's advancement);
4 in such a case the right to demand a non-official language as a school medium becomes meaningless or even counter-productive;
5 a further 'psychological' factor is added when the state and its instruments propagate negative attitudes toward the non-official language and its speakers (Webb 1990: 2).

Although these implications are quoted most often only in the context of Afrikaans losing its official status to English, they are equally valid in considering the need for granting official status to African languages in a dispensation which is inclusive of all cultural groups. In the present dispensation, Afrikaans- and English-speaking South Africans are privileged by the official recognition of their languages while it is speakers of African languages who suffer the disadvantages mentioned above.

LANGUAGE AS INDEX TO DIVIDE AND RULE

The official recognition of Afrikaans and English only was central in the Apartheid government's intention to create a South African nation characterized by Western European culture while dividing the African majority into ethnic minorities in the land of their birth.

Language was often the only basis on which Africans were classified into ethnic groups, stripped of their South African citizenship and forcibly removed to Bantustans (McLean 1990: 2). Ironically, such action, ranging from forced removals through to Bantu Education, has often been interpreted as support for the language rights of Black people (McLean 1990: 2). Few other countries in the world have attempted through legislation to separate demographically different groups on the basis of their vernaculars. In South Africa the vernacular became the basic feature of state nationalism (Brown 1988/9: 34).

Apartheid language policy further entrenched ethnic division by not making African languages accessible to non-speakers, thereby blocking communication between different ethnic groups. Language has, thus, been used as an effective barrier between those classified as Whites, Coloureds and Indians on the one hand, and those classified as Africans on the other. Separate group areas and education systems ensured that a number of generations of South Africans classified as White, Coloured and Indian would grow up unable to communicate in an African language, or to identify with African culture. African culture was thus mystified while the members of the dominant group promoted stereotypes of Africans as 'savages' not deserving to be included as an aspect of the 'civilized' world.

LANGUAGE AND POWER RELATIONS

The Anglo-European culture imposed by the Apartheid government not only symbolized centuries of oppression through slavery, colonial conquest and, later, Apartheid, but also contained ideological baggage antagonistic to being African and working class.

Frank Meintjies (1989: 15) first showed through several examples how language reflects, entrenches and reproduces power relations between White employers and Black workers; for example, the use of words such as 'boy' and 'girl' to refer to Black men and women, employment contracts for Black workers which contain terms such as 'obedience' and 'discipline' and criminalize 'latecoming' and 'talking back', as well as the differential use of the label 'thief': theft is used with reference to workers' misconduct, while 'fraud', 'corruption', 'embezzlement' and 'improper conduct' refer to management misconduct. Meintjies (1989: 16) pointed out, however, that 'Language is not inherently oppressive; its role is defined by the people who wield it and the social forces which act upon it'. Language is, therefore, an active terrain of struggle upon which the forces of Apartheid act to subjugate the Black majority, and which the forces of liberation should strive to transform. A democratic government should, through corpus planning, eliminate overtly racist discourse. Editors, journalists, writers and educators should be vigilant in eradicating language uses which perpetuate the ideologies of racism and patriarchy.

AFRIKAANS AND POWER RELATIONS

According to Trudgill (1974) oppression through language can take a number of forms. Most obviously, governments can discourage or prevent groups of people from using their native language for political reasons; Afrikaners suffered this form of oppression under British rule. Concern with their language rights in opposing British linguistic imperialism provided a focus and support for emergent Afrikaner nationalism in the last quarter of the nineteenth century (Reagan 1985). When the Nationalist Party came to power in 1948, however, it appropriated Afrikaans and used it to impose its value system on the broader South African community (Davids 1987; Du Plessis 1988). Thus, Afrikaans became linked with White power politics (Louw-Potgieter 1991: 329) and became known as 'the language of the oppressor'. Resistance to Afrikaner nationalist dominance and to the imposition of Afrikaans in African schools culminated in the Soweto riots, one of the outcomes of which was the withdrawal of Afrikaans as medium of instruction from Black schools (Steyn 1987).

The appropriation and politicization of Afrikaans by right wing Afrikaner ideologues resulted in the stigmatization of Afrikaans and decreased the likelihood of its spread as a lingua franca (Cluver 1991: 10). Present fears by some Afrikaners that Afrikaans would die out if it lost its official status are misguided and make sense only when Afrikaans is viewed as the language of the Afrikaner. The survival and growth of Afrikaans resides not in its official imposition, but rather in the recognition of all its varieties and cultures, in the opening of the language group boundaries to all its speakers, and in its capacity to rid itself ideologically of its racist connotations.

EFFECT OF OFFICIAL STATUS ON AFRIKAANS DEVELOPMENT

The use of Afrikaans as a language of government from 1925 onwards created a need for it to be standardized and lexically developed to enable its speakers to compete effectively with English speakers. Milestones in the development of Afrikaans include:

1 the founding of the 'Suid-Afrikaanse Akademie vir Taal, Lettere en Kuns' (1908),
2 the publication (1917 onwards) of the *Afrikaanse Woordelys en Spëlreëls*,
3 the creation of the Vaktaalburo (technical language bureau) in 1950, and
4 the implementation of 'Christian National Education' (CNE) and the 'mother tongue principle' in 1948 (Reagan 1985).

All of these institutions excluded Blacks and enabled Afrikaners to conduct their affairs in their mother tongue up to the highest levels of state, social, and technological functions.

AFRICAN LANGUAGES NOT DEVELOPED

The mother tongue principle never produced the advantages for speakers of African languages that it did for English and Afrikaans speakers within South Africa. The government never intended to develop African languages into fully standardized languages but to limit them to use within the African family, cultural group, the Bantustan and the school (Cluver 1991: 16).

In line with its policies of mother tongue instruction within Bantu Education, the government took up the task of developing African languages. Language boards were created to expand the vocabularies of the larger African languages for use in secondary and tertiary education and in the mass media (Cluver 1991: 16). This happened without the democratic participation of Africans and was therefore rejected by the ANC (Brown 1988/9: 42). Thus, the government's efforts to develop African languages were perceived by African leaders as an attempt to keep Africans in primitive tribal bondage (Lithuli 1962). At the time, the ANC had not entirely dismissed the notion of the development of African languages. Instead it was more concerned with the participation of African people themselves in the development of their languages (Brown 1988/9: 42).

Inherent in the promotion of different African languages for cultural affirmation was also a potential for inter-tribal division and conflict. The proposal to develop a unified orthography for closely related African languages for the purpose of promoting unity amongst Africans, as well as to facilitate the development of one or more standard African languages, emerged in the 1930s (Tucker 1929: 200) and again in the 1940s (Nhlapo 1945). More recently Alexander (1989) has revived the proposal for the unification of related African languages as part of a strategy for nation-building. A criticism of this position is that unification of languages through language planning will not in itself create unity amongst speakers of the different languages. Social psychological evidence in this regard indicates that speakers of different languages will converge only if perceived benefits outweigh costs (Giles, Bourhis and Taylor 1977). Acceptance of this strategy by the different speech communities is therefore crucial to its effectiveness.

Another perspective, emerging from within the Communist Party in the 1940s and endorsed by the influential Soviet Africanist Prof. I. Potckhin, argued for the development of all African languages. The Pan Africanists within the liberation movement argued instead for Swahili as lingua franca. Neither of these positions was taken up by the ANC during the 1950s, who were satisfied with choosing English as a unifying language in opposition to government attempts to promote tribalism through language differences (Brown 1988/9: 42).

More recently it is becoming evident that the choice of an ex-colonial language for the purpose of national integration makes possible only horizontal integration. This involves the combination of the educated élites from the various linguistic groups which may comprise only 10–15 per cent of the population. The alternative, vertical, integration would enable the integration of the élites with the masses and allow the vast majority of the people who have no access to the official language to participate in the social, economic and political system. This sort of integration is only possible through an African language (Bamgbose 1991).

In the ANC's present constitutional proposals, the right of all South African languages to enjoy equal status is affirmed. Similarly, Willemse has argued for the development of all South African languages:

> In a liberated South Africa the state and government, fully representative of the African majority, must be charged with the responsibility to protect and develop African languages.... The state

must also be charged with putting in action processes that would facilitate the development of multi-lingualism in South Africa, be that in terms of education, official media or commerce.
(Willemse 1991: 7).

The development of multilingualism is not limited to the achievement of equal status for different language groups. Through the development of individual bilingualism and multilingualism, it aims to overcome the barriers of inter-ethnic communication. The advantages of bilingualism for English and Afrikaans speakers in South Africa are undeniable and correlate with a reasonable standard of living achieved by the majority of these speakers. Where African languages are concerned, however, the diversity of languages has often been seen as a problem. It has been pointed out, however, that in the African situation a person who speaks several languages should be regarded as a better integrated citizen than one who is proficient in only one language, even if it happens to be the official language (Bamgbose 1991). In the meetings and conferences of the liberation movement in South Africa during the 1980s and 1990s, such multilingual individuals have performed an invaluable service in translating between the various languages prevalent to enable the masses to participate in the deliberations.

BANTU EDUCATION AND MOTHER TONGUE INSTRUCTION

In accordance with the stated aims of Bantu Education, not to educate the 'Bantu' 'above the level of certain forms of labour' (Verwoerd 1954, quoted by Meintjies 1989: 17), oppression through language initially took the form of encouraging diversity for the purposes of divide and rule by retribalizing all Africans into separate ethnic groups. Black people, therefore, regarded mother tongue instruction, not as a valuable democratic right, but as an attempt to isolate them from the ruling élite, from possibilities of advancement, from access to international literature and to other contacts (Trudgill 1974). Whereas Afrikaans- and English-speaking White South Africans could achieve social and economic mobility through mother tongue proficiency, the dissatisfaction of Africans with mother tongue instruction within Bantu Education, is well documented (Bunting 1964; Hirson 1981; Troup 1976).

Reagan (1985) challenged these objections to the 'mother tongue principle' drawing parallels with progressive and anti-imperialist education systems in other African countries. It has been cautioned, however, that international theories regarding the efficacy of mother tongue programmes should not be generalized uncritically to South African society (McLean 1990:4; Cluver 1991: 17). In spite of the fact that Reagan pointed out in the same paper that language planning is political, his criticisms of Apartheid language policy within Bantu Education were treated in an apolitical manner. In justifying Apartheid language policies Reagan (1985) overlooked the fact that they were imposed upon a disempowered population. As McLean (1990: 5) correctly pointed out 'a language policy is not intrinsically good or intrinsically bad. It is good or bad ... in terms of its human consequences within the specific sociopolitical milieu which it occupies.'

In the case of Africans, the consequence of Apartheid language policy was the denial of human rights. Language rights must proceed beyond initial mother tongue instruction. Individuals should have the right to use, speak, publish, be educated, and be employed, in the languages of their choice. All South African languages should be promoted and developed ultimately to deal with all the functions of language within speech communities as well as within the broader South African society. Multilingualism should be a conscious and state-aided endeavour (Willemse 1991). Only then will mother tongue instruction reap the pedagogic benefits advocated by linguists such as Reagan (1985).

ARGUMENTS ABOUT ENGLISH AS LINGUA FRANCA

It is not unusual for newly independent post-colonial countries to choose a lingua franca which is highly developed and ex-colonial (Brown 1988/9: 41). In the 1930s and 1940s the prevailing view within the liberation movement was that English should be the lingua franca as it would cut across ethnic divisions. This stand was taken by the ANC in opposition to the state, which supported the development of African languages for the purpose of divide and rule (Brown 1988/9: 41). More recently the potential of English for the fostering of national unity has been advocated by Alexander (1989) and Meerkotter (1985: 89). Alexander (1989), however, argues for English as lingua franca in the short term, with the longer term elaboration and unification of the Sotho and Nguni languages for this purpose. Meerkotter, on the other hand, argues for English as sole national lingua franca.

The use of English and the development and recognition of African languages as official at national and/or regional levels are inseparable. Recent perspectives on second language acquisition show that the learning of a second high status language is optimal when the first language is not threatened (Padilla *et al.* 1991: 125). At a more pragmatic level, it has been argued that the adoption of English as sole national lingua franca would militate against the development of African languages

(Dirven 1990; Willemse 1991). For these reasons, both for political and educational purposes the use of English as a national lingua franca should not occur at the expense of other languages in South Africa.

ENGLISH AND THE DANGER OF 'THOUGHT CONTROL'

English, because of its liberal ideology and status as a world language, is more acceptable as a second language – hence the widespread preference amongst Africans for English as a language of wider communication and educational medium. It also gains support from being a popular educational medium. Due to international economics, many textbooks are published in English. Willemse argues, however, that while English proficiency provides access to the international world, there is also the danger of a concomitant internationalization of thought control through the 'world' language (Willemse 1991).

Njabulo Ndebele (1986) in a keynote address to the Jubilee Conference of the English Academy of Southern Africa, warned against uncritical complacency regarding the role and future of English in South Africa. Within the context of the development of English as a world-language, Ndebele is critical of the desire of native speakers of English to maintain control over English in order to spread their influence. He draws a further link between the colonial relationship between European and African cultures in South Africa and the relationship between English and African languages. He states that the future cannot be defined solely by those who have previously wielded power to their exclusive advantage. Ndebele argues for the development of a new South African English which should be freed from 'the functional instruction of corporate English of American and British imperialism' (Ndebele 1986).

ENGLISH AS ÉLITIST

Further problems connected to the adoption of English as a national lingua franca concern its potential for entrenching unequal class relations. English is acquired through formal education and tends to be used by relatively educated speakers. Increasingly in South Africa, the distribution of English is less a feature of race than of class (McLean 1990: 9; Dirven 1990: 22). Access to English is regulated by class features, since its primary agent of dissemination is education, and its secondary agent is contact, which is more likely to occur between first language English speakers and the African urban middle class than the African rural working class (McLean 1990: 9).

Redressing the problem depends on a broader restructuring of South African society. Solutions include making English more accessible (e.g. through adult education and increasing opportunities for access to education, contact with first language English speakers), changing the status of English and the African languages by encouraging a 'difference' rather than a 'deficit' view of devalued varieties, elaborating the African languages, as well as raising the socio-economic status of African language speakers (McLean 1990: 9).

UNITY IN DIVERSITY IN A DEMOCRATIC NON-RACIAL SOUTH AFRICA

A clear distinction must be drawn between the narrow nationalism which Apartheid represented and progressive conceptions of national diversity. Oliver Tambo articulated this distinction in his address to FRELIMO in Mozambique during its Fourth Congress. He conceived of a future South African nation 'in which sovereignty will come from the people as a whole and not a collection of Bantustans and racial and tribal groupings organized to perpetuate minority power' (quoted by Jordan 1988: 117). Jordan further argued that, 'The nation . . . is not defined by skin colour or racial designation; its parameters are set by individual acts of voluntary adherence, which require submergence of other loyalties in favour of this larger unit' (1988: 118).

Although diversity should be recognized, people should not be assigned to eternally frozen categories. A democratic state should not legislate involuntary adherence to externally defined ethnic groups. It cannot legislate on diversity, neither can it abolish affinities based on such groups (Jordan 1988: 119). Whilst much has been written about the national question (Van Diepen 1988) such an alternative vision of a nation has not been popularized. People have lived through the Apartheid construction of group identity, of which language was often the only index. Many South Africans have internalized these racial labels and representations. While the Population Registration Act has been repealed, the racial labels and discourse continue to entrench racial differentiation. In this regard, politicians, educators and other opinion makers, at least those who are serious in their endeavour to develop non-racialism in South Africa, should not entrench race differentiation through unnecessary references to such labels in their speeches.

IMPLICATIONS FOR A NEW LANGUAGE DISPENSATION

In a new language dispensation, different language and cultural groups should not be set up in competition with one another. All major languages in a region should enjoy the advantages of official recognition. A South African national should be able to speak all the major languages in a particular region. In the Western Cape, for example, Afrikaans, English and Xhosa could become prerequisite for state jobs which involve communication with the public. Such a policy would not only produce more employment for Xhosa language teachers but would also provide incentives for non-speakers to learn Xhosa and seek opportunities for contact across ethnic barriers. Language would thus cease to be a barrier in inter-ethnic contact.

Educational and other state institutions should emphasize the multicultural and multilingual nature of the South African nation. Regional official languages should be taught in all schools by mother tongue speakers. Languages spoken by smaller speech and cultural communities should, wherever possible, be taught as subjects in schools.

The elaboration of languages should be performed by speakers of those languages, and resources should be pumped into the development of African languages in order to redress historical inequalities.

Even if English were to be decided upon as the national language of wider communication for pragmatic and economic reasons, this should not happen at the cost of developing African languages. Special emphasis should be placed on educating children within a multicultural context, in which tolerance for different cultures within the South African nation should be promoted. A South African English, which reflects all its users, should be developed and ways should be found to make English accessible beyond formal education.

CONCLUSION

I have attempted to show how language has been used through policy and planning by the Apartheid regime to complement Apartheid legislation and create a society consisting of a dominating Anglo-European White minority and a host of tribal and ethnic groupings (so-called national groups) held firmly in place socially, geographically, and linguistically. This structure has been entrenched within the various education departments to such an extent that the government hopes it can safely repeal Apartheid legislation because the social construction of ethnic groups, and the concomitant status relations between them, will continue to be reproduced.

With the present dispensation, the rights of communities to be educated in their mother tongues and within their own cultural environments will continue to maintain separate ethnic groups, while differential status and resource allocation between Afrikaans and English speakers on the one hand, and speakers of African languages on the other hand, will ensure that Africans either remain within their respective cultural communities or assimilate within the 'national' culture on terms or standards dictated by the White minority.

Mother tongue instruction would continue to ensure direct access to national resources for Whites while social mobility for Africans would be dependent on mastering a second higher status language and cultural environment. Thus, inequality between Whites and the majority of Blacks will continue to be entrenched. The aforementioned scenario obtains in the present stage of reform where, for example, traditionally White and Coloured educational institutions are being opened to African children in the absence of a multicultural educational environment.

At its national conference in 1992, the ANC adopted a human rights and language policy which emphasizes the right of the individual to communicate in the language of her/his choice, as well as the recognition, development and promotion of all the languages and cultures which make up South African society. Realization of this policy depends on the extent to which ordinary people, community organizations, churches, educational organizations, and trade unions recognize the role that language has played in dividing South Africans into ethnic groups and in entrenching inequality between White and Black groups. They need to recognize that language is one terrain in the struggle for building non-racialism and place the language and national question on their agendas. This struggle needs to be conducted within the classroom and the family, where attitudes towards languages are formulated. Unless people at the grassroots level develop alternative conceptions of the South African nation and consciously strive towards the removal of barriers to inter-ethnic communication and the achievement of equality, race discrimination will continue to reproduce itself through language.

REFERENCES

Alexander, N. (1989) *Language Policy and National Unity in South Africa/Azania*, Cape Town: Buchu Books.
Bamgbose, A. (1991) *Language and the Nation: the Language Question in Sub-Saharan Africa*, Edinburgh: Edinburgh University Press.
Brown, D. (1988/9) 'Speaking in tongues: Apartheid and language in South Africa', *Perspectives in Education*, 10, 2: 33–46.
Bunting, B. (1964) *The Rise of the South African Reich*, Harmondsworth: Penguin.
Cluver, A. B. de V. (1991) 'Language planning models for a post-Apartheid South Africa', *Language Problems and Language Planning*, 15, 2: 1–37.
Davids, A. (1987) 'The role of Afrikaans in the history of the Cape Muslim

community', in H. du Plessis and T. de Plessis (eds.) *Afrikaans en Taalpolitiek*, Pretoria: HAUM.

Dirven, R. (1990) 'Contact and conflict linguistics in Southern Africa', in K. Chick (ed.) *Searching for Relevance: Contextual Issues in Applied Linguistics in Southern Africa*, Durban: South African Applied Linguistics Association.

Du Plessis, L. T. (1988) 'Politiek en die ontwikkeling van Afrikaans', *Tydskrif vir Letterkunde*, 26: 75–80.

Giles, H., Bourhis, R. Y., and Taylor, D. M. (1977) 'Dimensions of Welsh identity', *European Journal of Social Psychology*, 7: 29–39.

Hirson, B. (1981) 'Language in control and resistance in South Africa', *African Affairs* 80, 319: 219–37.

Jordan, P. (1988) 'The South African liberation movement and the making of a new nation', in M. van Diepen (ed.) *The National Question in South Africa*, London and New Jersey: Zed Books.

Lithuli, A. (1962) *Let My People Go*, London: Collins.

Louw-Potgieter, J. (1991) 'Language and identity', in D. Foster and J. Louw-Potgieterin (eds.) *Social Psychology in South Africa*, Johannesburg: Lexicon.

McLean, D. (1990) 'Guarding against the bourgeois revolution: some aspects of language planning in the context of national democratic struggle', paper presented to public symposium on 'Language Planning' held at the University of the Witwatersrand on 2 February 1990.

Meerkotter, D. (1985) 'Moving towards monolingualism in a multicultural society: an educational perspective', *Journal of Language Teaching of the South African Association for Language Teaching* 19, 3: 88–95.

Meintjies, F. (1989) 'Language and labour', *Staffrider* 8, 3/4: 15.

Ndebele, N. (1986) 'The English language and social change in South Africa', Keynote Paper delivered at Jubilee Conference of the English Academy of Southern Africa, 4–6 September 1986.

Nhlapo, J. (1945) *Nguni and Sotho*, Cape Town: African Bookman.

Padilla, A. M., Lindholm, K. J., Chen, A., Duran R., Hakuta, K., Lambert, W. and Tucker, G. R. (1991) 'The English Only Movement: myths, reality and implications for psychology', *American Psychologist* 46, 2: 120–30.

Reagan, T. N. (1985) 'Language planning in South African education: a conceptual overview', *Journal of Language Teaching of the South African Association for Language Teaching* 19, 3: 71–87.

Steyn, J. C. (1987) 'Afrikanernasionalisme en Afrikaans', in H. du Plessis and T. du Plessis (eds.) *Afrikaans en Taalpolitiek*, Pretoria: HAUM.

Troup, F. (1976) *Forbidden Pastures: Education under Apartheid*, London: International Defence and Aid Fund.

Trudgill, P. (1974) *Sociolinguistics: an Introduction*, London: Pelican Books.

Tucker, A. N. (1929) *The Comparative Phonetics of the Suto-Chuana Group of Bantu Languages*, London: Green and Col (reproduced by Greg International Publishers, Westmead).

Van Diepen, M. (ed.) (1988) *The National Question in South Africa*, London and New Jersey: Zed Books.

Webb, V. (1990) 'Human rights, language policy and the linguistic situation in South Africa', paper delivered at a conference on 'Sociolinguistics in Africa', held at the University of Witwatersrand between 30 January and 2 February 1990.

Willemse, H. (1991) 'A position paper on language policy in a new South Africa *New Observations* 83: 6–8. New York.

9 Dismantling the Tower of Babel
In search of a new language policy for a post-Apartheid South Africa

Nhlanhla P. Maake

This paper addresses the problems of language in relation to development and government policy in South Africa, where there is now an urgent need, coupled with other social, political and economic needs, for a new language policy, especially given the history of that country, where the domination of one group over others has had far-reaching implications for African languages and cultures.

My purpose is not to set out the history of language politics in South Africa, fascinating as that history is, especially the rise of the Afrikaans culture, language and state, *Afrikanerdom*, from a defensive position at the turn of the nineteenth century to an imperial posture from the middle of the twentieth century. My bias here is to look towards the future rather than the past, though in South Africa more than in many places the present can only be fully understood in the context of current historical legacies.

LANGUAGE DISTRIBUTION

In South Africa the question of the role and place of African languages is an urgent one. Some of the views which have been expressed with regard to other parts of Africa by neo-conservatives who want to return to African languages on the one hand, and 'progressives' who want to intensify the use of the languages of Europe on the other, are not appropriate to South Africa/Azania's unique position.

I wish to link my discussion to two representations of 'language'. The first is taken from the Old Testament, to illustrate how differences of language can be used to divide people, and the second is drawn from the New Testament, illustrating how language can be used in a constructive way for the general good.

It has been suggested by observers that Africans in South Africa/ Azania have a negative attitude towards their languages because these languages enforce division between different ethnic or tribal groups, and that certain languages belong to certain political enclaves, for instance, that *isi*Zulu is the language of the Inkatha Freedom Party and *isi*Xhosa the language of the African National Congress. This view is commonly reinforced by simplistic reports on the current faction fights in South Africa. This view grossly neglects the complexity of patterns of language use and my intention is to consider the place of African languages in South Africa currently, and how these are destined to play a no less significant role in future development – technological, industrial, social, economic and political, in post-Apartheid South Africa. The term 'African languages' here will be used with specific reference to the nine indigenous languages: Zulu, Xhosa, Swazi, Northern Sotho, Southern Sotho, Tswana, Ndebele, Tsonga and Venda, and exclude the two 'official' languages, Afrikaans and English, which are basically languages of European origin but which by now have become indigenous, in the case of Afrikaans divorced to some extent from its origins in Dutch.

However, though the speakers of these latter languages have become natives through permanent settlement for now more than three centuries, they have, to their own detriment, deprived themselves of the opportunity to become an integral part of Africa by waging wars against and segregating themselves from the native inhabitants, forming a privileged and oppressive ruling class ever since their forebears moved to the Cape in the seventeenth century.

At present the speakers of African languages constitute 68.2 per cent of the population of South Africa. The distribution of the speakers of African languages within South Africa is as follows: Zulu is spoken in Natal and Kwa-Zulu; Xhosa in the Cape Province and the 'homelands' of the Transkei, Ciskei and part of the Eastern Cape; Swazi in the 'homeland' of Ka-Ngwane; Northern Sotho in the northern Transvaal, in and around the area designated the 'homeland' of Lebowa, stretching as far south as Warmbad and the Pretoria region; Southern Sotho in the 'homeland' of QwaQwa and the major part of the Orange Free State up into the area north of the Vaal river and the southern part of the Pretoria-Witwatersrand-Vaal triangle; Tswana is spoken in the fragmented 'homeland' of Bophuthatswana and the intervening areas, the south-western part of Transvaal and north-west Orange Free State; Ndebele in the 'homeland' of Kwa-Ndebele, stretching to the eastern Transvaal; Tsonga and Venda are spoken in the far north of the Transvaal, parts of which form the 'homeland' of Gazankulu and the so-called 'independent homeland' of Venda. The boundaries are not so clearcut, and in our general outline of this mapping we take into consideration the discussion of frontiers and boundaries presented by Fardon and Furniss in the introduction to this book.

It would be reasonable to expect that South African black society would by now be thoroughly mixed in terms of languages, given the history of South Africa and the movement of population occasioned by, among other things, the destruction of the Xhosa chiefdoms (1850s) and the mighty Zulu kingdom (1879), the discovery of diamonds in Kimberley in 1867 and gold in Johannesburg in 1886, the Land Act of 1913 which deprived the African population of their land and land-ownership, leaving them with little more than 10 per cent of the land, and the taxes which were imposed forcing Africans into urban areas to earn cash through the sale of their labour. Such mixing was, however, obstructed by the Nationalist Government's 'homeland' policy, which reversed the flow, moving people from the urban back to the rural areas, and restricted the tide of potential urban dwellers with laws like the Urban Areas Consolidation Act of 1945, which was enforced with the use of the notorious Pass Laws. Many people were removed en bloc from urban areas and 'repatriated' to the homelands; in this way the language map was kept almost intact and stable.

The government made great efforts to keep each language group to itself after the destruction of mixed areas like Sophiatown, Lady Selborne, Marabastad, Eastwood, District Six, and others. In the new townships sections were demarcated for and allocated to individual language groups. But, as irony would have it, although this situation led to a strong assertion of the African languages, as each group was developing in artificial isolation from other groups in its own area, at the same time the concentration of these languages in the industrialized areas led to the inevitable mixing of people who spoke different Bantu languages in churches, work places, social gatherings and other situations, which even the most stringent prohibitions could not contain. A new generation of children was born which could identify with more than one language group. The folly of trying to keep people within the same cultural family was exposed as a shameful fiasco in industrialised areas, for there was nothing to be gained for the Africans in creating tribal laagers. Apartheid succeeded only in separating Blacks from Whites, because an overwhelming majority of Whites wanted that separation – the honesty of the Afrikaner provided a convenient scapegoat for what the English-speaking community tacitly approved of and supported.

English and Afrikaans have been recognised since the Union of South Africa in 1910 as the two official state languages. Africans had to acquire knowledge of these languages as a means of finding employment, and at no time has it ever been the policy of government, including the White South African Party and others before 1948, to foster the knowledge of English among Africans to a high level. Communication between the two groups, Africans and Europeans, as the Whites called themselves, was always a one-way monologue, where the African had to understand only enough to carry out instructions as a servant and unskilled labourer. In other words, the idea of functional multilingualism as suggested by Mateus Katupha in this book, was the lot of the African language speakers.

Since the Act of Union, Africans were educated in missionary schools, but when the National Party came to power the task of educating Africans was grudgingly removed from the mission schools, who had all along been performing their Christian duty to the displeasure of the Union Government by producing English-speaking intellectuals. Among such intellectuals were the founders of the first African-organized political movement, the African Native National Congress, such figures as Sol T. Plaatje, Walter Rubusana, Pixley ka Isaka Seme, John L. Dube, Sam Makgothi, and Saul Msane, and the later founders of the Pan-Africanist Congress, such as Robert Mangaliso Sobukwe, Anton Mziwakhe Lembede, Zaphania Mothopeng and others. It was the rise of such intellectuals which provoked the National Party of the Afrikaners into limiting the education of the Africans, so that their intellectual advancement should not be a threat to the state, and lest they write *Mene, mene, tekel ufarsin* 'your government is divided and its days are numbered' on the walls of the buildings which house the Pretoria Government, as invisible fingers wrote on the walls of the palace of King Darius in the Old Testament.

LANGUAGE POLICIES OF THE PAST

When the National Party came to power in 1948 one of its major aims was to gain for Afrikaans ascendancy over English. The first target of this policy, and the pawns in it, were the Africans, whom Dr Verwoerd, the architect of classic Apartheid, described as 'Black Englishmen'. His aim was to make Africans occupy a lowly place in the economic and social life of South Africa. As one of the means to this end he introduced the Bantu Education Act Number 47 of 1953. The official reasoning behind it was that it would replace the missionary system of education which alienated Black students from their fellows who had not had the opportunity of Western education.

Instead of enabling the majority, Bantu Education was meant to disable the minority who were championing the rights of Africans and all underprivileged classes. The main grievance against Bantu Education among Africans was that the system as a whole was meant to isolate Africans from economic development in the country. Their position was to be that of perpetual hewers of wood and drawers of water for Whites. As Dr Verwoerd, then Minister of Bantu Affairs, put it:

> The number of detribalized Natives must be frozen . . . . Natives from the country districts and reserves will in future be allowed to enter the white towns and villages only as temporary workers, and on the termination of their service contracts they will regularly have to go back to their homes.
>
> (quoted in Pelzer 1966: 10)

This education system was only a part of larger machinery, and it is on this matter that many observers misunderstand the attitude of Azanian Africans towards African languages.

When the Act came into force there was strong objection to it – its control mechanisms, school organization, the syllabus, and all. The question of language was naturally on the agenda, since one of the ways in which this system sought to implement its objectives was through the medium of African languages in schools. Objections were made therefore not against the use of African languages *per se* but against their use as part of the system which was meant to hold back Africans from advancement. Africans were thus caught in a dilemma, since rejection of Bantu Education *ipso facto* meant disowning or neglecting their own languages. It was a painful position to be in, and its consequences remain painful.

The dilemma of the Afrikaner is also of note. On the one hand he was concerned with the advancement of the Afrikaans language and culture, to carry on the struggle of the *Genootskap van Regte Afrikaners*, 'the Fellowship of True Afrikaners', which was started in 1875; and at the same time he wanted to use the advancement of African languages and cultures to keep Africans under control and in isolation, distanced from their common identity as *Abantu/Batho* 'a people' or 'people'. Hence, he had to re-define the word *Bantu* and give it negative and derogatory connotations militating against any sense of unity:

> And the Lord came down to see the city and the Tower, which the children of men builded. And the Lord said, behold, the people *are* one, and they have all one language . . . . Come, let us go down, and there confound their languages, that they may not understand one another's speech.
>
> (Genesis 11: 5–7)

At the same time it must also be stated that this policy inadvertently and paradoxically helped Africans to achieve what was done so expressly for Afrikaans. Notwithstanding its many drawbacks, the language policy strengthened African languages to some extent, without creating much of the division which was originally intended.

REGULATION AND CONTROL OF AFRICAN LANGUAGES

In order to enforce control over African languages the Central Bantu Language Board and its subsidiary committees were established, headed by Afrikaners. In 1977 this Board was replaced by 'autonomous' Language Boards for each of the languages and handed over to native speakers. However, these language boards still worked indirectly under the auspices of the Publications Control Board with its many machineries of censorship of writing in general. The aims of these Language Boards were, *inter alia*, to standardize the languages, prescribe books for schools, work with publishers to accept or reject manuscripts for publication, make orthographic rules, etc. They acted as an arm of censorship and thus stultified the development of African language literatures.

English-speaking universities were no less culpable. In their Departments of African Studies they excluded native speakers of African languages, except in some cases where the most highly qualified were employed in the lowest positions. They were true to Afrikaner aspirations of control, and African academics were denied positions in the liberal English universities, where less qualified Whites held senior positions.

Even up to 1975 when some liberal White schools introduced African languages in their curricula, native speakers were deliberately excluded as a matter of policy. These schools were content with employing White teachers, whose knowledge of the African languages was sometimes appallingly weak.

It is not surprising that the English-speaking community was never concerned about African languages. Even when it came to defending their own language against the Afrikaner onslaught they raised the feeblest of protests; as Mphahlele put it, they behaved like a eunuch goaded into a fight over a woman (Mphahlele 1984). They left the pain of having to learn Afrikaans and English to the millions of Africans whom they only met as a source of labour and who were forced to learn Afrikaans or English so that they could meet their employers', demands. No one could have put the case more eloquently than Dr Verwoerd:

> The economic structure of our country, of course, results in the Natives in large numbers having to earn their living in the service of Europeans. For that reason it is essential that Bantu students should receive [some] instruction in both official languages from the begin-

ning so that they can even in the lower primary school develop an ability to speak and understand them . . . . Instructions have already been issued to commence immediately the teaching of Afrikaans.

(Pelzer 1966:77)

For both the English and Afrikaans speakers it was a matter of Mohammed having to go the mountain because the mountain would definitely not go to Mohammed.

Let us sum up the position with regard to the politics of language in South Africa: Whites of all political and ideological persuasions have been so comfortable with the privileges which Apartheid offered them in the form of cheap Black labour that they found no need to learn African languages – they were in a situation which never demanded that they associate with the African working class as equals at any time. One renowned South African journalist summarized the position succinctly: 'Once, while addressing a group of three hundred pupils at an English-speaking high school in Johannesburg ... when I asked how many knew a black child outside the master-servant relationship, there were three hands' (Sparks 1991: 217).

One of the major organs controlling the way in which African languages are used is the South African Broadcasting Corporation (SABC), which is state-controlled and run by non-native speakers appointed by the Government. As the sole major broadcasting medium it has had a monopoly of control over broadcasting in African languages. The SABC took upon itself the task of imposing standards and directing the course of the development of the African languages, and the administrative headships of the African language services were, and still are, securely in the hands of Afrikaners.

The two main institutions of control, the Language Boards and the SABC, in their attempt to keep the languages 'pure', have set conservative standards which are not in keeping with the evolution of language in the new urban cultures. They served as instruments of control retarding the free development of expression, and constraining the content of the literature published and prescribed in schools. Both the SABC and the Language Boards are responsible only to the Government, the Department of Information and Department of Education and Training (Bantu Education) respectively.

While these two institutions work in one direction, in most urban areas new dialects, codes and registers have developed to such an extent that one has to be wary of any notion of a 'standard' version of any of the African languages. There have arisen a number of patois, called *Flytaal* or *Tsotsitaal,* which have evolved since the 1940s and 1950s in formerly mixed areas which now exist only in name. Variations of these dialects are as numerous as there are townships in the Pretoria-Witwatersrand-Vaal (PWV) triangle, and other areas.

FUTURE POLICY CONSIDERATIONS

If history has any lessons for the future, it should be clear to policy makers that language in South Africa should not be used to enforce segregation of one group from another, nor as a tool of domination or reinforcement of class, racial or ethnic distinction. Language must be allowed to be a tool by which people communicate in given situations without feeling superior or inferior in relation to the other language, and without being put at a disadvantage by it. South Africa's history testifies to the tragic consequences of such unequal relationships.

Language must be used freely, and without stigma, to express ideas. The Tower of Babel must be dismantled, a tower which has been in the process of construction since the enforcement of the use of English by the English Governors such as Lord Charles Somerset in the 1840s, and that of Afrikaans by the Afrikaner Government in the 1970s, which led to the catastrophic climax of 1976 when school students took to the streets in protest against the imposition of Afrikaans as the medium of instruction for at least half of the subjects taught in African schools.

Contrary to the views of some outsiders, who can neither understand nor speak any South African Bantu language, it is evident that the Nguni languages, either in the form of Zulu or Xhosa, are becoming more widespread and generally acceptable as the main vehicles of communication among Africans, without any implication of political domination by those who speak those languages as their first language. This is evident to anyone who can speak South African Bantu languages, and who travels in South Africa. It is particularly true in the Southern Transvaal, where, as a result of more than one generation of inter-marriage among African 'mother tongue language' groups, it is rare to find a monolingual *um*Zulu, *um*Xhosa, *mo*Sotho, etc.

The so-called Separatist Churches provide examples of multilingualism without friction. These African churches, like the Zion Christian Church (ZCC) of Bishop Lekganyane, St John's Apostolic Church of Bishop Masango and Bishopress Manku, the Nazareth Baptist Church of Isaiah Shembe, and many others, now boast a larger membership than the established churches, constituting 20.8 per cent of the population, which is over 5 per cent more than the largest established church, the Afrikaans Reformed Church. At no time has it been suggested that the use of African languages has caused division or friction among members of these churches. The ZCC's headquarters are in Lebowa, and although it uses mainly Northern Sotho as the 'official' language, it has members across the Republic of South Africa in the north, and in the Southern African states of Botswana, Lesotho and Swaziland where languages other than Northern Sotho are used. The Apostolic Church, with headquarters in Katlehong in the East Rand (Bishop Masango) and Evaton in the Vaal (Bishopress Manku), uses both Southern Sotho and Zulu, and the Nazareth Church uses mainly Zulu, its headquarters being in Natal/Kwa-Zulu. Multilingualism within these organizations has never been seen as a source of difficulty.

African intellectuals and political organisations have always been preoccupied with rallying support across 'tribal boundaries' and they have neglected the use of African languages as a means to achieve liberation. With a few early exceptions, like the ANC newspaper *Abantu-Batho*, African languages have always been perceived as a tool of division and therefore their potential ability to mobilize ordinary people was not exploited. The liberation movements were concerned with making themselves understood to Whites, who were a small minority in the liberation struggle. Most significantly, the South African economy would have gained immeasurably if the African language speakers' potential as artisans, engineers, and skilled labourers had been met half-way and their mother tongues utilized in a variety of vocational fields. It was the trade union movement in the 1970s, and more so in the 1980s, which brought African languages to the forefront of the struggle, because it was the workers themselves who pursued the struggle, not the intellectuals who spoke English, at home or in exile.

LANGUAGE AND DEVELOPMENT

For South Africa/Azania to develop its economic potential to the maximum no major language can be excluded from the schools, factories, industries, judicial and legislative institutions, and other aspects of the new socio-political infrastructure. The trade union movements have proved that in order to communicate with the majority of workers it is necessary to speak the African languages. This writer has been a translator of documents from Afrikaans and English for trade unions (especially during the Rowntree strike in the Eastern Cape in the early 1980s and subsequently), documents for self-help organizations in the lower income groups, and pension and provident fund documents. All this translation work was urgently required to meet the need to communicate with various African language-speaking communities, a further indication of the need to give African languages their rightful place.

The majority of the people in the factories, mines and industries, are African language speakers, and the numbers are swelling even in institutions of higher learning, which have hitherto been dominated by Whites (for example, the University of South Africa has 47,096 African language speakers against 37,213 English and 26,023 Afrikaans-speaking students registered for the 1991 academic year). It is, therefore, only the most myopic policy which will deny the special role of African languages in the future development of South Africa.

Participative democracy will never become a reality until people who have had no opportunity to master even the basics of Afrikaans and English have been educated to understand and participate in their own languages.

Language policy makers will need to take into account the geographical distribution of these languages as indicated above. A natural starting point will be to consider a 'semi-federal' arrangement of support for 'official' languages. In the Cape Xhosa and English could be designated official languages, and perhaps also Afrikaans since it is spoken by a majority of the Coloureds; in Natal and Kwa-Zulu (as one part of a unitary South African/Azanian state), Zulu and English would be official languages; in the Orange Free State Southern Sotho and Afrikaans would be the first two official languages, with perhaps English as the third; in the Transvaal, with its diversity of groups, divisions could be drawn such that English would be the overall official language but coupled with Zulu in the south (PWV), with Ndebele and Afrikaans in the east, with Northern Sotho from Pretoria to the North of Pietersburg or Bandolierkop, and further north with Tsonga. Beyond Gazankulu Venda would be the official language. (There are other minority languages which are spoken by sections of the South African population which must also be given due consideration in any new language policy, such as Gujerati, Hindustani, Tamil, Telugu and Urdu.)

Official languages will need to be given equal status in the educational, industrial, technological, economic, social, judicial, legislative, executive and political infrastructure. Each child should start school with at least two languages, and then, as and when circumstances demand, learn other languages. And, in my view, no person, South African or foreigner, permanent immigrant or migrant worker, should be allowed to teach in a South African school without evidence of the mastery of at least one South African Bantu language. Last, but not least, non-native speakers, together with the present government-controlled Language Boards, must relinquish their custody of African languages and hand back control to native speakers, of whom there are many qualified to work on the standardization and development of these languages.

The main argument against this 'semi-federal' structure would be that a lot of economic resources would have to be invested in developing so many languages. In my view no future government of South Africa, be it of the ANC, the PAC, Inkatha, National Party, South African Communist Party, or any coalition of these, can afford to leave unaltered the damage that earlier language policies have inflicted on millions of South African citizens.

Some political organisations have realized the need for a language policy, and have started to work on it. However, so far, no definite outline, except in the most general and tentative terms, has emerged. Often the task of working on language policies is in the hands of individuals whose knowledge of the language situation is minimal and who do not know the languages themselves. As we approach post-Apartheid South Africa/Azania the need for an enlightened language policy is becoming ever more pressing. Having started with the Tower of Babel let me conclude with words from the Acts of the Apostles:

> And suddenly there came a sound from heaven like a rushing mighty wind, and it filled all the house where they were sitting. And there appeared unto them cloven tongues as of fire, and it sat on them. And they were all filled with the Holy Spirit, and began to speak with other tongues, as the Spirit gave them utterance.
>
> (Acts 2: 2–4)

REFERENCES

Mphahlele, E. (1984) 'Prometheus in chains: the fate of English in South Africa', address to the English Academy of Southern Africa, Johannesburg, 27 April.

Pelzer, A. N. (ed.) (1966) *Verwoerd Speaks: Speeches 1948–1966*, Johannesburg: APB Publishers.

Sparks, A. (1991) *The Mind of South Africa*, London: Mandarin Paperbacks.

10 Healthy production and reproduction
Agricultural, medical and linguistic pluralism in a Bwisha community, Eastern Zaïre

James Fairhead

INTRODUCTION

Conversations in one Bwisha village often mix Kinyabwisha (Kinyarwanda), Kiswahili and French, within as well as between words, phrases and sentences. This paper examines this linguistic pluralism in the context of medical/agricultural pluralism and political pluralism. Rather than focus on languages *per se*, the paper examines discontinuities in the ways Banyabwisha[1] understand and respond to human and crop health problems, and on related discontinuities in the ways they claim legitimacy in political action. The analytical strategy, therefore, is to focus on the frames of reference which orientate language use (cf. Fardon and Furniss) and to show what this reveals about the articulation between the different 'languages' which Banyabwisha draw on and mix.

The paper looks at some specific developments in linguistic practice associated with the articulation of different 'languages' such as the use of loan words and new constructions. It shows why these need to be understood in relation both to changing technical knowledge (e.g. in crop health therapy), and to the political and economic changes in which technical understanding is embedded.

Such an 'ethnography of linguistic interaction' should contrast with and complement discussions of the pros, cons and possibilities of policies to promote particular languages as part of 'development'. This example of how linguistic interaction is locally politicized and the roles which technological issues play in conditioning this, will help us consider both how language 'development' issues interact with technological ones, and how local people might interpret language policy.

The paper examines the idioms and frames of reference which cultivators use to describe soil fertility and crop health, drawing a strong contrast between those considered 'Bwisha', making sense within particular political relationships, and those distinguished as 'non-Bwisha', making sense in other political contexts. It is therefore necessary to begin by outlining the current political complexity of village life.

PROLIFERATION OF POLITIES

In 1910, inhabitants of north-west Rwanda, Bufumbira (in south-west Kigezi, Uganda) and Bwisha (in eastern Zaïre) were divided into their respective nation states. At that time, their quasi-autonomous territorial patrilineages were linked through marriage alliance and exchange networks, and shared a similar history and common language (Kinyarwanda). Senior family ancestors, the spirit of a cult heroine, and the Rwandan monarch (*Mwami*) were respected as the major actors who ensured prosperity, as were local officials who mediated relations with them. Respect was payable in labour, tributary payments, and military allegiance. Between family, cult and royal authorities there was an uneasy coexistence. For example, Nyabingi, the cult heroine, was at times the organizational focus of dissent from Rwandan monarchy.

Structures of authority have since multiplied. For Banyabwisha they have come to include the Belgian, and now Zaïrian state, the 'customary chief' installed for indirect rule, the Catholic and assorted Protestant churches, Islam, coffee estates, and NGO development projects. All these polities are currently represented in the study village, where villagers deal with their lineages, five important local churches, the village development committee, the village committee of the Zaïrian state party (MPR), the village chief of the traditional administration, and the neighbouring coffee estate. The strength and legitimacy of these different polities draw on the very different ways in which they protect people and land, and influence personal and soil health and fertility.

DISCONTINUITY IN BWISHA MEDICAL PLURALISM

When ill, a Munyabwisha patient and caring friends and relatives must make some tough decisions. Whatever the proximate cause, many conditions can ultimately be the work of a poisoner/sorcerer (*umurozi*), a disgruntled ancestor (*umuzimu*), or a chance incident which provoked the ill-fortune which it evoked symbolically (*umuziro*). It may be sufficient just to treat the symptoms, and most people would start there, either asking around for news of a good local specialist for the problem, or attending a clinic. But this is not necessarily the most prudent approach. Whether for serious, strange, or persistent illnesses, it may be necessary to treat the underlying cause, either by soliciting the help of a diviner and other specialists to whom one may be referred, or the help of a Christian/Islamic god. Therapeutic decisions are, however, further complicated by a strong distinction drawn locally between specifically Bwisha conditions (*ikinyabwisha*) and conditions for which western medicine may be appropriate (*ikizungu*). Distinguishing between these causal domains can be crucial. One fearful patient considered that mistakenly using *ikizungu* medicine to treat a Bwisha condition would be fatal.

In diagnosis, certain symptoms are clearcut, but often the character of their cause is less obvious, so the symptoms cannot be properly recognised, let alone interpreted and treated. There are, however, 'divinatory' tests which help to identify the necessary interpretive framework. Whilst specialist diviners can be consulted for this, people usually test themselves first. A standard and common test is to drink an emetic which will induce vomiting only if Bwisha sorcery/poisoning is responsible. Many will attend a clinic only if this has a negative result.

Distinguishing between these frames of interpretation is just as relevant to understanding crop health. Putrefaction of a bean crop may be attributed to proximate causes, such as excessive rainfall which has not been compensated for in management techniques, or the presence of a menstruating woman whose periods are known to be damaging. In the same way, poor (or fantastic) crops can be attributed to sorcery, ancestral malice, or the legitimacy and practice of territorial chiefs.

Explanations and treatments within these different frameworks of analysis draw on very different concepts of cause, origin and contagion, and of responsibility, culpability, chance and intention. They have different specialists (e.g. paramedics, *umupfumu* 'diviner-healers') to whom villagers can go if their condition defies self-diagnosis and treatment. And these specialists use characteristically different methods and instruments of investigation, and have very different styles of treatment. Historical changes in these different discourses have influenced attitudes towards different languages, and their use.

UNDERSTANDING CROP HEALTH: HOT AND COLD, MOIST AND DRY, HARD AND SOFT

Villagers sometimes consider the influences on plant growth in terms of temperature (heating and cooling), and humidity (moist and dry) and consistency (hard and soft). But explanations in these idioms contrast strongly with those in another explanatory idiom in which crop success (and personal health) is related to *ivitamin*, or nutrients. I will argue that a stark contrast between these different idioms is associated with the very different forms of legitimacy which structure village society and politics.

Villagers often describe the determinants of plant growth in terms of the interaction between soil temperature, moisture and consistency, and try to balance these attributes in crop management. Decaying vegetation or cow dung noticeably give off heat, just as they would if burnt, but more slowly, and over a longer period. Steady decay of such organic matter, like the sun's heat, is thought to warm the soil, and such warmth in the soil is considered to encourage crop growth. If they can, farmers prefer to cultivate decaying vegetation into the soil rather than burn it, and burning vegetation is considered a waste.[2] Nevertheless, too much decaying vegetation in the soil can 'burn' germinating seedlings, turning the crop yellow and harming it. In such circumstances it is better to burn off the excess, or at least to wait for a week or two after cultivating the vegetation into the soil, to allow the initial 'heat' to dissipate before sowing. A balance must be struck, and this underlies the skilful manipulation of field weeds, crop residues and vegetation accumulation during more or less prolonged fallows in local soil fertility management practices (cf. Fairhead 1990).

At the higher, cooler and wetter altitudes further up the Rift Valley slopes and towards the Virunga volcanoes, sorghum and bean crops take several months longer to grow and beer ferments in three days, not one (cf. Pottier and Fairhead 1991). When cool things happen more slowly. Rain water is considered cooling and so, for example, as the rains set in after the long dry season, they cool the land. Consequently, it is good to sow early in the season especially in land which does not keep its heat (where there is less decaying vegetation). Sometimes farmers say that a crop is growing poorly because a 'stream' in the soil is cooling the roots. Crop putrefaction, like poor growth, is often attributed to this cooling effect of water. The verb 'to rot' (*kubora*) also means 'to be soaked to the bone'. When a bean crop putrifies in the field after prolonged and untimely rain, it can be described as going completely cold (*kuhororoha*). Equally, if rain or dew drops remain on a bean leaf or a bean flower for long, they 'cool' it, causing it to putrify. Such putrefaction can also be likened to the effects of pouring boiling water over a leaf, exemplifying the notion of moisture and temperature balance in explanation.

Moisture and decayed organic matter are important factors which influence the third key component in local site productivity evaluation: soil consistency. Both moisture and decaying organic matter soften soils. A hard soil is considered to be both less productive and more difficult to cultivate and control weeds in. Soils can be considered hard for several reasons. Firstly, the reddish clay subsoil (*kahuhuma*) may be nearer the surface and reduce the softer texture of the the black topsoil (*urukara*). Secondly, as the soil dries out it hardens. Thirdly, the tough and extensive roots of certain difficult weeds (e.g. *Imperata spp.*, *Pennisetum spp.*, *Agrostis spp.*) can make the soil difficult to hoe. Controlling these weeds, and thereby softening the soil, is necessary in order to grow a successful crop. Fourthly, soils low in decaying organic matter tend to be hard. The more decaying vegetation in the soil, the softer and more fertile they become. These four factors are usually conflated in the general ascription of consistency. Although farmers do distinguish between the different reasons for softness (and distinguish exceptions to these norms, e.g. 'soft because of over-cultivation'), this property can rarely be reduced to a single cause, and the general ascription of softness is more useful.[3] This interpretative framework drawing on temperature, moisture and soil consistency can (or at least could) link causes of crop health with social and political affairs, with kin and ancestral relationships and with political legitimacy.

PROCREATION, PRODUCTION, POLITICS AND PUTREFACTION

As is also the case in neighbouring regions, it is considered the duty of a political chief or monarch not only to 'warm the land' but also to prevent it from overheating.[4] *Kuteka*, meaning to rule, also means to 'warm up' or 'to cook'. Peace, which a successful ruler should ensure, is itself a state of warmth, and the term *umutekano* unites these two meanings. Looked on another way, peace is also a state of coolness: *amahoro*, 'peace', derives from the verb *kuhora*, 'to cool'. Political leadership and the distribution of 'warmth as fertility' are linked through the two words which mean fertilizer. The first, *ifumbira*, derives from the term *ifumba*, which is the bundle of dry herbs in which one wraps smouldering embers to distribute fire. The second, *ingabulire*, is the noun form of the verb *kugabulira*, which means 'to distribute pasture or food as a chief'; a necessary attribute of good rule. It shares a common root with the term *umugabo*, meaning 'man'; that is to say a man who has a child. *Ingabulire* simultaneously connotes the distribution of manure in the field, the distribution of fertility emanating from the most senior chief, which in Rwanda is the Monarch, the *Mwami*, and the role of men in generating such fertility. As will become clear, the chief lies at the focal point of a veritable 'economy of heat, moisture and softness' which transcends and links things agricultural, things reproductive and things political.

At the core of this 'economy of heat' is the association between sexual intercourse, heat and fire. To make fire, one rubs a firestick (*urugabo*, meaning male) into the receptacle hole of another stick (*urugore*, meaning female). The sexual act, fire-making and fire itself are central to both family and royal procedures used to ensure the reproductive success of crops or people. First we shall examine sowing procedures, then reproductive understanding, then the role of the political leaders.

The family procedures[5] to ensure successful sorghum or millet cropping were observed by Lestrade in the 1930s (1972: 253–7). The evening before sowing, a senior man mixes the seed with other protective objects in a barrel (*ikicuba*). Protective items include (a) plants such as 'spontaneous reproduction' (*umutobotobo*), 'success' (*umuganashya*), 'desire' (*umwifuzo*), 'family' (*insina*, 'banana shoots'); (b) manure from both a cow untainted by the death of a parent or offspring (evoking life), and a hippopotamus (evoking high yields), and (c) 'slag from a forge' evoking virility. The officiant's wife places some sorghum porridge and her spatula in a serving basket, and puts this in the storage bin; an action evoking productivity. Then, dressed in sheepskin (*inyabuhoro*, also meaning 'origin of peace/coolness'), the officiant solicits success from the family ancestors. Husband and wife then have sexual intercourse, whilst married adult children refrain. The next day, the officiant ties some roof thatch around a burning ember taken from his family fire. Carrying this wrapped fire (*ifumba*, cf. *ifumbira*, 'fertilizer') and the protected seed, he leads the sowing group to the field, followed by his wife who carries the hoes, and helpers who carry extra seed and beer. The fire is put in a hole dug in the field to shelter it. It must not go out. The field is sown, and on completion further ancestral solicitation is made. On the way home, the wife walks in front, with her husband behind carrying the hoes. No one may cross a stream or wash in cold water. The fire is returned to its origin and the hearth fire must not go out until the crop germinates. All married family members have sexual intercourse. These procedures generate and maintain the heat needed for the growing crop. As we shall see now, this management strategy is not only a preoccupation throughout the reproductive cycle of both crops and people; it also links these cycles.

We have seen how heat and moisture (rain) soften the soil (*kuregea*). This softening procedure is central to local understanding of fertility. For example, farmers attest that only after such softening does the fertility of a fallow become apparent. Farmers can accelerate the softening of fallowed land by laborious cultivation, clod breaking, crumbling and root extraction. When they lack the time for this, they often plant peanuts which do better in harder soils, and wait a season until the land has gradually softened before sowing millet.[6] Such softening is equally important in human fertility. Just as hard dry land is infertile, so a hard, dry woman is infertile. A 'dry woman' is one who can produce no vaginal secretions (*umunyaza*) during sex, and who can produce no breast-milk (Taylor 1988).[7] One term (*igihama*) is used to describe both the agricultural and human condition.

Central to human reproduction is the need for both male and female secretions (*itanga*, 'gifts of the self') to mingle, preferably during orgasm. The two fuse to produce a common product, a child.[8] Considerable effort is made during a woman's upbringing and in the sexual act itself to ensure that women enjoy sex and produce vaginal secretions (Taylor 1988). In short, reproduction necessitates the coming together of fluids under warm conditions; of softened earth and rain in crop production, and of vaginal secretions and sperm in human reproduction. Fundamentally, these conditions are not just important during the sexual act or during sowing, but must be maintained throughout the reproductive cycle. During pregnancy, more frequent sexual intercourse (*gukurakuza*) is necessary as this actually constitutes or builds the child (Taylor 1988, 1990). Equally, growing crops are improved by maintaining fire in the house, having frequent sex, and working in the field. At weeding, for example, fire is again taken to the field, this time wrapped in straw from the conjugal bed.

The need for partners to make love persists after giving birth because a woman must be warmed for her to convert hard body fat to liquid milk (Taylor 1990). There is, however, an eight-day interval between the birth and the first and (obligatory) post-partum love-making. During these eight days, a good husband will make a point of bringing his secluded wife wood for the night fire (Lestrade 1972). A couple must also make love after preparing the first post-harvest sorghum porridge. If a woman has not eaten this with her husband, any adulterous acts she engages in while he is away will kill him.[9] Whereas a husband's heat and semen constitutes the child, adulterous love-making can burn (overheat) the uterus, and dehydrate the child (Taylor 1988). Unsurprisingly, adultery is considered to be poisoning. Equally unsurprisingly, its effects are not restricted to people. If a woman sows sorghum in her husband's absence, her subsequent adultery would either kill the crop or, if the crop grew, kill her husband. Other forms of malicious poisoning (*uburozi*) cool a woman's blood and thus make her dry and unfit either for sex or for nourishing a child. Cures 'warm' the blood to improve vaginal secretions or lactation.[10] For example, a cold woman afraid of sex (*intinyi*) can be taken discreetly to a blazing forge to heat her. This is a dangerous thing for a normal woman to do; a 'taboo' (*umuziro*) (Lestrade 1972: 40).

In principle, reproductive cycles must not be mixed. The produce of one season cannot be mixed with the produce of another (Lestrade 1972:

262), just as the sexual liaisons of one season or of one child cannot be mixed with another. Furthermore, as a woman's menstruation represents an infertile part of the human reproductive cycle, it is not surprising to find that growing crops can be devastated by a menstruating woman (Bigirumwami 1984).[11]

Whilst this 'economy of heat' links crop production and human reproduction, the chief also plays a central role. We do not know the procedures of Bwisha's chiefs, but we do know those of the Rwandan *Mwami* who were Bwisha's overlords from the seventeenth century (d'Hertefelt and Coupez 1964). The *Mwami* tactically manipulated water and heat to distribute 'peaceful warmth' and rain to soften the lands of his followers. In procedures to overcome problems in the kingdom, the fire lighter is a key implement, and fire-making linked with love-making are crucial and complementary elements. In these procedures, the *Mwami* would normally light a fire with grasses drawn from everywhere in the country to associate all Rwanda with the heat (ibid: 330). Epidemic illnesses and other disasters were sometimes attributed to the pollution of the royal fire: a fire kept perpetually alight by its guardians at the royal court. To put the polluted royal fire 'back on its path', the *Mwami* would extinguish it using water from the rivers Abundant and Incalculable, mixed with some milk. He would then light a new fire and have sexual intercourse with a new wife (ibid: 65). The importance of fire and water is made clear in the procedures the *Mwami* used to remove the skins of the dynastic drums; drums which controlled the fate of the kingdom. To do this he had to soften the skin binding with hot water. Seemingly to avert the dangers of over-heating the kingdom, the king would first mix the boiling water (drawn from the river Abundance) with some cold water (drawn from the river Incalculable) to create peaceful tepid water. He would then sprinkle some cold water on the drums, saying 'here is cold water/peace (*ubu n'ubuhoro*); let the drums, men, cows and land have peace'. Only then did he use the hot water on the drum to loosen the binding.[12]

The *Mwami* used similar methods to afflict his enemies and those who would not pay tribute with harmfully extreme conditions. In one case, for example, as the king was about to set off on a journey, two burning embers of the royal fire were wrapped for transport (*ikifumba*, cf. *ifumbira*, 'fertilizer'). One of these fires was maintained in his honour, but the other was extinguished with water from the river Groan (*Bugongi*), as the king, to paraphrase him, said 'would that we make Bushumbi, Burundi and Bunuabungo and all places not paying tribute groan on the drum' (ibid: 133).[13]

Links between crop production and human reproduction are equally apparent both when a person dies, and when a year dies; that is, when the dark phase of the annual *Gicurasi* moon begins. Both human and seasonal funerals divide into two stages: mourning (*kwirabura*, when things are black) and the end of mourning (*kwera*, when things become white again). During the black phase (three days for a woman, four days for a man, five days for a season and much longer for a *Mwami*) no one associated with the deceased may marry, cultivate, let cattle copulate and many other things. Any progeny would be diabolical and would need to be destroyed. Only when mourning, for whatever reason, is properly finished (*kwera*), could one take up cultivation again and go on to expect good harvests and personal fertility. The term *kwera* also describes these good harvests, just as the term *kwirabura* describes poor ones. Poor harvests could result from problems relating to a deceased person associated with that land, or more generally, from problems associated with the season.

To sum up at this point, it is clear that Bwisha agricultural explanations have extremely strong pragmatic elements, but this does not mean that we can consider Bwisha farming description to draw on 'natural explanation', unless we are extremely careful in our definition of natural. Technological explanations are integrated with political and social thought, and the linkages are inscribed in vocabulary, language and practices. It is through this 'economy of heat and consistency' that we can understand why rituo-political leaders could be accredited with responsibility for the agricultural prosperity of those living within their jurisdiction, and why royalty considered the claims of others to control fertility to be a political threat (Schoffeleers, 1978).

IVITAMIN: ANOTHER EXPLANATORY FRAMEWORK

But in Bwisha, people do not necessarily consider it to be people who present alternative claims to fertility and thus usurp power. A new comprehension of fertility complicates things. When I lived in Bwisha from 1986–8, farmers did talk about their farming in terms of heat, moisture and consistency, but the links with family and political affairs seemed not to be in evidence. When talking in a substantive way about fertility, people usually described it in terms of *ivitamin* (from French *'la vitamine'*), and *ivitamin*'s local synonym (in farming) *imboreo* (from the Kiswahili, *mboleo*).[14] But why do people prefer to use these borrowed terms even though they are speaking in Kinyabwisha? Why do the Kinyabwisha terms *ifumbire* or *ingabulire* not seem right?

In some ways, the use of the term *ivitamin* does parallel fertility descriptions in terms of *ifumbire*. Nowadays, indeed, the old term *ifum-*

bire has often come to be used synonymously with *ivitamin*. But the political and ecological associations of the new term are very different; *ivitamin* does not belong to an economy of heat and consistency, but to the economy of money with which we are perhaps more familiar. *Ivitamin* acquires its existence or status as an object within a very different structure of presuppositions, and, when invoked, evokes the relevance of these. For those seeking a clear theoretical statement in terms of social theory, Foucault (1972) might have argued that *ivitamin* is an object emergent within a very different discursive formation. Before drawing on some of Bwisha's political and economic history to explain discontinuities between these two lived-in economies or 'discourses', it is important to recognise how *ivitamin* is used. To do this I want to dwell on aspects of crop and human nutrition.

Bwisha's inhabitants tend to consider themselves to have 'states of health' which, if bad, can lead to illness. They have several ways to evaluate their state of health, and one potent indicator is the amount of blood (*amaraso*) they have. Too little blood, and one is weak, dizzy and susceptible to illness. But a balance must be struck; too much blood, and one can be tense, get headaches and also fall ill. The same idiom and the same need for balance is used for plants. For example, if bean plants have too little sap then they are weak, uncompetitive with weeds, and yield poorly. Too much sap, and they become 'over-vigorous' (*gufura*), and are liable to putrefy and yield badly. In this state, a plant almost forgets what it is for, which is to produce flowers and seeds, not leaves.[15]

These descriptions are compatible with the ideas about reproduction described earlier. Within this understanding, the quantity of blood was just as important an indicator of states of health. Both the white semen and women's white secretions which fuse to create and build the child are derived from red blood which has been purified (Taylor 1990). Foods which increase blood consequently increase virility. Today, villagers usually say that levels of sap or blood are influenced by the amounts of *ivitamin* available. *Ivitamin* is the term used for 'goodness', whether in soil or foods. The more *ivitamin* in food or soil, the more sap or blood it will engender. Too little *ivitamin* leaves a plant low on sap and weak; too much will encourage too much sap, and engender over-vigorousness. Where there is too much *ivitamin*, farmers may switch to crops which grow better in these conditions, or to crop varieties which are less vigorous (more controlled) in their growth patterns. Choosing crop varieties to suit soil conditions, or altering soil conditions to suit crop varieties are matters of great skill. Farmers consciously improve the efficiency of *ivitamin* use by placing decaying organic matter in the right place at the right time (cf. Fairhead 1990).

To overcome insufficient *ivitamin* in the soil where they were cultivating perennial coffee, certain villagers approached me privately to try out western fertilizers: *ivitamin*. They had gained some familiarity with fertilizers during the period when they were used by large-scale colonial and post-colonial coffee plantations and, these days, local representatives of the United Nations Food and Agriculture Organisation (FAO) promote fertilizer use, although they seem only to assist large plantations. Following a similar logic, people who consider themselves to be low on blood now visit the local paramedic for an *ivitamin* injection, if they can afford it (injections go straight into the blood). Otherwise they buy the *ivitamin* tablets available at the market, or try to eat certain foods said to have more *ivitamin*. Such foods include local foods known to give strength (i.e. millet, sorghum, beans and, most of all, meat) as well as foods which health extension workers have suggested contain *ivitamin*, such as fruit, vegetables and several western foods such as sweet tea, coffee and bread.

This concept of *ivitamin* has now become central to local notions of crop health and the recycling of organic matter. Decaying vegetation releases *ivitamin* to the soil (*kutanga ivitamin*), and growing plants acquire it. Significantly, in this construction it is decaying plants which 'give of the self' (*kutanga*). The involvement of any other agency in the process is marginalized. In this way, the nutrient cycle which influences crop production is now conceived of in isolation from, and independently of, the social and political elements of the economy of heat and consistency.

Intriguingly, the linguistic construction of the soil having (*gufite*) something in and of itself that makes it fertile is generally used only in relation to *ivitamin* or *imboreo*. Past constructions relating to fertility identify that the soil is something (e.g. hot, soft, warm, productive) or that it has had something done to it (e.g. has had vegetation spread over it, has been worked a lot, has had cattle grazing on it), but not that it possesses something which is the agent of fertility. Thus when using the old terms, rather than say 'the soil has a lot of *ifumbire* (*bufite ifumbire nyinshi*)', one would use the passive of the verb *kufumbira* (not the noun *ifumbira*) to say that 'the soil has been spread with *ifumbire*'.

The distinction between understanding fertility in terms of heat and in terms of *ivitamin* is shown in the different metaphors which two farmers used to describe poor fertility in one field. One farmer said there was a stream flowing under the soil surface, cooling the roots. Another inferred that the nutrients had been lost from the soil, using the verb 'to pour off the water that beans have been cooked in' which connotes a separation of goodness and its washing away (this water is often fed to goats).

I could not have contrasted more strongly the understanding of fertility in terms of *ivitamin* with understandings within the economy of heat and consistency. But it is not immediately obvious why the concept of *ivitamin* should not just have become incorporated into the existing agricultural and medical conceptual framework in the way that, for example, highland Maya have incorporated modern scientific disease notions and cures into their 'traditional' classifications of hot and cold.[16] Bledsoe and Goubaud (1985) criticize the way researchers have represented the intersection between indigenous healing systems and western medicine, showing that there is a tendency for researchers to assume: (a) that the two medical systems are discrete; (b) that their integration is awkward; (c) that they can conflict or compete with each other and (d) that they can coexist and play complementary roles in a pluralistic system of choices. Bledsoe and Goubaud question the assumption that western and indigenous medical systems are discrete or discontinuous, arguing that this is an ethnocentric vision and that, for the user, western medicine and indigenous medical systems may be analytically integrated. They examine how Mende have reinterpreted certain kinds of western pharmaceuticals as appropriate for indigenously defined sicknesses and cures.

I would disagree only insofar as to say that local interpretations can include an understanding of discontinuity between analytical and therapeutic systems. However, to understand the existence of such discontinuity we should not look just to the radically different intellectual logics of the the different explanatory and therapeutic frameworks. These are more epiphenomena than causes. Is any 'intellectual system' (therapeutic or otherwise) so systematic that it cannot incorporate new ideas and objects, albeit reinterpreting them in the process? No, the emergence and existence of such intellectual discontinuity for the user requires a more positive explanation; one that is rooted in particular historical, political and economic circumstances, and in the perpetual reinstantiation of that history in the current political and economic structures which are its living legacy.

THE ORIGIN AND ENDURING NATURE OF EXPLANATORY AND THERAPEUTIC DISCONTINUITY

The explanations of agricultural, political and familial phenomena in the first part of this paper could be seen to 'speak to each other', to use the computer idiom. When reflecting on explanations and therapeutics within this field of compatibility Bwisha people refer to it as *ikinyabwisha* (meaning 'things of Bwisha'). They contrast this with a field of experience, explanation and therapeutics which they refer to as *ikizungu* (meaning 'things of Bazungu'; of White outsiders). Whilst *ikinyabwisha* is also the term for the local language dialect of *kinyarwanda*, and whilst French is an *ikizungu* language, my argument is that these fields of experience do not map onto linguistic boundaries. Nevertheless, the distinction and discontinuity between *ikinyabwisha* and *ikizungu* seems to be fundamental to modern Bwisha thought and life, to explanation and therapy.

In origin, this discontinuity or frontier initially had a strong geographical form. During Belgian rule (effectively 1927–60), Bwisha was divided into land that remained under customary authority (known as *isheferi*), and land that was alienated from customary authority and jurisdiction, and came under state control. European coffee farmers purchased this land (*iplantasion*). Plantations had (and still have) very different political, juridical and fiscal structures from non-alienated land. They introduced new farming techniques, and alien crops and varieties. They used western fertilizer (*ivitamin*), and used chemical sprays (also an *ikizungu* medicine, *umuti*). What Banyabwisha made of such fertilizer one can only speculate. How those whose land had been alienated felt when such fertilizer was applied to it is not known. Nevertheless, Banyabwisha who were forced to work in these plantations (and 70 per cent of them did by 1959) would walk to and from this *ikizungu* world daily.

Discontinuity between the *ikizungu* and *ikinyabwisha* world also originated and persists as a result of the particular way that western health care has been established. Predictably, and in keeping with the times, this was instituted in total independence of, and confrontation with, local medical practices. It was made available through the plantations (which needed labour) and church institutions (which needed converts). Health care was not always voluntary. Vaccinations and sleeping sickness monitoring were, for example, imposed in much the same way as employment or religion. But the distinction between *ikizungu* and *ikinyabwisha* in health practices no longer allowed the two discontinuous domains to be distinguished in a purely geographical way. People's bodies became subjected to the two worlds. And to the best of my knowledge, the *ikizungu/ikinyabwisha* distinction did not become imaged in a divided bodily geography. Rather, the distinction emerged in a strong contrast between *ikizungu* and *ikinyabwisha* illness; hence the divination techniques with which this paper began.

The origins of this discontinuity are enduring, as, for example, in the discontinuity that is maintained within the structures of land ownership, and instantiated in village and regional land disputes. Those living on their ancestral lands can claim 'inalienable' rights to it for *ikinyabwisha* reasons outlined above. But where I lived, there were only a few people with such claims to village land. Land is now bought and sold and, in many ways, people consider the land they cultivate to be privately owned either by themselves or their husbands or their landlords. True, fathers, uncles and brothers can still have claims to one's private land, and true, wives have durable rights to their husband's land. But village men no longer consider that they need to respect or pay tribute to those from whom they acquired their land. Indeed, most judge that it is those who purchase land now who deserve respect. Power rests in money, not land. Those who cede (sell) land and who use it to acquire political authority as a result are nowadays imaged as weak. Other villagers live on squatted land which they have come to consider as theirs by right. After three years of unchallenged squatting, they can gain durable land rights, even if this is never the case in *ikinyabwisha* thought. Indeed within *ikinyabwisha* reasoning, it is foolhardy to squat and cultivate a place deserted by old occupants, because assistance of living descendants of the land ancestors was a prerequisite both for successful cultivation and family life (cf. Lestrade 1972: 229). But those who claim land through purchase or 'ownership' seem not to think their own or their crops' health to be much threatened by ancestral spirits of dead previous occupants or by their political chiefs. When it is, such intervention is defined as poisoning (*uburozi*), and the Bible and Christianity afford some protection against the newly defined ancestor 'devils' and those who would use diabolic powers.

Understanding fertility in terms of the restricted cycling of nutrients (*ivitamin*) makes sense and is appealing for many land users. *Ivitamin* is a substance which soil or people can have more or less of, which in and of itself renders them strong and their soil fertile. Like land, fertility in the form of *ivitamin* is the sort of thing that can be purchased. Reliance and dependence on rituo-political superiors is avoided. Bluntly, *ivitamin* is an understanding of fertility which is compatible with the open market for land. The monetary economy which now constructs land ownership and health care has also come to define the origin of productivity. Like modern money in Bwisha society *ivitamin* is also gender neutral. It not only disengages understandings of soil fertility from wider political control, it also disengages it from household relations, which, as described earlier, were once so integral to crop and human fertility understanding. Whitehead (1981) has argued that when money becomes an index of value of men's and women's produce and labour, men's and women's tasks in agricultural production become more comparable. This is true in Bwisha, but understanding soil fertility in these new ways has been a necessary intellectual corollary.[17]

It is important to stress that *ikinyabwisha* and *ikizungu* 'discourses' are *not* associated with different categories of persons, nor are the discourses in some way mutually exclusive in the sense of a Kuhnian paradigm shift. The discourses may clash in land or allocatory disputes, but they do not directly 'compete' for 'the right logically to exist'.

Every villager, of no matter what tenurial status, has an ambiguous relationship with 'the state', the church and all things *ikizungu*.[18] This ambiguity can be identified in land tenure worries which are ever present for villagers. For example, state administrative apparatus and the 'traditional' chiefs have an uneasy coexistence. Whilst the state claims rights to all land, and the authority to dispossess all people of land or political authority, many chiefs and those with traditional land claims are unwilling to accept the state's authority over 'their' land and people. And given the weak local implementation of state law, so-called 'traditional' chiefs (especially the *Chefs de Collectivité*) tend to get the upper hand. A recent government report, for example, accuses the chiefs of wrongfully using their customary jurisdiction to dispossess their subjects of their land, forbidding them to build permanent homes, and denying them all right of land ownership (Katuala and Mwramba Tshibasu 1986: 89). Both the state and other institutions, such as the Catholic church, the village MPR, and non-Governmental development organisations (NGOs), which (can) support the rights of small-holders against their chiefs, fall clearly within the *ikizungu* field of experience.

These conflicting signals from the divided higher authority are reflected in local land classification. Sometimes villagers categorize their land as *isheferi* (i.e. under customary authority) relative to the plantation, so stressing their autonomy from the exactive neighbouring plantation which they associate with state-endorsed land alienation. However, at other times they may classify their land as state land (*ileta*) as opposed to the chief's land, so stressing their autonomy from traditional chiefs.

This is perhaps a superficial expression of a much deeper rooted ambiguity. We have seen that many villagers have social and economic reasons to evade and denigrate 'customary' authority, whether as a result of their personal tenurial status (as land purchasers or squatters) or more generally as gender independent rather than gender interdependent farmers (Fairhead 1990). But for everyone there are also many social and practical reasons for asserting authority. Both husbands and wives, for example, need to assert different sorts of customary authority in married and family life to prevent ridicule and to gain the respect of each other and their peers. A Protestant minister's wife who diagnoses herself as ill from *ikinyabwisha* causes cannot ignore this even if for moral or religious reasons she does not seek the therapy of *ikinyabwisha* specialists. Whilst she may suggest that many specialists are charlatans, she does not suggest that what they deal with is in the realm of fiction. For her it is very real, and very evil. She may rely on self-treatment with local (not *ikizungu*) medicines and prayers. Equally healer-diviners themselves who find that they have *ikizungu* ailments may well seek the medicine of paramedics.

In short, these discourses coexist and endlessly structure relations of authority and dissent. Attempts to live on one side of this intellectual frontier and to present the other side as non-existent are inconceivable.

SOME CONCLUDING THOUGHTS: LINGUISTIC PLURALISM AND DISCOURSE

Bwisha's customary chiefs and authorities sometimes associate the erosion of their power with things 'French', explicitly forging an association between the French language and *ikizungu* phenomena. One chief put it this way ' "People of French"[19] are destroying this country. They prevent my people from doing compulsory labour' (Seruraho 1979: 50). But it is really only within the 'two dimensional' and 'conflatory' rhetoric of political speeches that an identity between language and discourse can be forged, and even then, such a conflation is most unstable.

Banyabwisha do distinguish their language, Kinyabwisha, as discontinuous from other languages spoken in the region such as French, Kinande, Kikiga, Kiswahili. Within Bwisha itself, certain dialects are described. Equally, things *ikinyabwisha* are also contrasted with things *ikizungu*. But crucially, these two notions Kinyabwisha (language) and *ikinyabwisha* (economy of heat) – of language and of explanatory coherence – do not map on to each other. The latter bounds a particular 'form of life' in which words and gestures can acquire particular sorts of agency. The former bounds a language which anyone can learn. For Banyabwisha, the objects and phenomena constituted within the *ikizungu* discourse were no less 'natural' phenomena, for being different to *ikinyabwisha* phenomena. Misinterpretation could kill. And, as we have seen, today's Kinyabwisha language can, of course, describe these things, albeit with borrowed words and constructions.

For the purposes of this book, I would like to make three other concluding remarks. Firstly, putting analytical stress on discourse rather than languages *per se* (cf. Fardon and Furniss) has implications for the ways 'borrowed' words are conceptualized. Rather than ask how borrowed words are loaned from one language to another and how they are considered part (or not) of that language, a better question might ask how different frames of reference integrate and render compatible (or not) concepts from different languages.

Secondly, the focus on discourse might alter how we consider the relationship between African and European languages. Although linguistically Kiswahili clearly resembles Kinyabwisha more than French, when considered in terms of the historical circumstances of their use, as we have seen, Kiswahili can have more in common with French than Kinyabwisha. This exemplifies a problem in drawing too strong an analytical distinction between horizontally and vertically related languages based, perhaps, on the phylogenetic 'horizontal' relationship between Bantu languages and the unequal vertical relationship between these and the languages of colonialism.

Thirdly, as academics, we should not conflate discourse with language in the two dimensional way of Bwisha politicians. We should not (necessarily) look for political relations in languages and their interactions, and expend too much energy in promoting or politicizing this or that language. By focussing on 'which language', we might have been overlooking the existence of what are much more fundamental local political and technical debates.

ACKNOWLEDGEMENTS

This paper is based on fieldwork in Bwisha, Kivu, Zaïre (1986–8). I am grateful to inhabitants of the village where I lived, to the Economic and Social Research Council of Great Britain who funded the research, and to the International Centre of Tropical Agriculture's (CIAT's) Great Lakes Bean Improvement Programme with which I collaborated.

NOTES

1. Banyabwisha literally means 'people of Bwisha', a small chiefdom in eastern Zaïre which borders on north-west Rwanda and south-east Uganda.
2. Ash is somewhat anomalous. Burnt, and no longer able to generate heat, it nonetheless enhances plant growth. Local associations with ash show its ambiguous position. A 'cold ash' translates as 'a wolf in sheep's clothing'. Ash (*ivu*) is associated with a chameleon (*uruvu*) and with the notion of 'origin' (*amavu*).
3. Certain linguistic usages and translations are derived from Jacob (1984–7).
4. Richards (1939) described this for the Babembe.
5. I use the term 'procedures' with care. These have been termed rituals, but this places the actions within a 'religious' sphere, whereas it appears to me that we are dealing with the manipulation of natural processes.

Healthy production and reproduction

6 The longer fallows of the past left the land relatively soft, and less work was needed.
7 For analysis of Rwandan understanding of sexuality and reproduction, I draw heavily on Taylor (1988 and 1990).
8 As well as meaning to give, *kutanga* means 'to go in front'. Recall that at the sowing procedure a man goes in front of his wife to the field, and a woman goes in front on the way back (Lestrade 1972: 253–7). A similar act is replayed by the *Mwami* in royal sowing procedures (d'Hertefelt and Coupez 1964: 139).
9 The intercausality between human reproductive and crop productive cycles helps us understand why dry women and barren (e.g. non-menstruating) women were once put to death (d'Hertefelt and Coupez 1964: 260). Their existence undermined the fertility of the land (Taylor 1990: 1025).
10 The use of cooling, heating, dampening and drying materials is current in indigenous medicine and magic (Lestrade 1972: 26).
11 Gottlieb (1982) provides an example of why it is wrong to see menstrual blood *per se* as necessarily polluting. Rather, it is the confusion of reproductive cycles which is dangerous for both crop reproduction and human reproduction.
12 In one procedure to put out the royal funeral fire, water from the river Bubeho is used. Bubeho derives from the word *imbeho*, meaning 'cold'. This evokes peace (d'Hertefelt and Coupez 1964: 372).
13 These links make it clear why people fear boiling over (or spilling) cooking water on to the cooking fire, as it presages ill fortune (Lestrade 1972: 249). Similarly, if milk falls in the fire, the cow which produced it risks becoming ill. To reduce this risk, one must sprinkle the flame with cold water (Lestrade 1972: 28). It is clear why to take a pot off the fire means to remove problems, and why if a house burns down people consider fire to have become dangerous. It is clear also why both sex and cultivation are suspended until a specialist redresses the situation and gives back to fire its utilitarian and socially constructive role. These observations also help us to understand why, at critical 'hot' times for the country (e.g. during illness or epidemic), general sexual abstinence was necessary.
14 Banyabwisha have other *contextual* ways to describe places of differential fertility on which I do not dwell here. People describe places (a) where plants grow vigorously (*harashishe*) or not (*hatashyishe*); (b) where harvests are good (*kurumbuka*) or poor (*kurumba*); (c) where productivity is low (*uburumbe*) or otherwise; (d) where there has recently been a fallow or a build-up of vegetation (*umurare, ingando*); (e) where there has not been much recent cultivation (*nk'ingando*, like *ingando*), and (f) where cattle have grazed. Whilst these descriptions refer to the fertility status of a place, they gloss over the nature of fertility.
15 According to the dictionary (Jacob 1984–7), the term *fura* connotes getting lost, acting before thinking, and getting carried away with oneself.
16 Logan (1973), cited in Bledsoe and Goubaud (1985).
17 The use of the term 'necessary' here needs qualifying. There are many African examples where land has become commoditized but where the nature of fertility seems to remain understood within ancestral terms. Sometimes in these cases, land sale can either be delimited to descendants of common ancestors (e.g. mentioned in Riddell and Campbell 1986), or can be associated with blood pacts which unite buyer and seller (e.g. mentioned in White 1990). 'Commoditization' is not a universal phenomenon, but can take many

forms. This essay is examining the particular form which land commoditization has taken in Bwisha and hopes to understand how this is the result of a particular history.

18 Smith (1979) suggests that a similar dilemma exists in Rwandan thought. The saying 'to be in Rwanda is to keep taboos' (*kub'i'Rwanda n'ukwizirira*) can be matched with another saying: *kiriziya yakuye kirazira*, 'the church has uprooted [displaced] taboos'. Smith describes how people, when forced to transgress customary taboos, invoke the latter saying, less as a statement of reality, than as an excuse to break a particular cultural rule in the hope that it will not bring calamity. Banyabwisha have another way of doing this. When breaking customary norms, people may say that they are following 'Article 15'. Article 15 is the celebrated Zaïrian principle of 'getting-by' (*débrouillez-vous*), a principle advocated by (or associated with) the state. *Se débrouiller* has entered Kinyabwisha as *kwidebrie* via Kiswahili (*kujidebrie*). People invoke the principle, and implicitly, the support of the state, in their actions when they do something that they feel they really ought not to do.

19 These 'People of French' such as the church and NGO authorities consider themselves intellectuals, supporting the rights of poor small-holders.

REFERENCES

Bigirumwami, A. (1984) *Imihango n'imigenzo n'imizilirizo mu Rwanda*, Rwanda: Nyundo.

Bledsoe, C. and Goubaud, M. (1985) 'The re-interpretation of western pharmaceutical science among the Mende of Sierra Leone', *Social Science and Medicine* 21, 3: 275–82.

d'Hertefelt, M. and Coupez, A. (1964) *La royauté sacrée de l'ancien Rwanda*, Tervuren: Musée Royal de l'Afrique Centrale.

Fairhead, J. (1990) 'Fields of struggle: towards a social history of farming knowledge and practice in a Bwisha community, Kivu, Zaire', unpublished Ph.D. thesis, University of London (SOAS).

Foucault, M. (1972) *The Archaeology of Knowledge*, London: Tavistock.

Gottlieb, A. (1982) 'Sex, fertility and menstruation among the Beng of the Ivory Coast: a symbolic analysis', *Africa* 52, 4: 32–47.

Jacob, I. (1984/85/87) *Dictionnaire Rwandais-Français de l'Institut National de Recherche Scientifique*, 3 vols, Butare: INRS.

Katuala, K. K. and Mwamba Tshibasu (1986) *Les grands conflits foncières du Nord Kivu: philosophie, action préventive et rectificative et rapport de la Commission Foncière Sous-Regionale*, Goma (Zaïre): MPR.

Lestrade, A. (1972) *Notes d'ethnographie du Rwanda*, Tervuren: Musée Royal de l'Afrique Central.

Pottier, J. P. J. and Fairhead, J. (1991) 'Post-famine recovery in Highland Bwisha, Zaire: 1984 in its context', *Africa* 61, 4: 537–70.

Richards, A. I. (1939) *Land, Labour and Diet in Northern Rhodesia: an Economic Study of the Bemba Tribe*, London, New York and Toronto: Oxford University Press for the International African Institute.

Riddell, J. C. and Campbell, D. J. (1986) 'Agricultural intensification and rural development: the Mandara mountains of North Cameroon', *African Studies Review* 29, 3: 89–106.

Schoffeleers, J. M. (1978) 'Introduction', in J. M. Schoffeleers (ed.) *Guardians of the Land: Essays on Central African Territorial Cults*, Gwelo, Zimbabwe: Mambo Press.

Seruraho, N. (1979) 'L'autorité coutumière et le développement du Bwisha' (travail de fin d'études, ISP, Bukavu, Zaire), unpublished MS.

Smith, P. (1979) 'L'éfficacité des interdits', *l'Homme* XIX, 1: 5–47.

Taylor, C. (1988) 'The concept of flow in Rwandan popular medicine', *Social Science Medicine* 27, 12: 1343–8.

—— (1990) 'Condoms and cosmology: the "fractal" person and sexual risk in Rwanda', *Social Science Medicine* 31, 9: 1023–8.

White, L. (1990) 'Bodily fluids and usufruct: controlling property in Nairobi, 1917–1939', *Canadian Journal of African Studies* 24, 3: 418–38.

Whitehead, A. (1981) 'I'm hungry mum: the politics of domestic budgeting', in K. Young, C. Wolkowitz and R. McCullagh (eds.) *Of Marriage and the Market: Women's Subordination Internationally and its Lessons*, London: Routledge and Kegan Paul.

11 Minority language, ethnicity and the state in two African situations

The Nkoya of Zambia and the Kalanga of Botswana

Wim van Binsbergen

INTRODUCTION[1]

Language differences often provide an anchorage for ethnic identity. Ethnic self-articulation tends to have a linguistic component: propagation of the language spoken by a national minority in the face of lack of recognition of that language in a nation state's language policy covering such domains as formal education, the judiciary, contacts between the state and its citizens in general, political discourse, freedom of expression and the media. Language policy – even if appealing to 'objective' considerations of linguistic analysis, constitutional equity and socio-economic development – is often formulated and implemented in a political and ideological context partly defined by ethnic parameters. In the present paper I shall briefly trace, and contrast, the ethnic aspects of the language situation in two contemporary African communities: the Nkoya of central western Zambia, and the Kalanga of north-eastern Botswana. The choice of these two cases is inspired by more systematic considerations than personal preference alone: while my own current anthropological and historical research happens to concentrate on these two communities, their choice here is strategic. In terms of their linguistic, ethnic and political situations within their respective nation states, Nkoya and Kalanga are in some respects comparable, yet they display striking differences with regard to the role language has played in their respective processes of ethnicization in the twentieth century. Thus, the comparison may have *heuristic* value in highlighting some of the crucial variables that inform the interplay between language, ethnicity, the state and development, even though I take it for granted that a two case comparison can never in itself yield viable generalizations.

Comparative empirical data concerning the two languages, and the ethnic groups of the same names which focus on these languages, are compiled in an elaborate matrix (Appendix) which has the disadvantages of being condensed and schematic but the advantage of accommodating

Minority language, ethnicity and the state 143

Figure 11.1 The Nkoya and the Kalanga in Southern Africa

more information than could otherwise be presented in an article. Granted this descriptive background, my discursive argument will be selective.

My argument is set, implicitly, against the background of studies of ethnicization and inter-ethnic relations in Zambia and Botswana. While the relevant literature on Zambia is considerable (including classic studies in this field by Mitchell and Epstein),[2] the multi-ethnic dimension of contemporary Botswana society has been largely ignored by scholarship. Researchers have themselves internalized the image of a peaceful, ethnically and linguistically homogeneous, thoroughly Tswana country – an image propagated by the national élite under conditions of Tswana linguistic and cultural hegemony. The notable exception is the considerable attention paid to the plight of the Khoi-San (locally called Sarwa), under conditions of social humiliation and economic exploitation at the hands of the Tswana.[3] The claim to homogeneity of Botswana has also been accepted by linguists (e.g. Alexandre 1972: 89).

THE NKOYA OF WESTERN ZAMBIA[4]

The scattered minority language we call Nkoya today (with its constituent dialectal variants such as Nkoya-proper, Mashasha, Lushange, Lukolwe, Mbwela), with about 30,000 speakers in central western Zambia, is generally accepted to be the language of people who formed part of an early movement – like so many others in the past half millennium – from southern Zaïre into the savanna of South Central Africa from c. AD 1500.[5] On the strength of political and cosmological notions deriving from their Zaïrean homeland (Kola), some of these immigrants began to involve the local population (in part consisting of earlier immigrants) in a process of state formation, from the late eighteenth century, if not earlier, which led to the creation of a number of small polities (along lines clearly discernible from recent research) in which Nkoya was the court language. Most probably, the language, and the people identifying themselves by reference to it, were known early on not as Nkoya but as Mbwela. The origin of the name Nkoya itself remains somewhat obscure: it is associated with a forested area near the Kabompo/Zambezi confluence, and it later became the toponym for the entire region (roughly coinciding with today's Kaoma district) where Nkoya is spoken by the majority of the population; it may well be a dialectal variant of the magical name of Kola itself. Whatever the case, our first record of its use for the political élite of one of these polities dates back to c. 1840: in the praise-name under which a female ruler, Mwene[6] Komoka, acceded to the major Mutondo royal title. Only a few years later these polities, on the eastern fringes of what later (e.g. in Max Gluckman's famous anthropological studies) became known as Barotseland, were made tributary to the Kololo state, through which immigrants from what is today South Africa had supplanted the earlier Luyana administration. The original Luyana ousted the Kololo immigrants again in 1864 but largely retained the latter's southern Sotho language, amalgamating it with their original Luyana to form today's 'Lozi' language. It was in the context of political incorporation into the Lozi state that 'Nkoya' (in its Lozi form Mankoya, which was also extended to become the name of a district capital, to be renamed Kaoma in 1969) became the name of one particular Lozi 'subject tribe' and of the latter's language – myopically uniting, under this Lozi-imposed label, not only a certain dialectal variation but also several encapsulated polities which had never before identified themselves as 'Nkoya'. Favoured by the colonial state which was imposed in 1900, Lozi administrative and judicial subjugation, social humiliation and economic exploitation of the people in the eastern Barotseland fringe actually increased during the colonial period. While the Luvale (another 'subject tribe', to the north of the Lozi core area) were allowed to secede from Barotseland and form a district of their own, Lozi colonization of Nkoyaland went on through the creation of a Lozi court at Naliele near Kaoma in the 1930s, where the son of the Lozi *Litunga*, 'king', was put in charge of the newly created Mankoya Native Authority; Mwene Mutondo Muchayila, who opposed these developments, was ousted from office and for ten years (1948–58) exiled to a remote part of Barotseland – only to return to office in the years 1981–90. Under the unifying impact of this shared negative experience within an overall administrative and political framework, it was in the period around World War II that the name 'Nkoya', now reflexively used by the people themselves, became a rallying cry for an increasingly comprehensive ethnic identity facing a common perceived ethnic enemy, the Lozi, whose language, used in the Lozi indigenous administration including the courts, had become a main instrument of control and humiliation.

Nkoya was a minority language in the Barotseland Protectorate, the indigenous administration of which retained considerable autonomy under colonial rule. Meanwhile, throughout Northern Rhodesia (now Zambia) – of which Barotseland formed part – seven languages had come to be recognized by the state as vehicles of formal education, broadcasting, the judiciary, and state/subject interaction: Bemba, Tonga, Nyanja, Lozi (throughout Barotseland and in the region of Livingstone, the early colonial capital in the south), Lunda, Luvale and Kaonde. At Independence, the colonizer's language became the country's official language. For fear of 'tribalism' and in the service of 'nation-building', in the first decades after Independence no language other than English was used in state–citizen communication – a practice observed so strictly that President Kaunda addressed crowds in his native Chinsali district not in the local Bemba language but in English. Nkoya found itself among the sixty-odd languages or dialects in Zambia to which no official status was accorded. Thus, the Nkoya language had become doubly peripheral: a minority language vis-à-vis Lozi, that remained dominant in most formal situations including education, local government and the courts in Barotse (later Western) Province, and vis-à-vis English. Also peripheral in terms of participation in the modern economy, minimum access to national markets of labour, produce and power (while the regional spheres were totally dominated by Lozi speakers), in the 1960s the Nkoya ethnic identity (defined by speaking the Nkoya language, and by allegiance to local chiefs – the encapsulated heirs to the independent polities of the eighteenth and nineteenth centuries) was characterized by great resentment of continued Lozi domination and by rejection of the independent nation state of Zambia which (from the parochial perspective of Kaoma district) had allowed itself to be captured by the Lozi aristocracy.

Circulation of people over great distances has been a normal feature of the social organization of Nkoya rural society, in which young men and women move between villages in search of kinship-based patrons and spouses, until they become less mobile by middle age. The geographical scope of this intra-rural migration has extended beyond the areas where Nkoya is spoken by the majority of the population, and as a result many Nkoya were and are bilingual or trilingual in the languages of western Zambia. Since the beginning of the twentieth century, the local language and ethnic situation has considerably diversified; Lozi domination facilitated the immigration of Lozi speakers into the fertile and well-watered, sparsely populated lands of Nkoya; Angolan immigrants (speaking such languages as Luvale, Luchazi, Chokwe and Mbundu and ethnically identifying by these same names) also flooded into the region from the late 1910s. As a result, Nkoya soon became a minority means of expression even at the newly-created district capital. The influx of immigrants (whose agricultural and hunting methods tended to be more modern and aggressive) created pressure on local land for the first time in history. Encapsulated within the Lozi indigenous administration (which moreover controlled part of Nkoyaland directly, through Lozi *indunas*),[7] Nkoya chiefs were unable to curb this invasion. After Independence (when their power was further eroded by the institution of Local Courts over which the chiefs no longer had formal control)[8] the selective granting of land to ethnic strangers was adopted by the chiefs as a means of gaining prestige and additional income. Appointed as members of the new Rural Council, which after Independence supplanted the Lozi-controlled Mankoya Native Authority, the chiefs facilitated a major development project, which led to a massive agricultural scheme in the eastern fringe of Kaoma district attracting thousands of ethnic strangers from all over western and southern Zambia in what was to become the new rural town of Nkeyema. Not only did this further diversify the local language situation, it also confirmed the Nkoya as linguistic and economic underdogs, serving – usually in a language other than their own – immigrant farmers on their own lands as casual labour, or pursuing, in their nearby villages (and then in their own language), the meagre yields of an eroded historical agricultural production system which, because of the depletion of the forests, could be supplemented by the time-honoured techniques of hunting and gathering to a diminishing extent.

In this linguistic, ethnic, political and economic desolation, from the 1920s, the local Nkoya-speaking groups found an ally in Christian missions and (since the local Catholic Mission was rather Lozi-orientated) especially in the fundamentalist evangelical South African General Mission, which shifted to Nkoyaland from an increasingly hostile Angola. In its wake, the mission brought Mbundu immigrants to the district, thus contributing further to its ethnic and linguistic differentiation; however, in the context of this mission, ethnic strangers would adopt Nkoya as a second language. Establishing excellent relations with the Nkoya chiefs, the mission pioneered literacy in Nkoya, published school primers, had hymns and part of the Bible translated into Nkoya,[9] and was largely responsible for the creation of a climate in which peasants would go about their Christian activities and their social contacts (especially in the form of letters to the many relatives who were temporarily absent as labour migrants) in their native language. A remarkable form of ethnico-religious discourse emerged, in which local Christian leaders would also be the articulators of the budding Nkoya ethnic identity, and improvised prayers in Nkoya would mix pious and political elements in fervent evocations (full of predictable biblical parallels) of their ethnic plight at the hands of the Lozi. In this context the first Nkoya pastor, Rev. Johasaphat Shimunika (1899–1981), nephew and son-in-law of the first Mwene Mutondo to be baptized, was not only largely responsible for Bible translation but also collected Nkoya oral traditions, collating them into passionate statements of Nkoya ethnic identity and anti-Lozi manifestos, which circulated among the Nkoya from the late 1950s. I have recently edited a published version of his main work, *Likota lya Bankoya*, 'The history of the Nkoya people' (van Binsbergen 1988, 1992a: parts II and III).

Away from their rural homeland, Nkoya labour migrants had no choice but to reproduce the peripherality which was their fate at home. A few years of mission education in Nkoya hardly compared with the splendid educational facilities, in the empowering languages of Lozi and English, which the Lozi aristocracy had managed to attract and develop in the centre of Barotseland. The Nkoya's small numbers and lack of specialized skills made it impossible for most of them to capture substantial portions of the urban labour markets, which were controlled by the Lozi and other dominant ethnic groups. Occasional urban success often involved ethnic and linguistic 'passing', dropping the (still only emergent) Nkoya ethnic identity for that of Lozi or Bemba, and loosening the home ties. The majority of the many Nkoya labour migrants however remained insecure strangers in town, and continued to rely heavily (in times of unemployment, illness, bereavement and personal conflict) on such security as the intensive (and costly) cultivation of rural ties would accord them. Regrettable as this state of affairs may be judged from the perspective of personal achievement in modern, capitalist relations of production, it was largely responsible for the continued vitality of Nkoya rural society. Persistent investment of migrants' cash in rural-based institutions (kinship, marriage, chieftainship, old and new cults of affliction) allowed Nkoya rural society to remain the relational, symbolic and therapeutic power-house of dispersed Nkoya-speaking individuals, and thus a viable basis for an increasingly vital Nkoya ethnic, linguistic and cultural identity.

Twenty years ago, when I started research among the Nkoya, they still felt the lack of recognition of their language to be the major sign of their powerlessness at the national and regional level, which they interpreted exclusively in terms of Lozi oppression. Primary school teaching was no longer in the hands of the mission but had become the responsibility of Government, and as a result it took place in the recognized language of Western Province and Livingstone, Lozi. Very few Nkoya primary school graduates found their way to secondary school and fewer still matriculated: this happened largely because educational success depended on the mastery of two languages (Lozi and English) hardly used in the Nkoya rural milieu, but also because the number of children attending school was low, and the regularity of those who did attend poor – due to the Nkoya's emphasis on boys' hunting and musical skills, and girls' domestic chores and puberty ceremonies. In the collective Nkoya consciousness a large and sinister place is occupied by a district educational officer, inevitably (like the majority of local teachers) of Lozi identity, who allegedly rounded up and burned virtually all Nkoya school primers. Neither was the Nkoya language used in any of the provincial or national media. Since the early nineteenth century the Nkoya royal orchestra had been a standard element in court culture all over western Zambia, and as a result the folklore programmes of Zambia Broadcasting Corporation often featured Nkoya songs. Requests for Nkoya-language programmes, however, were systematically turned down by reference to the country's formal language policy. Nkoya speakers occupied only the most lowly jobs at the district headquarters and UNIP party office, and any dealings between Nkoya villagers and the outside world, for administrative, medical or judicial purposes, would have to take place through the medium of Lozi, of which only half the adult men and very few women had more than a smattering. Political meetings, too, had to be conducted in Lozi or English. At one such meeting, held in preparation for the 1973 national elections which for the first time brought a Nkoya (Mr J. Kalaluka)[10] into Parliament, the District Governor (of eastern Zambian extraction), when challenged why the meeting could not have been held in Nkoya, spoke out in anger: 'This nonsense has to stop. Chief, you must control your people. There is no Nkoya. Nkoya does not exist!'

Various processes combined to change this situation substantially in the course of two decades, even if Zambia's language policy formally remained the same. The integration of the Barotseland Protectorate, its traditional ruler the Litunga and the Lozi aristocracy, into the independent state of Zambia had been difficult, and had had to be bought on the onerous conditions of the Barotse Agreement. One section of the Lozi aristocracy had promoted UNIP in Barotseland, which had been a reason for many Nkoya to side with UNIP's rival, the African National Congress (ANC),[11] in addition to short-lived political organizations of a specifically Nkoya nature. The commitment to the struggle for Independence had been massive among the Nkoya, not so much out of disgust with the colonial state (whose blessings were to form a standard topic of conversation among the Nkoya in the post-Independence period – despite the fact that Lozi domination had been greatly reinforced by the colonial state) but in the hope that Independence would bring the end of Lozi domination. Until the late 1960s the Lozi played a major role in the successive factional coalitions around which Zambian national politics revolved. The prohibition against habitual labour migration from Barotseland to Rhodesia and South Africa increased ANC sympathies among the Lozi, at a moment when UNIP was already contemplating one-party rule. The Lozi were outwitted and divested of their political power at the national level, and UNIP found in the Nkoya welcome allies in an otherwise hostile province.

The Nkoya's ethnic claims for access to regional and national representative bodies, restoration of the prestige of their traditional leaders, and increased development efforts in their area, were met to a considerable extent, and such few Nkoya as could be considered to constitute a traditional and modern élite (e.g. the royal chiefs, and Mr Kalaluka) soon found themselves in a position where, as brokers between the modern world and local villagers, they could combine ethnic mobilization with personal economic and political advancement. UNIP branches, and ward and village development committees mushroomed, and for the first time the repertoire of UNIP political songs was translated and sung in the Nkoya language. Political meetings in favour of the ruling party were held locally in the same language. The enhanced economic opportunities in Nkoyaland increasingly contrasted with the bleak situation of many Nkoya migrants in the declining economy of Zambia's towns, and people began to remigrate home.

Moreover, at the national political and ideological level, the earlier universalist insistence on English and fear of 'tribalism' gradually gave way to considerations of authenticity and pluralism, and the more the impoverished and disintegrating Zambian state proved unable to mobilize popular support on the basis of services and benefits extended to citizens, the more passionate and desperate became the appeal to a composite cultural heritage to which each ethnic and language group was now seen to contribute, even outside the established happy few of the seven state-recognized languages.

While the political acceptability of the Nkoya language increased, at the major Christian mission establishment in Kaoma district the work on the translation of the Bible continued steadily. Largely under the supervision of Rev. Shimunika until his death, and subsequently under that of his former associates, draft translations were made of the entire Old Testament, and these were discussed at general conferences which the church organized in Kaoma and Lusaka in the late 1980s. Although the text has been ready for publication for some years now, and a subscription campaign has been launched, funds are still lacking to place a print order.

While this translation work, and the enthusiasm it generated over the years, clearly testifies to the vitality of the Nkoya language, the organizational framework for the text consultations was no longer exclusively that of the mission and of the Evangelical Church of Zambia which it has engendered. Instead, the editorial processing of the Bible translation in recent years, as well as similar consultations in the context of my edition of Rev. Shimunika's *Likota lya Bankoya*, has taken place within the context of a new Nkoya ethnic association.

Ethnic associations, which had thrived in Northern Rhodesia but then been discouraged after Zambian Independence, became viable again after 1980. With restored ethnic pride, the return of educated manpower to the rural homeland, and the fruition of the ethno-historical seeds which Rev. Shimunika had sought to plant for so many years, the time was ripe for the *Kazanga* cultural society to be launched in the early 1980s. The society derived its name from an ancient Nkoya institution, the king's first-fruits festival, which (partly because of the connotations of ritual murder which it shares with all royal ceremonies in the Nkoya context – among others) had rarely been held in the twentieth century. While continuing (in vain, so far) the campaign for the Nkoya language in the media and schools, joining hands with Nkoya politicians in their attempts to further the cause of Nkoya chieftaincy, and formalizing an economic and social support structure for rural–urban migrants on a modest scale, the society's main project was to develop a newly 'bricolaged' form of *kazanga* as an annual festival, bringing together all Nkoya chiefs (especially the four royal ones, who historically would meet rarely, each, instead, observing a strict avoidance in his own area), and presenting to the crowds of urban and rural Nkoya, other locals, government officials and hopefully tourists, a densely packed programme encompassing the entire (if slightly orchestrated, folklorized, and electrified) repertoire of Nkoya music and dance (van Binsbergen 1992b).

Thus the festival was to form the Nkoya answer to the famous Lozi *Kuomboka* ceremony, which has attracted large crowds since the beginning of the twentieth century. At the second *Kazanga* festival, in 1989, the triumph of the Nkoya language could hardly have been more complete: not only did the junior Minister of Culture, Lazarus Tembo (of eastern Zambian background, once Zambia's most popular folk singer, and a blind man), attend in his official capacity, but he seized the opportunity to be the first high-ranking state official ever to address a local crowd in Nkoya – mispronounced and apparently off the cuff, but in reality touch-read from the braille notes hidden in the Minister's pocket. The previous night the state had declared a 100 per cent devaluation of the Zambian Kwacha, and villagers who later that week went shopping at the district capital returned to their homesteads empty-handed since their money could no longer buy even what little was available in the shops. But the state could not have chosen a more effective way to impress the Nkoya with, in Mr Tembo's words, 'how much we have to be thankful for'.

In October 1991 the Kaunda era came to an end when UNIP lost the national election to the new MMD coalition party, and Mr F. Chiluba became state president (Baylies and Szeftel 1992). The Nkoya of Kaoma district were divided. During his last year of office, President Kaunda had successfully intervened to protect Nkoya chieftaincies against the Litunga's mounting aspirations, and this is a major reason why UNIP remains a remarkable presence in the area. However, especially among the peasants, there was and still is considerable support for MMD. The new administration offered new national level opportunities to politicians from the area, some of whom are full Nkoya, and others who are not but make a point of expressing themselves in Nkoya to further cultural and traditional-political aspirations as articulated by the *Kazanga* society. Gradually shedding their underdog image, the Nkoya are becoming increasingly deft at the situational manipulation of their ethnic identity at the regional and national level, and begin to command considerable political resources. At the regional level, ethnic antagonism now occasionally gives way to a more comprehensive ideology of ethnic solidarity between the groups of western and northwestern Zambia – as against the ethnically dominant centre and especially north (Bemba, Aushi), on which the Chiluba administration leans heavily. Although it is too early to make predictions, it does look as if the upward movement of Nkoya identity in the 1980s will continue under the new regime.

THE KALANGA OF NORTH-EASTERN BOTSWANA

Like the Nkoya language, the western Shona dialect cluster known as Kalanga, today extending from north-western Zimbabwe all the way into the North Central and North East districts of Botswana (where it mainly exists in the form of the Lilima dialect), boasts a considerable local presence. While much of the history of this language and of the ethnic group who are identified by it remains to be written,[12] it is a well-established fact that Kalanga, already called by that name, was the state language of the Changamire state which in the late seventeenth century succeeded the Torwa state; the latter produced the archaeological complex known as the Khami culture, and was closely associated historically with the earlier extensive state system centring on the famous site of Great Zimbabwe.

When, as an aspect of the Zulu expansion, the Changamire state was supplanted by the Ndebele state in the early nineteenth century, Kalanga speakers lost their association with dominant political power. The southern part of the Kalanga area then found itself in the overlapping and competing spheres of influence of the Ndebele state, in the north-east, and an expanding Tswana polity, to be known as Ngwato, to the south. While these powers were more or less in balance, the relative no-man's-land on the Tati river became a major area for White prospecting and mining, agricultural enterprise and urban settlement: the Tati district, later known as the North East district, was focussed on the new town of Francistown. Land alienation and the general implantation of the capitalist mode of production went on there on a scale unequalled elsewhere in the Bechuanaland Protectorate during the colonial period. Attempts to annex the Protectorate as a whole for South Africa failed as did attempts to incorporate the Tati district into the Southern Rhodesia of which it was so reminiscent. After Botswana's Independence (1966), administrative formalities made the Botswana/Rhodesia boundary more difficult to cross. Under UDI, and during the Zimbabwe war of liberation and its violent aftermath in south-western Zimbabwe (when local Kalanga suffered along with the Ndebele under the ZANU state's aggression), the experiences, and political and cultural concerns, of Kalanga on either side of the border increasingly diverged. Yet massive emigration of war and post-war refugees, dispersed by violence in Zimbabwe as much as attracted by the post-Independence economic boom of hitherto tranquil and rustic Botswana, kept the lines of contact open.

In at least one respect the Zimbabwean Kalanga immigrants found an unpleasantly familiar situation in Botswana: their ethnic and linguistic identity made them, along with the original Botswana Kalanga, stand out as politically and socially suspect in a country which for fear of appearing disunited, emphatically proclaimed itself a monolithic Tswana state: through the adoption of Tswana as its national language, by its ruling party's (BDP – Botswana Democratic Party) populist imagery centring on the Ngwato royal family (whose one-time heir apparent, Sir Seretse Khama, was to be BDP's leader and the country's first president), and by the very name of Botswana, i.e. 'Tswanaland'. In Botswana, Kalanga is very much a minority language, in which no formal education is offered, which is not used in the media, is practically inadmissible for use in courts of law except in outlying villages, and in which hardly any published material circulates.

The Kalanga (comprising c. 120,000 speakers or 13 per cent of the population (Picard 1987: 5)) constitute the largest non-Tswana-speaking group in the country, but by no means the only one: for example, in the north, north-west and west, Mbukushu, Yei, Koba, Ndebele, Subiya, Herero, etc., defied ethnic and linguistic classification as Tswana, as did the Khoi-San (called by their Tswana name 'Sarwa') scattered all over the country. The Kgalagadi are a borderline case in that their language is similar to standard Tswana but, as a separate branch of the Sotho-Tswana peoples, they are not counted among the eight constitutionally recognized Tswana groups,[13] and they share with the Sarwa a history of serfdom and humiliation at Tswana hands (Gadibolae 1985; Mautle 1986).

Under the Protectorate, the Tswana had formalized a model according to which the country's entire territory was neatly parcelled up among themselves, each 'tribal' area administered by a hereditary chief. Consolidating the realities of Ngwato expansion in the second half of the nineteenth century, the area where the Kalanga lived (with the exception of most of the North East district, which had become freehold land of the Tati Company) fell under the *kgotla* ('tribal' headquarters, court) of the Ngwato chief (*kgosi*). Kalanga traditional authorities were incorporated into the Ngwato indigenous administration as mere village headmen (sing. *kgosana*, 'little chief'). At Independence, the Tswana chiefs' constitutional and juridical status was redefined as complementary to the modern central state and its democratic institutions. A House of Chiefs was instituted as the apical structure of tribal administrative and judicial organization and, in terms of the Constitution (Republic of Botswana 1983), only senior members of the Tswana tribal administrations qualify for membership. Kalanga activists read into this section of the Constitution a denial of the existence, within the national territory, of languages other than Tswana, and of ethnic groups other than the eight Tswana-speaking ones.

In that part of southern Kalangaland which lies in present-day Botswana, the influx of relatively small offshoots of non-Ngwato Tswana groups (primarily the Khurutshe, since the late eighteenth century, and the Rolong in the early twentieth century)[14] and of non-Tswana recent immigrants from the north and east had turned the ethnic and linguistic situation of north-eastern Botswana into a complicated mosaic. Kalanga ethnic identity and language, which had such a long local history, had considerable but not unanimous attraction for these immigrant groups: Khurutshe in the village of Ramokgwebane, and Rolong in the nearby Moroka, soon adopted Kalanga, whereas the offshoots of the same groups in Makaleng, Tonota, Matseloje and Borolong retained their original ethnic identity and their Tswana tongue (Schapera 1952; van Waarden 1988; Malikongwa & Ford 1979). The Khurutshe *kgosana* of Makaleng came to represent the local population, including the Kalanga, in the Ngwato indigenous administration and in the House of Chiefs. This meant that the Kalanga were and are not represented, in their own right, in the far from nominal traditional political structures of the country (cf. Gillett 1973; Silitshena 1979).

Especially in the second quarter of the twentieth century under the rule of the regent Tshekedi Khama (Seretse Khama's paternal uncle), Ngwato overlordship in north-eastern Botswana was resented and often challenged, especially over church matters (Benson 1960; Chirenje 1977; Wylie 1991). Not unusually in Protectorate Botswana, the Ngwato administration did not permit any Christian diversification and upheld the monopoly of, in this case, the London Missionary Society. In this part of Protectorate Botswana African independent churches, which were already flourishing in South Africa where thousands of Botswana labour migrants became acquainted with them, inevitably acquired overtones of ethnic and tribal defiance of Ngwato dominance. The Tati concession, however miserable in other respects, offered a White-controlled sanctuary from Ngwato rule, and it is here that 'Christian Independency' first flourished in the country. In the historical consciousness of contemporary Kalanga in Botswana much is made of the high-handed way in which a particular immigrant Kalanga group around John Nswazwi, defying Ngwato overlordship both in religious and in tributary matters, was beaten into submission by Tshekedi's regiment in 1947.[15]

The Kalanga's reliance on agriculture rather than animal husbandry made their children more easily available for schooling than, for instance, the Tswana, whose school attendance had to be balanced against the need to herd cattle. In the Protectorate period, ideas and people moved freely between Bechuanaland and Rhodesia, and while educational services (or any other services to be provided by the colonial state and the indigenous administrations it upheld) were kept at a minimum in the Protectorate, Christian missions in nearby Rhodesia were flourishing: they translated the Bible into Kalanga, and offered a great many Kalanga both the formal education and the ideological outlook that provided the basis on which to advance in colonial society, while increasingly challenging the premises of inequality on which that society was based (Bhebe 1973). The great Zimbabwean politician Joshua Nkomo is very much a product of this situation (Nkomo 1985). But so are others (e.g. Mssrs K. Maripe, T. Mongwa, P. Matante, D. Kwele) who later, as commercial entrepreneurs, Kalanga ethnic activists and national level politicians, were to play a prominent role in the modernizing and highly proletarianized situation of Botswana's north-east, with its rapidly growing town of Francistown. After 'Christian Independency', Francistown became the cradle of the first major independence party, the Botswana People's Party, which from its outset was highly critical of Tswana ethnic, administrative and linguistic hegemony (cf. Nengwekhulu 1979; Murray et al. 1987).

It testifies to the complexity and situationality of ethnic identity that most of these leaders could, and did, adopt other, non-Kalanga, idioms of mobilization. Nkomo could identify as Ndebele as much as Kalanga, and it is in the former identity that he gained world-wide renown. Maripe completed a doctorate in industrial relations in Belgium and, long before gaining local prominence as a Kalanga novelist and as BPP president, stood out as a trade unionist active not in Botswana but in the Federation of Rhodesia and Nyasaland (Meebelo 1986: *passim*); in other words he could have identified, and probably did at one time, as Zimbabwean and even Zambian. Mongwa, Francistown's BPP mayor in the mid-1980s, is Pedi as much as he is Kalanga. Matante was prompted to form the BPP through his membership of the South African, African National Congress (ANC), and he was moreover active as the leader of an independent African church in Botswana; so we might have heard from him as a South African black politician or as a minister of religion. All this reminds us of the fact that appeal to an ethnic idiom in the context of formal, national-level politics is not the expression of primordial attachments ingrained through socialization in early childhood – as first-generation studies of ethnicity in Africa and the Third World in general tended to stress (cf. Geertz 1963) – but is often the deliberate and strategic choice of a particular political instrument, identity and career from among alternatives.

After Independence, Botswana rather unexpectedly saw an economic boom – largely based on the diamond industry (in which South African capital and expertise was wisely matched with Botswana state control) and the beef export industry – against the background of open economic relations with South Africa guaranteed by a Customs Union putting Botswana (along with Swaziland and Lesotho) in an awkward but economically favourable position among the Southern African front-line states. The BDP Government, which gained power democratically in the drive for Independence and has retained it ever since, therefore had plenty to offer to the Botswana state élite and to the population at large, and prudently but consistently delivered enough to ensure stability, economic progress and popular support. In the process, the multi-party system was nominally encouraged and gained the country international esteem and donor support. In reality, however, with every national election which was held at the constitutionally stipulated times, the impotent opposition parties – including the BPP and the BNF (Botswana National Front) – increasingly became an ornamental fringe to a *de facto* one-party, populist and rather authoritarian political regime (cf. Picard 1987; Holm & Molutsi 1989). Repeatedly, when the outcome of democratic elections led to opposition majority at the district and town-council level, the dilution of representative bodies by state-appointed BDP representatives, and the persuasion of elected opposition representatives to cross over to the BDP while retaining their seats, proved to be standard tactics to retain or regain BDP control.

This situation was not entirely unlike Ngwato/Kalanga relations in the nineteenth century and under the Protectorate: occasional and dramatic Kalanga challenges to Ngwato hegemony did not preclude the fact that the ordinary, and widely accepted, situation was one of peaceful accommodation, where the Kalanga, as 'Northerners', had their assigned place in the Ngwato polity, not only in distant homogeneous Kalanga villages at a distance from the Ngwato capital, but also in the Ngwato heartland, even in specifically Kalanga wards at the capital (Schapera 1952, 1984, 1988).

A remarkable contradiction between implicit ethnic accommodation and occasional overt ethnic confrontation can be observed at this point. Challenge to Tswana hegemony and explicit proclamation of Kalanga identity became more and more bitter as standard expressions of political opposition to the BDP. That political opposition in the struggle over state control had to be phrased in an ethnic and linguistic idiom was also due to the fact that such religious and class oppositions as had unmistakably arisen at the level of people's consciousness, were still not sufficiently well articulated to serve as a basis for mass mobilization. In independent Botswana, a class idiom is mainly propagated by the BNF, in intellectualist Marxist terms which fail to attract mass support. Of course, the unsettled nature of class contradiction as a basis for mass mobilization has, until quite recently, been a general theme in post-Independence politics throughout Africa. In fact, however, the Kalanga's relative educational and entrepreneurial success had led to a situation where a disproportionately large percentage of BDP politicians at all levels (including Cabinet Ministers and MPs) happened to be Kalanga, who as a condition of political eligibility and respectability played down their Kalanga identity and allowed Tswana ethnic and linguistic hegemony in the country to go unchallenged.

Thus the very people who, being affluent and relatively well-educated, might have been involved in the production and consumption of Kalanga symbolic culture (in the form of literature, drama and ethno-history) inside Botswana, tended to have vested interests in not doing so. Maripe's Kalanga novels are nowhere to be bought in Botswana. Copies of the 1929 Bible translation in Kalanga could be seen for years rotting on the shelves of the Francistown Bookshop along one of the town's main shopping streets. Kalanga oral-historical traditions, folklore and proverbs were largely left to foreign researchers and had no market inside Botswana. It is commonly believed that it is an offence to publish books in Botswana in any language other than English and Tswana; not being a jurist, I have no information on whether there is any law under the Constitution which limits freedom of expression in such a way. The insights which modern scholarship, mainly on the basis of Zimbabwean material, have gained into the splendour and historical depth of Kalanga history, highlighting its intimate link with the glorious Zimbabwe state and the widespread Mwali cult which is among Southern Africa's major religious expressions,[16] have so far never managed to percolate back into the publicly-articulated ethnic consciousness of the Botswana Kalanga. There is an amazing contrast between the riches of Kalanga history, and the poverty of the Botswana Kalanga collective historical consciousness which seldom reaches beyond the Nswazwi episode, never taps the sources of ethnic pride history has so abundantly to offer, and even reproduces the erroneous Tswana view[17] that the Kalanga in Botswana are merely recent immigrants enjoying, but dishonouring, Ngwato hospitality! Such inspiration as could have been derived from ethnic identification with the Zimbabwean Kalanga across the border[18] seems scarcely to have been tapped after Independence. While assistance through personal kin networks was offered to Kalanga victims of the Zimbabwean war of liberation and its atrocious aftermath (mainly in the form of accommodating illegal immigrants in Botswana), at the public and national level the border communities went out of their way to dissociate themselves from such violence as spilled across the frontier, stressing – not always spontaneously – that their first allegiance was to the Botswana state and not to an international Kalanga ethnic identity.

The increasing entrenchment of Botswana Kalanga within the national territory of Botswana was one of the reasons for the Kalanga Bible Translation Project in the mid-1980s, headed by White Lutheran missionaries recruited from Germany and the USA, and with strong organizational backing from the Lutheran mission in South Africa. Justifications for the project included the incomplete nature and linguistic defectiveness of the existing translation of 1929, whose orthography, moreover, was judged inadequate. Draft translations were undertaken in the Project Office variously based in the town of Francistown (1987–8), the village of Zwenshambe (1988–9), and Francistown again (1989–present). The actual translation work is mainly in the hands of Kalanga native speakers with post-secondary education, assisted by advisory committees throughout the Botswana Kalanga area. Attempts to expand the project into a revitalization of Kalanga language and culture in general have so far not taken off, and the project has been severely hampered by conflicts over external, White control, conditions of service, and the conflicting national cultures and management styles of the various missionaries involved. So far the project's main achievement has been the development of a new standardized Lilima orthography in consultation with Botswana native speakers.

In the course of the 1980s, Kalanga ethnic and linguistic identity developed into a major issue, but within the Kalanga community more so than between Kalanga and Tswana. Students at the University of Botswana founded the Society for the Propagation of the Ikalanga Language (SPIL) with amazingly little government opposition: the required registration with the Registrar of Societies was virtually routine, even though this was to be the only overtly ethnic association in the country and one obviously not propounding Tswana hegemony.[19] On various occasions, SPIL branches and individual members (never the entire association as such) challenged the Kalanga members of the Government to speak out in favour of the teaching of African languages other than Tswana, and to identify publicly as Kalanga instead of submitting to Tswana hegemony. This led to major outcries, in which the official position with regard to the exclusive use of Tswana for the sake of national unity and efficiency was repeatedly expounded and defended, and local BDP politicians clamoured – in vain, so far – for the prohibition of the SPIL.

However, to date, the SPIL initiative has failed to engender massive ethnic support. It has remained a pastime of middle-class people whose command of Tswana usually equals that of Kalanga, and whose children have often been raised to have Tswana or English as their first language. With the exception of the few and irregularly produced issues of the mimeographed journal *Tjedza*, 'Light', the society can boast little literary or cultural production. Its annual meetings are enlivened by performances of dance troupes but, expert and exciting as their repertoire is, their very presence brings out the dilemmas of ethnic mobilization along Kalanga lines in Botswana: traditional dancing is part of the general primary and secondary school curriculum throughout the country, the movements and songs hardly stand out as specifically Kalanga, and to the extent to which elements are borrowed from territorial and possession cults these, too, combine Kalanga references with Ndebele, Venda and even Tswana ones.

My reading of SPIL is that it primarily reflects a struggle, within the Kalanga middle-class community, between those whose acceptance of Tswana hegemony has paid off in terms of political and economic power – in other words has allowed them a share in state power – and those (typically younger, perhaps slightly better educated and perhaps with slightly stronger roots in their rural home communities and the latter's traditional leadership) whose access to political and economic power so far has been frustrated and who, through insistence on a Kalanga ethnic idiom, seek either to capture their own share of state power, or at least to discredit the state, proving it to be less universalist, and more ethnically particularistic, than its constitutional pronouncements would suggest. But these ideological expressions mobilize less support in a context where, *de facto*, numerous individual Kalanga have had more than their fair share in the capturing of the Botswana state – even if they could not publicly claim to have done so under the ethnic label of Kalanga.

SPIL emphatically declares itself to be a non-political society. Churches find themselves in a similar position, and it is noteworthy that – even though my Botswana research has come to concentrate on the religious domain – I have no evidence of linguistic and ethnic antagonism playing a dominant role in churches and non-Christian cults in north-eastern Botswana today. Multiple and situational ethnic and linguistic identity, code switching, the mixture of songs and texts from Kalanga, Ndebele, Tswana (and even Shona and English) in the course of one religious event, and the accommodation of potential ethnic opposition within an encompassing idiom of religious transcendence of disunity are the catchwords to describe the local religious situation.

Having concentrated on urban research, I do not really know to what extent this pattern in the religious domain corresponds with a relative absence of group conflict along ethnic lines in other spheres of life in the *rural* communities of north-eastern Botswana today. My impression – not supported by extensive fieldwork – is that their ethnic and linguistic diversity, particularly the Kalanga/Khurutshe distinction of long local standing, has no negative impact on social relations; bilingualism, intermarriage, patterns of residence, and the frequent passing of Khurutshe (of the Mpofu totem) as Kalanga, support this view. However, my extensive participant observation in the *urban* setting of Francistown shows the nature of relations in religious contexts, as described above, to be in contrast with other contexts in which there are ubiquitous, petty confrontations on language and ethnic issues, in relationships between neighbours and between friends, on the work floor, in access to the informal sector of the economy, in amorous matters, in drinking and nightlife, and in the conceptualization of social relationships in terms of sorcery. These frictions are clearly reflected in the cases tried at the urban customary courts. As an urban society, Francistown is saturated not only with African/White but also with Tswana/Kalanga conflict, in which ethnic stereotypes and the failure or refusal to learn and understand each other's language often adds an awkward dimension to casual interaction between strangers.

In the face of this conspicuous inter-ethnic conflict in everyday urban life, it is remarkable that the political efficacy of Kalanga ethnic mobilization has remained so slight. While closely linked to the Kalanga cause and always vocal on minority language rights (National Executive Council 1984, 1988; Maripe 1987), the BPP's nationwide aspirations have prevented this party from identifying too narrowly as a one-'tribe' affair. Daniel Kwele's Botswana Progressive Union (BPU) was founded specifically because his being Kalanga prevented him from assuming the national leadership of the BNF (which has a strong regional backing in the south of Botswana); and until his death in 1990 his pronouncements were the most militant and unashamedly pro-Kalanga among contemporary Botswana politicians. Never really successful, the performance of BPP and BPU in the 1989 national elections was extremely disappointing. There is little to suggest the imminent failure of the BDP strategy of Tswana hegemony, populism, and co-option of potential opposition, as long as the state élite remains in a position to 'deliver'. The country's language policy is likely to remain as it is. In the long term, however, the diminishing diamond resources, the impact of continued drought on Botswana's problematic agriculture, the paradoxically negative effects for the Botswana economy of the dismantling of Apartheid in South Africa, increasing rates of inflation and unemployment, the increasing public arrogance of the Botswana military, and the wave of democratic change and popular participation in many other (far less liberal) African countries since 1990, may yet bring Botswana to a critical point where language and ethnicity are turned into effective political capital (Bernard 1989).

DISCUSSION

Despite many superficial correspondences, comparison of the trajectories of Nkoya and Kalanga reveals considerable underlying differences. First the correspondences: as a result of the *mfecane* upheaval which affected the entire Southern African subcontinent in the nineteenth century, in two regions a Bantu language of considerable local antiquity, and sharing both structural and lexical continuity with adjacent languages,[20] is confronted by a Sotho language (of a very different group of Bantu languages, and unintelligible to speakers of Kalanga and Nkoya) originating from the south and carried by a group of such power that it relegates the other local language to minority status;[21] in the colonial and post-colonial period this minority status is formalized in a national language policy and implies exclusion of the language involved from the state's political and administrative practice; the dynamics of state formation and hegemony, and the introduction of Christianity as a literate world religion, then engender an ethnic consciousness largely focussing on language; the recent political and economic history of the people who carry the minority language casts light on the extent, direction, degrees of organization, cultural and ethno-historical elaboration, and success, of the language-centred ethnic strategies of each group. At this level of generality a similar story could be told for scores, if not hundreds, of languages and ethnicities in the modern world. Only on closer scrutiny, are systematic differences between the Nkoya and the Kalanga trajectories highlighted, which suggest crucial underlying variables.

Difference in scale

Difference in scale is very manifest: the 30,000 Nkoya speakers constitute less than 1 per cent of the Zambian national population, while the 120,000 Kalanga speakers constitute 13 per cent of the Botswana population. That the Kalanga are almost twenty times larger, as a national percentage, than the Nkoya cannot be ignored if we want to understand the differences between Kalanga and Nkoya in terms of access to the modern state and economy, education, and privileged class positions.

The absolute numbers also suggest disparities as potential markets for missionary efforts, book production and marketing, and for creative talents to be mobilized in literary production, even though it cannot be said that the Botswana Kalanga have done better than the Nkoya in these respects.

The definition and historical restructuring of national political space

The number of hierarchical politico-administrative levels between minority speakers on the ground and the nation state, and the changes this set-up has undergone in recent constitutional history – in other words the definition and historical restructuring of national political space – is a significant variable.[22] In the course of the last two centuries, Nkoya speakers have had to accommodate themselves within two states which relegated their language to minority status: first the Kololo/Luyana state, which constituted the highest level of political organization until 1900 (much was retained by the Barotse indigenous administration under colonial rule), and whose majority language (in terms not of numbers but of power relations) was that of the Lozi élite; and subsequently the colonial and post-colonial state, whose majority language was, and has remained, English. The Lozi did not manage to perpetuate their Protectorate in the form of a seceded post-colonial state of Barotseland – an option seriously contemplated by many at the time (cf. Mulford 1967; Caplan 1970), and still lurking around the corner today – but had to accept integration within the Zambian state on terms which were increasingly similar to those applying to other regions in the Zambian territory. This meant that the Lozi, having increased their ethnic and political domination over the Nkoya during most of the colonial period, failed to capture the wider post-colonial state; their own Lozi language was relegated, in political and administrative status, from the supreme level of state language to an *intermediate level* as one of the seven state-recognized regional languages under the hegemony of the official national language, English. After 1964 it was the decline of Lozi power at the national level that offered the Nkoya room to enhance their linguistic status and their chieftaincies, to engage in ethnic organization and cultural and ethno-historical revitalization, and to start, as an ethnic group, on a centripetal movement vis-à-vis the nation state and its development initiatives.

From the point of view of the redefinition of national political space, the Botswana Kalanga trajectory has been fundamentally different: if Tswana domination in south-west Kalangaland (i.e. north-east Botswana) in the nineteenth century and under colonial Protectorate conditions was rather similar to Lozi domination in Nkoyaland during the same period, subsequent differences between the Nkoya and Kalanga linguistic and ethnic trajectories owed much to the fact that (as a result of international political and economic relations prevailing in the subcontinent since the late nineteenth century, but also because of the undeniable presence of a Tswana language majority over a huge part of what today is Botswana and the Republic of South Africa) no intermediate level emerged: the Tswana did capture the post-colonial state of Botswana, managed to impose their language as the national language for use in its state institutions along with English, retained their hold on the state throughout the post-colonial period by a dexterous utilization of democratic institutions and international esteem, and thus ended up in a position incomparably more powerful than that of the Lozi in Zambia today.

Tswana as a national and as a regional language

There is a clear contradiction between (1) Tswana as a national, state-backed language on the one hand, and (2) Tswana as just another regional language at the sub-national level of north-eastern Botswana, spoken by Khurutshe locals and southern urban immigrants, on the other.

This contradiction explains some of the inconsistencies in the patterns of ethnic animosity (in everyday urban life), ethnic accommodation (in everyday rural life, if my reading of the scanty evidence at my disposal can be supported), transcendence of ethnic opposition (in the religious domain), antagonism over language in the formal political domain of party politics, and the failure of mass mobilization over minority language issues and Kalanga ethnicity in general. Tswana national political hegemony empowers speakers in certain state-defined situations in north-eastern Botswana: BDP politicians addressing a political rally, judges in the urban customary court, civil servants in offices, schoolteachers, broadcasters; but (because of the effective constitutional functioning of the Botswana state, which makes it difficult to mobilize state power openly for particularistic personal interests) such empowering is far less relevant in the day-to-day contacts between urban neighbours who are ethnic strangers, and between rural fellow-villagers who know that despite their different tongues they have shared a local history for a century or more. We must resist the temptation to consider ethnic phenomena in the national political domain and those in the local domain as necessarily converging on the same categories of ethnicity.

Traditional rulers

Traditional rulers have played a very different role in the ethnic and linguistic trajectories of the Nkoya and the Kalanga. Although Nkoya perceptions cast the Lozi as their main ethnic enemies, the fact remains that some Nkoya royal chieftainships survived the incorporation process, and not as mere village headmen (as among the Kalanga), but as senior members of the Lozi indigenous administration, sharing (albeit to a lesser extent than their Lozi counterparts, and at the cost of considerable contestation) in the financial proceeds of the 1900 Barotse Treaty and the 1964 Barotse Agreement. Nkoya chiefships have largely retained their regalia, royal enclosure, palace, subsidized orchestra, and paid councillors, throughout the colonial and post-colonial periods until today.[23] The creation of the Naliele Lozi court in the 1930s as a tangible expression of Lozi internal colonization was greatly resented, but it provided an administrative continuity when its Mankoya Native Authority became Kaoma Rural Council, with the chiefs (or their Prime Ministers) as appointed members – a situation again persisting today. Thus the chiefs could continue to function as foci of cultural, ethnic, linguistic, and historical identity, and at the same time act (in collusion with their junior relatives: Nkoya modern politicians such as Kalaluka) as political brokers bringing together their people and the state. Among the Botswana Kalanga, Tswana domination effectively and from early on rooted up everything of this nature, so local ethnic consciousness remained without a traditional political focus, which might have served as a tangible connexion with the splendid political history of the Kalanga over the past 500 years or more.

An important lesson is to be learned here in terms of the appreciation, from the point of view of national integration and development, of the potential role of ethnicity and of traditional leaders as foci of ethnic consciousness. *One cannot blindly generalize that all sub-national identity is divisive and leads to centrifugal tendencies away from the state – as has often been maintained both by African politicians and by political scientists.* Under specific circumstances, which empirical sociological and historical research has to identify, the road to increased participation in the state and its development efforts leads via ethnicity and traditional leaders – as in the case of the Nkoya. One can only speculate how different Botswana Kalanga ethnicity would have been today if Ngwato hegemony had not eclipsed Kalanga traditional leadership, or if the latter had been restored when the opportunity to do so arose at Independence. My guess would be that Kalanga ethnicity in Botswana might be more vocal and vital today and less of a backroom middle-class pastime, that the status of the Kalanga language would have been higher – so that a Kalanga élite could be more loyal to it, and that Kalanga identity and Kalanga language would have developed into respectable sub-national expressions with their own recognizably loyal place in the Botswana nation state, as vehicles for qualified integration rather than centrifugal disruption (as they are seen by the Tswana today). It is for profound reasons that the position of Kalanga traditional rulers in Botswana today is analogous to the position of the Kalanga language today: powerless, peripheral, without organic place on the national scene. And just as the 1980s have rediscovered the importance of traditional rulers for an understanding of the contemporary African state and its defects, it is likely that the near future will see the same for minority languages.[24]

The state has a discourse not only on language, but also in language

Given the three-tiered complexity of the Nkoya ethnic situation (local level/Barotseland/national level) Nkoya ethnicity could grow to become centripetal vis-à-vis the state; given the two-tiered make-up of the Kalanga situation (local level/national level), Tswana capture of the state meant that any Kalanga ethnicity opposing the Tswana would have to be centrifugal vis-à-vis the state. This is an important reason why language policy in Botswana is inflexible in a way it did not prove to be in Zambia. Speaking Nkoya does not directly threaten the constitutional premises of the Zambian state, but refusing to speak Tswana can very well be interpreted as a subversive act. Of course, there is plenty of room for semantic mystification here: it is only by sleight of hand that BDP politicians manage to convince their audiences that (a) whoever is constitutionally a Motswana[25] (which includes all Botswana Kalanga except the most recent immigrants), is (b) linguistically and ethnically a Motswana (which leaves out 30 per cent of the citizens of Botswana), and therefore (c) would not wish to speak any other language than Tswana!

Here we are confronted with the highly significant fact, often overlooked in discussions of language policy and ethnicity, that the state has a discourse not only on language, but also in language – so that the premises of élite power are subjectively implied in the very social constructs that, in terms of language policy, are being negotiated under the pretence of disinterested objectivity. Language policy in Botswana may formally be enacted in English documents, but it is largely prepared, thought out, and discussed in Tswana.

It is probably due more to naivety than to cunning that semantically twisted syllogisms of the above kind are propounded time and again in the national political discourse in Botswana: the identification of the Botswana state with Tswana ethnicity and the Tswana language is generally perceived by the actors as a social reality, and whoever challenges that reality threatens to destroy all the undeniable blessings which make Botswana stand out as a stable and affluent country in a lost continent (cf. Good 1992). Whoever is loyal to these underlying premises, and shows such loyalty by submitting to Tswana hegemony in public behaviour, is apparently welcome to use whatever language he likes in the privacy of his home. Of course, sophisticated Kalanga activists (like Dr Maripe, or the lawyer Mosojane – member of a Kalanga royal family, BPP presidential candidate in the 1984 national elections, BPP national secretary, SPIL member, and in daily confrontation with the Botswana state on behalf of his clients, in court and in correspondence with the Registrar of Societies, etc.) have on numerous occasions pointed out the constitutional flaws in this attitude (cf. Maripe 1987; National Executive Council 1984, 1988), but to no avail. The fact that most of their fellow-Kalanga in the same educational and income bracket have chosen to submit to Tswana hegemony is a major reason why the non-Kalanga state élite can afford to ignore the principled constitutional argument and perpetuate the existing language policy.

One country or two

Speaking of national political space, we also realize that the difference in the Nkoya and Kalanga trajectories has to do with the concrete geographical location of their speakers' homelands on the map. For the purpose of the present argument I have slightly simplified the Nkoya situation so as to assume that all Nkoya speakers fall within Lozi territory – ignoring the less prominent royal chieftaincies of Mwene Momba and Mwene Kabulwebulwe outside Zambia's Western Province; it is no simplification however to maintain that the entire Nkoya-speaking rural population is found in the heart-land of western Zambia. People speaking languages close to Nkoya are found in southern Zaïre and in eastern Angola (Mbwela, Ganguela), but present-day Nkoya speakers, even their ethno-historical specialists, are virtually unaware of these connexions which – as I have argued in detail elsewhere (van Binsbergen 1992a) – certainly do not inform their ethnic consciousness. Kalanga, by contrast, is spoken in western and southern Zimbabwe as well as in adjacent north-eastern Botswana. Without going into a discussion of Zimbabwe Kalanga ethnic and linguistic accommodation to the other Shona languages of that country, to Ndebele expansion since the nineteenth century, to Tonga and other trans-Zambezian languages, it is clear that the trajectory of Kalanga ethnicization, since the creation of the Bechuanaland Protectorate and especially after Independence in 1966, must be seen in the light of their incorporation into an entirely different national political space. Botswana Kalanga define themselves not so much – through inclusion – by reference to Zimbabwean Kalanga (with whom they continue to entertain kinship, marital and ritual ties), but – through opposition – to Botswana Tswana, particularly the Ngwato. This must be part of the explanation why cultural and linguistic production among the Zimbabwe Kalanga seems hardly to filter across the border and why the exciting insights of Zimbabwean history (but relating to a time when the Botswana/Zimbabwe border did not exist, and much of the Kalanga-centred state system lay in north-eastern Botswana) fail to be incorporated in Botswana Kalanga consciousness. There is an additional reason on the Zimbabwe side: although Kalanga is a western variant of Shona, and the latter is the majority language (numerically and politically) of Zimbabwe, the Kalanga language's status in Zimbabwe (and hence its organization and resources) is weak and problematic since it is identified, by the political centre, with anti-ZANU tendencies in the (largely Ndebele) south-west of the country. The Botswana/Zimbabwe border has increasingly hardened into a real boundary, even to the extent of the expansion and growth, to a level of considerable local autonomy, of Botswana branches of the Mwali cult, which continues to have its centre in the Matopos hills south-east of Bulawayo; the influence of this cult on trans-border linguistic continuity may be limited since its personnel is multi-ethnic and its archaic ritual language is not today's Kalanga.

The Botswana Kalanga mainly speak the Lilima dialect, which is the standard for SPIL and for the Kalanga Bible Translation Project of the Lutheran church in Botswana. The insistence on a new Lilima orthography, which (as arbitrary as all orthography) is emphatically different from the Zimbabwean conventions, and the enormous investment in the translation of the Bible into this dialect following this new orthography (even when the New Testament is largely available in a 1929 translation; Ndebo 1985), must be understood as an attempt at manifest localization or Botswana-ization: to claim and define a place for Botswana Kalanga within the national political space of Botswana, with as little reference as possible to a Zimbabwe which, in Botswana eyes, is poor, conflict-ridden, criminal, violent, non-Tswana, in short subject to negative stereotypes. There is a strong element of artificiality and uprootedness in this accommodation to Botswana political space, and one cannot really be surprised if the exercise has not, so far, led to the general cultural revitalization the White expatriate Lutheran missionaries had expected. Instead the Kalanga Bible Translation Project (with close links with SPIL in terms of personnel) is ridden with conflict over White control and African initiative; as if the opportunity to put one's 'own' language on the Christian and publishing map, condescendingly offered by the missionaries at great expense and effort, is not sufficiently redeeming in its own right.

The objectification of language

Bible translation, among the Nkoya and the Botswana Kalanga, is an example of the convergence between ideological expansion of a world religion, and the linguistic and ethnic processes at the local level. The Nkoya case shows the potential, the Kalanga case the limitations of this convergence. What happens to a language when it is committed to writing, pummelled into the desired orthographic shape, scrutinized for its potential lexically and syntactically to convey the alien images of an imported world religion with its alien theological classifications and nuances? We have seen how this Christian/ethnic convergence in the language process can be illuminated by the idea of a national political space, in which the language is to claim and fill a specific niche given prevailing political and language-policy conditions. However, the same phenomenon could also (cf. Fardon & Furniss 1991) be described as *reification* or *objectification* – at the hands of academic linguists, missionary linguists, administrators and educationalists but also and primarily at the hands of native speakers themselves (cf. Fabian 1986).

In the process, a language is named, standardized, variants become perceived as dialects and subsumed under the general chosen name (a form of hegemony in itself, but one we cannot go into here), and the lexicon has to be deprived of some of its capacity endlessly to incorporate new matter from adjacent language communities: for language defines itself by opposition to other languages at the local scene, so some linguistic forms will have to become marked as one's own and others as alien. More than any other part of institutionalized culture, language is encoded in formal rules whose infringement can immediately cause puzzlement, ridicule, rejection or a breakdown of communication among listeners and readers. This capability of encoding and displaying identity or alienness in social interaction, incidentally, must be one of the reasons why, among all possible culturally produced materials, it is primarily language on which ethnicity feeds and thrives. Lexical and syntactic purism is one of the hallmarks of ethnicity. For example, when I edited the *Likota lya Bankoya* manuscript in consultation with a few readers' committees of native speakers of the Nkoya language, the latter insisted that Rev. Shimunika's Nkoya text be cleansed of all anglicisms and Lozi-isms, even when these were totally accepted in contemporary spoken Nkoya and the 'purer' alternatives were felt to be awkward, obsolete or not generally understood.

It is impossible to assign a definite starting date to the process of linguistic objectification, even with reference to a specific language and access to historical linguistic data. It is difficult to see how any language could maintain a minimum stability and persistence over time, without which it would not deserve the term language, if objectification did not already exist in some inchoate form. One thing can be said in this connexion, however: the model of the nation state, in which a unique language coincides with state power, is alien to most pre-colonial African contexts. Eighteenth and nineteenth century states in central western Zambia outside the Zambezi flood plain were multilingual and multi-ethnic; political power was not linguistically or ethnically marked to the extent it was to be in the Lozi state; and there are indications that, as a result, language boundaries were more fluid – as if the objectification process was still in an early stage. Certainly the objectification process is very much intensified in a context of political and economic incorporation – the very cradle also of ethnicity.

When selected elements of collective symbolic production (e.g. a language, a cult, a vision of the past) are drawn into the orbit of a group's identity formation in inter-ethnic relations, these elements tend to be objectified to the extent of fossilization. For the social analyst like myself, who is not a linguist, there is even the risk of overlooking the dynamics of language and treating it as if it were an independent variable in the ethnicization process, rather than being shaped itself in that very process. Both Nkoya and Kalanga are relatively ancient linguistic presences in the region where they are found today. A discussion of the historical linguistics of these languages is beyond my competence, but it is important to realize that we have identified at least two contexts in which objectification is particularly manifest: when the language becomes a focus of an emerging ethnic identity, and when language is committed to writing for the first time, often in a context of the dissemination of a world religion.

Identity, commodity and proletarianization in the context of language

In the objectification process the named, standardized and purified language becomes imbued with an 'emotive relevance', a socially constructed sense of identity and of opposition vis-à-vis other, rival expressions at the local and regional scene. It is for this reason that I cannot entirely go along with David Parkin's otherwise illuminating idea of approaching language objectification in Africa (specifically on the Swahili coast) as a form of 'commodification': as if the language becomes a commodity which is cut and dried, strictly demarcated and regulated like an industrial product, freely exchangeable – and disposable – in a market of money, power and prestige.

The ethnicization process, viewed here as the ideological and organizational response to incorporation in a national political space, inevitably implies alienation: identity has to be constructed only when it has become problematic, in the face of the intrusion of an otherness so massive and powerful that it can no longer be encapsulated by means of the usual mechanisms through which the local society accommodates newly-born members, in-marrying spouses, strayed travellers and other isolated individuals. In the modern world, such alienation often springs from material disempowerment, in the process of the imposition of alien political power (e.g. the colonial state) and the world-wide penetration of the capitalist mode of production. In the process people lose (give up, often) much of what they then subsequently realize was once their own: a supportive kinship system, expressive art forms, a symbolically powerful and meaningful cosmological order. This is the familiar context for a discussion of commodification (cf. van Binsbergen 1992b).

Perhaps in the final analysis, the Botswana Kalanga's underplaying of language, the submission to Tswana linguistic hegemony and the lack of success of Kalanga ethnic mobilization along language lines, could be explained in terms of the Kalanga language (in the highly proletarianized situation of north-eastern Botswana) having become a commodity, easily exchanged for another (Tswana) whose higher market value is undeniable. In such a context one makes a fool of oneself if one publicly cherishes a despised minority language as a vehicle for literary expression, or evokes the splendour of a medieval state which has long since disappeared and which cannot be linked in other than negative terms to the present dominant group (the Tswana) in the local nation state.

Perhaps it is also as a result of proletarianization that Kalanga ethnicity primarily *expresses itself in the political domain* rather than in the cultural, literary, religious or ethno-historical domain. One of the most disconcerting aspects of symbolic life in Botswana today is that local historic (i.e. African) culture is largely absent from public life; it is allowed to enter public discourse only in the very form (fossilized, commodified) which Parkin stresses for language in the contemporary context. In order to be acceptable for public consumption (I use this word purposely) historical elements of African rural culture (e.g. the traditional judicial process in the *kgotla* or village court, which features in official discussions of the very different modern customary courts)[26] have to be selected, taken out of context, deprived of their meaning, reduced to textbook truisms, and then added as harmless ornaments (as duly processed packages of 'identity') to a consumerist life-style whose principal reference group is the urban middle class of nearby South Africa, known in detail through the media and personal exposure. The prominence of this pattern among the Botswana population especially in the urban areas is striking, even if we realize that the difference with other African societies is only a matter of degree. The pattern's contradictions are particularly manifest in the racially-conscious environment of Francistown (cf. van Binsbergen 1993). The problem is not that historical African cultural forms – referring to a past rural order and its contemporary partial survival, real or imaginary – are not there and do not decisively inform people's ideas and actions, but that *they are largely censored out of public discussion*: they have gone underground, where they are safe from harassment by dominant White culture and its local, predominantly African representatives. The cult of the High God Mwali, the place of ancestors in everyday and ritual life, healing cults, sorcery, ritual violence, divination, the symbolic basis of family life and of production and consumption – only at the cost of personal commitment and patience greater than ordinarily required in other parts of the continent is the expatriate researcher allowed a glimpse of the extent to which the 'Kuwait of Africa' shares in a general African cultural orientation. Under such circumstances there is no premium on traditionalizing and historicizing symbolic production as a channel for ethnic expression[27] (the path the Nkoya have taken): instead, one confronts the formally organized texture of social power, in the thoroughly respectable, political domain, which is seen to be organized along modern principles of rationality.

All this sounds like praise rather than criticism of Parkin's idea. Yet, especially in a context of alienation and proletarianization, powerlessness in the face of an authoritarian state, and the shattering – in modern migrants' consciousness – of a village-orientated symbolic microcosm, *language for the native speaker tends to be the last refuge of owning and belonging, of competence and identity.* Cultural reconstruction and revitalization, such as is at the root of many ethnic movements in the form of literary and ethno-historical production, seeks to rebuild an imaginary world of belonging in order to combat the disowning that characterizes the ethnic group's collective experience in the outside world. But while this is eminently true for the Nkoya (whose language has been objectified, but certainly not commodified), it is far less true for the Botswana Kalanga. Straddling both urban and rural commitments, survival strategies and cultural expressions, the Nkoya were never effectively proletarianized, and the viability of their rural culture and their language testifies to this. But why have the Kalanga responded so very differently? Was it because they have been much more effectively proletarianized, deprived of the possibility of returning to any viable rural society, since land alienation, over-grazing and drought have led to the collapse of the local ecosystem? Or was it because, in their proletarianized condition, Kalanga success in the modern world, away from the lost village, has been incomparably greater than that of the Nkoya?

CONCLUSION: LANGUAGE POLICY AND DEVELOPMENT

Our argument has perhaps illuminated the role of language in the trajectories of two African ethnic identities, but does it also contain a lesson for language policy? One striking point which emerges is that under similar conditions of withheld state recognition, the two languages, Nkoya and Kalanga, and the ethnicities associated with them, have been able to traverse such different paths while the formal language policy in the respective countries remained unchanged. The existence of a restrictive Zambian language policy did not prevent the Nkoya from engaging in cultural and ethno-historical self-reconstruction, and on the Kalanga side we have seen plenty of reasons why, even if Botswana's language policy had been less restrictive, it would have been unlikely that the Kalanga would have produced a more enthusiastic ethnic and linguistic response. The specific nature of the existing *language policy* hardly explains what happened – instead, political and economic factors cast much more light on the correspondences and differences between the two cases.

In principle this means that the data presented in this paper do not in themselves suggest a particular ideal form for a national language policy in African states. The following remarks therefore, although inspired by my research, are basically personal. Much as I love the two languages discussed here, and would regret to see them disappear from the treasure of universal human culture, I do not think that the only, or even best, way to safeguard their future existence and to utilize their present potential for self-expression, communication and citizen participation, is to include them in a national level formal language policy. They must be acknowledged and accommodated in policy, but only at the regional and local level.

The following two situations bring out the dilemma:

1 a peasant farmer being forced to use any language other than his own in first-line administrative, medical, judicial and developmental con-

tact with the state (a situation which, however common in both Zambia and Botswana today, constitutes an infringement of his human dignity and human rights, and effectively prevents him from citizen participation), and
2 national level institutions (such as parliament, the university, the High Court) being burdened with a multiplicity of languages, which may boost ethnic pride but at enormous financial sacrifice and at the risk of international isolation.

The latter even suggests that the national political space within which ethnic and linguistic processes evolve (since this is the constitutionally defined space for the legitimate exercise of state power), might very well be too narrow for a meaningful language policy to be defined. Botswana, with only one million inhabitants, has risked isolating itself from international production and circulation in the intellectual, artistic, and technological fields, by allowing Tswana to be used at the national level beside English; Zambia's policy, of not allowing the use of any African language at the national level, seemed the better choice, but we have seen how the decline of the state is forcing it to compromise in this respect.

When the costs of thwarted citizen participation and frustrated ethnic pride at the local and regional level are weighed against the costs of consistent plurality of official languages in politics and public administration, formal education, industry, etc., we have to look for a formula which balances efficiency with equity: *a graded model* which insists on the use of one official language at the national level, while for the regional and local level makes generous provision for the use, preservation and propagation of such plurality of languages as actually exists within the national boundaries. In this way basic human rights are safeguarded; the obvious role of the mother tongue in alphabetization is recognized (even for reasons of efficiency no modern state can afford to waste the intellectual and technological potential of the youths who happen to have a minority language as their mother tongue); the requirements for effective local and regional communication in social, cultural, religious and political matters – surely essential in a democratic state – are met; and language-centred ethnic frustration is far less likely to threaten the stability and integrity of the state.

In post-colonial Africa, and in the world at large today, there are numerous examples to show that such a threat can be very real. A Kalanga activist like Kwele liked to see the Kalanga case in the same light, and his standard ethnic rhetoric included the phrase 'or else the guns will speak'. In the light of my analysis this prediction is, for the moment, somewhat unrealistic, but the experience of humiliation, on which such utterances are based, is both undeniable and unnecessary, and deserves our concern and our intellectual efforts.

The argument also has some bearing on the issue of development. In the first place symbolic reconstruction and social revival at the local and regional level – such as language-based ethnicization often entails – could be recognized, more than is the case at present, as an essential element of development. The practical design and implementation of a graded unitary/pluralist language policy as advocated above would qualify for an exciting form of development cooperation.

More often, however, development is conceived in terms of a population's increased economic opportunities. In this respect the lessons of my analysis are far from straightforward. Among the Nkoya, the postcolonial state's positive if partial and opportunist response to ethnic aspirations (a package including language, traditional leaders, modern representational bodies at the regional and national level) brought the Nkoya much closer, not only to the state, but also to a modernizing economy which is clearly developmental – even if most Nkoya villagers, as yet, have not exactly benefited from this type of development. Among the Botswana Kalanga, their relative access to a modernizing economy and to the state (albeit not specifically as Kalanga) prevented their ethnic and language aspirations from taking wing. In both cases one has the feeling that the state's formal language policy has remained rather irrelevant since it failed to make provision for the local level of peasants and poor urbanites; it is primarily at this local level (where plurality of languages is a reality, especially in Africa) that development is realized, or fails to be realized.

APPENDIX

Table 11.1 Nkoya and Kalanga compared

variable	Nkoya	Kalanga
1. basic language data		
Guthrie (1948) classification[28]	L62[29]	T16[30]
estimated number of speakers in national territory	30,000[31]	120,000[32]
percentage of national population	0.8 per cent	13 per cent
formalized dialectal variation	hardly	yes
orthography	not an issue, rather standardized	bone of contention between Botswana and Zimbabwean native speakers
close affinity with languages outside immediate language area	Lunda, Luvale; (Mbwela, Ganguela in Angola)	other Kalanga dialects in western and southern Zimbabwe (the Botswana Kalanga is identified as the Lilima dialect); other Shona languages (the Kalanga cluster is considered to be western Shona)
country where this language is spoken	Zambia	Zimbabwe, Botswana

Table 11.1 (continued)

variable	Nkoya	Kalanga
2. inter-language relations		
national official language	English	English/(Tswana)
state-recognized languages	Bemba, Nyanja, Lozi, Luvale Tonga, Kaonde, Lunda	Tswana[33]
regionally dominant language	Lozi[34]	Tswana
language most speakers in local rural area speak	Nkoya	Kalanga
language of official communication in local rural area	Lozi	Tswana
other languages in local rural areas	Lozi, Luvale, Luchazi, Kaonde, Tonga, Ila, Lunda, Mbundu	Tswana, Ndebele, English, Afrikaans, Shona, San
lingua franca of national urban centres frequented by native speakers	Lozi (Livingstone), Nyanja (Lusaka today), Bemba (Copperbelt, pre-WWII Lusaka)	Tswana/(Kalanga) (Francistown), Tswana (other Botswana towns)
3. ethnic self-perception		
language name in use as ethnic name since	late 19th century	17th century
is ethnic identity underpinned by historical consciousness?	yes, spanning the period 16th–20th century	yes, but mainly with reference to colonial period

Table 11.1 (continued)

variable	Nkoya	Kalanga
contemporary self-perception of ethnic group in terms of local precedence	claim historical precedence as the first group to arrive in central western Zambia from Zaïre	dim historical awareness, many members accept the erroneous Tswana claims as to the Botswana Kalanga being recent immigrants from Zimbabwe

4. inter-ethnic relations

variable	Nkoya	Kalanga
nationally dominant ethnic group	Bemba, Tonga, 'Nyanja', Lozi	Tswana
regionally dominant ethnic group	Lozi	Tswana
the language's status in national society	very low	low
main perceived ethnic enemy	Lozi	Tswana
when native speakers 'pass', they pass as	Lozi, Bemba	Tswana
economic position of average native speaker/member of this ethnic group	below national average	at or above national average

5. language and state institutions except formal education

variable	Nkoya	Kalanga
is it allowed to use this language in the lowest courts?	allowed but discouraged in testimony; judges prefer Lozi, clerks record in English	formally yes, but discouraged
can state officials use this language in dealing with the local population?	not until late 1980s	no

Table 11.1 (continued)

variable	Nkoya	Kalanga
is this language admissible for use in Parliament?	no	no
state attitude towards this language	reticent but increasingly positive	strongly negative and hostile
is this language used in broadcasting?	no, except in popular and traditional songs	no

6. language and formal education

language used in schools	Lozi (Nkoya only occasionally and informally)	Tswana (Kalanga only occasionally and informally)
school primers locally available in print	late colonial period: yes; 1960s–1980s: no; 1990s: reprinted	no
relative educational level of native speakers of this language	far below national average	well above average

7. politics and language

was this language ever the state language of a pre-colonial state?	yes, since late 18th century	yes, from 17th to early 19th century
is this language used in royal/courtly ceremonies today?	yes, locally by musicians and throughout western Zambia (since early 19th c.)	no, except at village level
is this language used in local-level traditional politics today?	yes, by the district's major traditional 'rulers'	yes, but not the district's major chief's court

Table 11.1   (continued)

variable	Nkoya	Kalanga
do representatives of this ethnic group have access to national-level traditional politics today?	yes	no
do representatives of this ethnic group have access to modern regional politics today?	limited but increasing	extensive
do representatives of this ethnic group have access to modern national level politics today?	limited	extensive
political party favouring this language	UNIP, MMD (ruling parties)	BPP, BPU (opposition parties)
is language an issue in oppositional political rallying?	it was in the 1970s, not any more	yes!
8. language and expressive culture		
literary works available in this language	none exist	some exist but none are available locally
pious literature available in this language	rather abundantly	no evidence except hymn book and part of New Testament
ethno-historical literature available in this language	yes	yes, but not available locally

Table 11.1 (continued)

variable	Nkoya	Kalanga
is this language served by an ethnic/linguistic society? (since)	yes, *Kazanga* (1983)	yes, SPIL (1984[35])
profile of that society's membership	primary school-teachers, local-level politicians, paramedics	university students, secondary school-teachers, highly-educated professionals
is there a periodical in this language?	no	yes, but moribund (*Tjedza*)
does linguistic self-presentation take place in conjunction with other cultural forms (music, dance)?	yes, emphatically so	yes, but problematically so
9. religion and language		
was this language first committed to writing by a Christian mission?	yes	yes
Bible translation (year)	New Testament and Psalms (1953); Old Testament recently completed in MS	Gospels and Acts (1929); new translation currently in preparation
language used in local churches	Nkoya, Lozi	Kalanga, Ndebele, Tswana
(main) hymn book in	Mbunda/Nkoya/Lozi	Tswana, Sotho; Kalanga
is there any church exclusively using this language?	no	no
is this language used in non-Christian cults?	yes, but together with Luvale and Lenje	yes, but together with Ndebele, Shona, Venda, Tswana

NOTES

1 Fieldwork among the Zambian Nkoya was undertaken in 1972–4, and during shorter visits in 1977, 1978, 1981, 1988, 1989 and 1992 (twice). Fieldwork among the Kalanga of Botswana was undertaken in 1988–9 and during shorter visits in 1990, 1991 and 1992 (twice). I am indebted to the African Studies Centre, Leiden, for the most generous encouragement and financial support; and to research participants, to assistants and Government officials in both Zambia and Botswana and to members of my family, for invaluable contributions to the research. An earlier version of this argument was presented at the conference on 'African languages, development and the state', Centre of African Studies (University of London) and EIDOS, London, April 1991; in this context, I wish to thank the conference organizers, Richard Fardon and Graham Furniss, and the participants, for stimulating discussions; and the African Studies Centre, Leiden, for financing my participation. Rob Buijtenhuijs made useful comments on an earlier draft.
2 Cf. Mitchell 1974, Epstein 1978, and references cited there; major recent additions to this literature are in Vail 1989, including Robert Papstein's (1989) analysis of Luvale ethnicity which has considerable parallels with the Nkoya case. I have given an overview of rural ethnicity studies on Zambia in van Binsbergen 1985; 1992a deals with the interplay between twentieth-century ethnicity and the production of images of the pre-colonial past.
3 Cf. Wilmsen 1988, 1989 and references cited there.
4 On the Nkoya, cf. Brown 1984; McCulloch 1951; van Binsbergen 1977, 1985, 1986, 1987, 1992a, 1992b; Clay 1945. On the Lozi and Barotseland (Western Province, Western Zambia) in general, cf. Gluckman 1943, 1951, 1968; Prins 1980; Mutumba Mainga 1973; Stokes 1966; Caplan 1970. The only linguistic publication specifically on the Nkoya language is Yasutoshi Yukawa 1987.
5 This is not only the Nkoya's self-image (cf. van Binsbergen 1992a), but also the opinion of, among others, the ethnologist McCulloch (1951: 93) and the linguist Fortune (1959: 26).
6 *Mwene*: 'ruler'; here: 'queen'.
7 *Induna*: 'office-bearer in the Lozi indigenous administration'.
8 Throughout the colonial period, those Nkoya royal chiefs whose chieftaincies had survived functioned as members of the Lozi aristocracy and in this capacity boasted their own courts; legal proceedings were by preference conducted in Lozi, but the use of Nkoya was not ruled out. Shortly after Independence (1964), the central state instituted Local Courts, with state-trained judges and assessors who *de jure* were independent from the chief (not *de facto*, since they were members of the local aristocracy and appointed in consultation with the chief). At an unofficial level, below the Local Court each valley would continue to have its court presided over by a senior member of the chief's council; proceedings there would mainly be in Nkoya. An interesting development in Nkoyaland in the late 1980s was the spontaneous, but state-tolerated, institution of *mabombola* 'palaver' courts at chiefs' palaces, administering a local customary law in the Nkoya language, but without any formal powers beyond reconciliation; cf. van Binsbergen 1977.
9 Testamenta 1952. A list of published texts in the Nkoya language is given in van Binsbergen 1992a: 441ff.

182 Central and Southern Africa

10 Mr J. Kalaluka is the son of a Lozi father and of a Nkoya mother, sister of Mwene Timuna Kahare. On his career, cf. van Binsbergen 1992a.
11 Not to be confused with the South African political organization of the same name, by which it was however inspired.
12 The Kalanga have received considerable ethnographic attention (especially in the work of R. P. Werbner (e.g. 1970, 1971, 1975, 1989, 1990), but much work remains to be done on their history (cf. Malikongwa and Ford 1979; Tapela 1976, 1982; von Sicard 1954). In recent years, the Botswana Kalanga have been the subject of extensive oral-historical and especially archaeological research by van Waarden (1988), and linguistic and ethnohistorical research by Wentzel (1983). Fortune was the first to describe the Kalanga language (Fortune 1949, 1956, 1969). Elements of Kalanga can also be found in the classic works of Doke (1931a, 1931b, 1954); a very early wordlist is Weale 1893. A first impression of the historical data on Kalanga as a language can be gleaned from Beach 1980: xi, 189, 243, 258–9, 265, 279 and *passim*. On ethnic relations in the area, cf. Masale 1985; on rural land alienation, cf. Schapera 1943, 1971.
13 In the Botswana constitution, the section on the House of Chiefs is the only part listing ethnic groups, and (as is clear from the context) exclusively with a view to defining the composition of that House; these groups are: Ngwata, Ngwaketse, Kwena, Tawana, Kgatla, Lete, Rolong and Tlokwa (Republic of Botswana 1983).
14 For the place of these groups among the Tswana see Schapera 1952, 1984. Khurutshe are a sub-group of the Hurutshe Tswana of neighbouring South Africa; the Rolong Tswana also originate in South Africa but are now found on both sides of the border in the south of Botswana. One particular, massive category of immigrants had no impact of its own on the language situation beyond swelling the numbers of the existing groups: labour migrants from Zambia and Malawi for whom Francistown was a major stop-over between South Africa and their homes, and many of whom settled permanently in and around Francistown. While some have retained or assumed a distinct ethnic identity (notably as 'Rotse', which refers to Barotseland), virtually all have adopted Kalanga or Tswana as their language.
15 For an official reading of the episode, where its scope and violence are relegated to minimum proportions, see Tlou & Campbell 1984. A recent reading is Wylie 1991: 162–72; also cf. Ramsay 1987. The topic is also currently covered in work in progress by such prominent historians as T. O. Ranger and N. Q. Parsons.
16 On the Mwali cult, cf. Blake-Thompson & Summers 1956; Daneel 1970; Fortune 1973; Werbner 1989.
17 Which meanwhile has found its way into authoritative textbooks widely available in Botswana, e.g. Tlou & Campbell 1984.
18 At present I have insufficient data on these developments in Zimbabwe. The developments hinted at are far from recent. Already in the late 1950s Fortune (1959: 8) wrote with reference to Zimbabwe: 'There are a number of *Kalanga* and *Lilima*-speakers who are anxious to preserve and develop their language and to have it as a medium in their junior schools'.
19 Registrar of Societies, Gaborone, file No. H 28/90/258; this society was registered on 7 August 1984; also cf. van Binsbergen, in press.
20 Cf. Guthrie 1948; Fortune 1959; the continuity on the ground was repeatedly

Minority language, ethnicity and the state 183

brought out in a practical sense in the course of my anthropological and historiographical field-work, when I found that my language skills, however limited, in Nkoya or Kalanga enabled me to communicate, albeit defectively, with local *non*-speakers of these languages.

21 There is an interesting concrete link between the Kalanga and the Nkoya situations: in the second half of the nineteenth century the Wankie area, the north-western extension of the Kalanga language region, was tributary to the Kololo and subsequently the Luyana, so that Holub (1879) could list Kalanga as another Barotse subject tribe.

22 For a related discussion of ethnicity in an idiom of space, cf. Amselle 1985.

23 This applies to the most senior Nkoya royal chiefs, Mwene Mutondo and Mwene Kahare, of Kaoma district. Outside the district, and outside Barotseland, the history of Mwene Kabulwebulwe and Mwene Momba has been rather different, but then they never suffered Lozi incorporation to the same degree as their Kaoma counterparts.

24 A point made by Richard Fardon at the conference where this paper was first presented; also cf. van Binsbergen 1987.

25 The usual term, in Botswana English, to denote the personal nominative of Tswanahood.

26 Cf. Roberts 1972.

27 On this point the Botswana situation as described has strong parallels with present-day South Africa, and reflects such dilemmas of cultural and symbolic reconstruction as have only very late in the liberation struggle gained explicit recognition and respectability.

28 Not being a linguist, I include this entry only in order to allow those who are, to identify the languages professionally. I am aware that the classification of African languages has evolved greatly since Guthrie's pioneering work (Greenberg 1963; Alexandre 1972).

29 Fortune contests Guthrie's classification even if it is close to Doke's (1954): 'There is need for a closer examination of the Nkoya-Mbwela languages, scattered as they are, and influenced by others, it is at the moment impossible to indicate the true position' (Fortune 1959: 27). Ohannessian & Kashoki's authoritative *Language in Zambia* regrettably does not reconsider this question and comfortably classifies Nkoya in a group of its own (H, comprising such minor dialectal variants as Nkoya, Lukolwe/Mbwela, Lushangi and Mashasha) (Ohannessian & Kashoki 1978: 20 and *passim*).

30 Also cf. Fortune 1959: 8-9.

31 Cf. Kashoki 1978: 20; van Binsbergen 1992a: 6; and references cited there.

32 Based on Picard 1987: 5.

33 Guthrie (1948) classification S21.

34 Guthrie (1948) classification K21, which however does not seem to do justice to the fact, well recognized by Fortune, that Lozi is 'a mixture of *Southern Sotho* and *Luyana*, now the lingua franca of Barotseland Protectorate and used in all African courts. It is mainly Sotho in morphology but has a great number of Luyana words which seems to be increasing . . . . The language Lozi, a combination of Sotho and Luyana, grew up between 1869, the date of the expulsion of the Kololo invaders, and 1919, at the Barotse court' (Fortune 1959: 41-2; cf. 1963). On Luyana, the original court language of the Luyana kingdom with striking parallels with contemporary Nkoya, cf. Givon 1971.

35 This was the year of official registration; considering the amount of time

needed to prepare for official registration, the actual founding initiative dated from 1981–2.

REFERENCES

Alexandre, P. (1972) *An Introduction to Languages and Language in Africa*, London, Ibadan, Nairobi: Heinemann.
Amselle, J.-L. (1985) 'Ethnies et espaces: pour une anthropologie topologique', in J.-L. Amselle and E. Mbokolo (eds.) *Au coeur de l'ethnie*, Paris: La Découverte.
Baylies, C. and Szeftel, M. (1992) 'The fall and rise of multi-party politics in Zambia', *Review of African Political Economy* 54: 75–91.
Beach, D. N. (1980) *The Shona and Zimbabwe, 900–1850: an Outline of Shona History*, Gwelo [Gweru]: Mambo Press.
Benson, M. (1960) *Tshekedi Khama*, London: Faber and Faber.
Bernard, St. (1989) 'Botswana: un multipartisme fragile et menacé?', *Politique Africaine*, 36: 125–8.
Bhebe, N. M. B. (1973) 'Missionary activity among the Ndebele and Kalanga: a survey', in A. J. Dachs (ed.) *Christianity South of the Zambezi, I*, Gwelo [Gweru]: Mambo Press.
Blake-Thompson, J. and Summers, R. (1956) 'Mlimo and Mwari: notes on a native religion in Southern Rhodesia', *Native Affairs Department Annual (NADA)* 33: 53–8.
Brown, E. D. (1984) 'Drums of life: royal music and social life in Western Zambia', unpublished Ph.D. thesis, University of Washington, School of Music; Ann Arbor: University Microfilms International.
Caplan, G. (1970) *The Elites of Barotseland 1878–1969*, London: Hurst.
Chirenje, J. M. (1977) *A History of Northern Botswana 1850–1910*, London: Rutherford.
Clay, G. C. R. (1945) *History of the Mankoya District* (Communication No. 4, 're-roneod' [sic] 1955), Livingstone: Rhodes-Livingstone Institute.
Daneel, M. L. (1970) *The God of the Matopo Hills – An Essay on the Mwari Cult in Rhodesia*, The Hague/Paris: Mouton for African Studies Centre, Leiden.
Doke, C. M. (1931a) *A Comparative Study in Shona Phonetics, Part IV*, Johannesburg: University of Witwatersrand Press.
—— (1931b) *Report on the Unification of the Shona Dialects*, Salisbury: Government of Southern Rhodesia.
—— (1954) *The Southern Bantu Languages*, Oxford: Oxford University Press.
Epstein, A. L. (1978) *Ethos and Identity: Three Studies in Ethnicity*, London: Tavistock.
Fabian, J. (1986) *Language and Colonial Power: the Appropriation of Swahili in the former Belgian Congo*, Cambridge: Cambridge University Press.
Fardon, R. and Furniss, G. (1991) 'Language and languages: frontiers and boundaries', paper read at the conference on 'African languages, development and the state', Centre of African Studies (University of London), and EIDOS, London, April.
Fortune, G. (1949) *Ndevo yenombe luvizho and other Lilima texts*, Communications from the School of African Studies, University of Capetown, New Series. No. 21.

—— (1956) 'A Rozvi text with translation and notes', *Native Affairs Department Annual (NADA)* 33: 67-91.
—— (1959) *A Preliminary Survey of the Bantu Languages of the Federation* (Rhodes-Livingstone Communication No. 14), Lusaka: Rhodes-Livingstone Institute.
—— (1963) 'A note on the languages of Barotseland', *Proceedings of Conference on the History of Central African Peoples*, Lusaka: Rhodes-Livingstone Institute.
—— (1969) '75 years of writing in Shona', *Zambezia* 1, 1: 55-67.
—— (1973) 'Who was Mwari?', *Rhodesian History* 4: 1-20.
Gadibolae, M. (1985) 'Serfdom (Bolata) in the Nata area', *Botswana Notes and Records* 17: 25-32.
Geertz, C. (ed.) (1963) *Old Societies and New States: the Quest for Modernity in Africa and Asia*, New York: Free Press.
Gillett, S. (1973) 'The survival of chieftainship in Botswana', *African Affairs* 72, 287: 179-85.
Givon, T. (1971) *The Si-Luyana Language* (Communication No. 6), Lusaka: Institute for African Studies.
Gluckman, M. (1943) *Organisation of the Barotse Native Authorities: with a Plan for Reforming Them* (Communication No. 1), Lusaka: Rhodes-Livingstone Institute.
—— (1951) 'The Lozi of Barotseland, N. W. Rhodesia', in E. Colson and M. Gluckman (eds.) *Seven Tribes of British Central Africa*, Oxford: Oxford University Press.
—— (1968) *Economy of the Central Barotse Plain*, (Rhodes-Livingstone Paper No. 7, reprint of the 1941 edition), Manchester: Manchester University Press.
Good, K. (1992) 'Interpreting the exceptionality of Botswana', *Journal of Modern African Studies* 30, 1: 69-96.
Greenberg, J. H. (1963) *The Languages of Africa*, Bloomington: Indiana University Press.
Guthrie, M. (1948) *The Classification of the Bantu Languages*, Oxford: Oxford University Press for the International African Institute.
Holm, J. and Molutsi, P. (eds.) (1989) *Democracy in Botswana*, Gaborone: Macmillan.
Holub, E. (1879) *Eine Culturskizze des Marutse-Mambunda Reiches in Süd-Central-Afrika*, Vienna: Königliche und Kaiserliche Geographische Gesellschaft.
Kashoki, M. E. (1978) 'The language situation in Zambia', in S. Ohannessian and M. E. Kashoki (eds.) *Language in Zambia*, London: International African Institute.
McCulloch, M. (1951) *The Southern Lunda and Related Peoples*, Oxford and London: Oxford University Press, Ethnographic Atlas of Africa.
Malikongwa, D. M. and Ford, C. C. (1979) 'The history of the Bakhurutshe (the Phofu group) and the Bakalanga of Botswana', unpublished MS, Institute of Adult Education, University of Botswana.
Maripe, K. T. T. (1987) 'Open letter to His Excellency Dr Q. K. J. Masire, President of the Republic of Botswana', n.p.: Botswana Peoples Party.
Masale, G. (1985) 'Ethnicity and regionalism in Botswana and their impact on elections: a case study of the North-East and Francistown', paper presented

at the workshop on preliminary results from the 1984 election study project at the University of Botswana, Gaborone, 16–19 May.

Mautle, G. (1986) 'Bakgalagadi-Bakwena relationship: a case of slavery, c. 1840–c. 1930', *Botswana Notes and Records* 18: 19–32.

Meebelo, H. S. (1986) *African Proletarians and Colonial Capitalism*, Lusaka: Kenneth Kaunda Foundation.

Mitchell, J. C. (1974) 'Perceptions of ethnicity and ethnic behaviour: an empirical exploration', in A. Cohen (ed.) *Urban Ethnicity*, London: Tavistock.

Mulford, D. C. (1967) *Zambia: The Politics of Independence, 1957–1964*, Oxford: Oxford University Press.

Murray, A., Nengwekhulu, H. and Ramsay, J. (1987) 'The formation of political parties', in F. Morton and J. Ramsay (eds.) *The Birth of Botswana: a History of the Bechuanaland Protectorate from 1910 to 1966*, Gaborone: Longman.

Mutumba Mainga (1973) *Bulozi Under the Luyana Kings*, London: Longman.

National Executive Council, Botswana Peoples Party (1984) *This Way Botswana: Botswana Peoples Party 1984 Election Manifesto*, Francistown: Botswana Peoples Party.

National Executive Council, Botswana Peoples Party Headquarters, n.d. [1988] *To the President of the Republic of Botswana*, Francistown: National Executive Council, Botswana Peoples Party Headquarters.

Ndebo Mbuya Yobuhe gwe Ndzimu: Four Gospels and Acts in KALANA [sic] (1985), Roggebaai, Cape Town: Bible Society of South Africa, third South African impression 1985, reprint of the first edition by the British and Foreign Bible Society 1929; first South African edition 1979.

Nengwekhulu, H. R. (1979) 'Some findings on the origins of political parties in Botswana', *Pula* 1, 2: 47–76.

Nkomo, J. (1985) *The Story of My Life*, London: Methuen.

Ohannessian, S. and Kashoki, M. E. (eds.) (1978) *Language in Zambia*, London: International African Institute.

Papstein, R. J. (1989) 'From ethnic identity to tribalism: the Upper Zambezi region of Zambia, 1830–1981', in L. Vail (ed.) *The Creation of Tribalism in Southern Africa*, London, Berkeley and Los Angeles: James Currey and the University of California Press.

Parkin, D. (1991) 'Language, Government and the play on purity and impurity: Arabic, Swahili and the vernaculars in Kenya', paper read at the conference on 'African languages, development and the state', Centre of African Studies (University of London) and EIDOS, London, April 1991.

Picard, L. A. (1987) *The Politics of Development in Botswana: a Model for Success?*, Boulder and London: Lynne Rienner Publishers.

Prins, G. (1980) *The Hidden Hippopotamus*, Cambridge: Cambridge University Press.

Ramsay, J. (1987) 'Resistance from subordinate groups: Babirwa, BaKgatla Mmanaana and BaKalanga Nswazwi', in F. Morton and J. Ramsay (eds.) *The Birth of Botswana: A History of the Bechuanaland Protectorate from 1910 to 1966*, Gaborone: Longman.

Republic of Botswana (1983 etc.) *Laws of Botswana: The Constitution of Botswana*, n.p. [Gaborone]: s.n. [Government Printer].

Roberts, S. A. (1972) 'The survival of the traditional Tswana courts in the national legal system of Botswana', *Journal of African Law* 16: 103–129.

Schapera, I. (1943) 'The native land problem in the Tati district', unpublished report to the Bechuanaland Protectorate Government (cf. Schapera 1971).
—— (1952) *The Ethnic Composition of Tswana Tribes* (Monographs on Social Anthropology No. 11), London: London School of Economics.
—— (1971) 'Native land problems in the Tati district', *Botswana Notes and Records* 3, 219-68.
—— (1984) *The Tswana*, London: Kegan Paul International in association with the International African Institute, enlarged reprint of the 1963 edition.
—— (1988) *Praise-Poems of Tswana Chiefs*, Cape Town and Oxford: Oxford University Press, 3rd impression (reprint of the 1965 edition).
Silitshena, R. M. K. (1979) 'Chiefly authority and the organisation of space in Botswana', *Botswana Notes and Records* 11: 55-67.
Stokes, E. (1966) 'Barotseland: survival of an African state', in E. Stokes and R. Brown (eds.) *The Zambesian Past*, Manchester: Manchester University Press.
Tapela, H. M. (1976) 'The Tati district of Botswana, 1866-1969', unpublished Ph.D. thesis, University of Sussex.
—— (1982) 'Movement and settlement in the Tati region: a historical survey', in R. R. Hitchcock and M. R. Smith (eds.) *Settlement in Botswana*, Gaborone: Botswana Society.
Testamenta ya yipya/Nyimbo [*Nkoya New Testament and Psalms*] (1952) London: British and Foreign Bible Society.
Tlou, T. and Campbell, A. (1984) *History of Botswana*, Gaborone: Macmillan.
Vail, L. (ed.) (1989) *The Creation of Tribalism in Southern Africa*, London, Berkeley and Los Angeles: James Currey and the University of California Press.
van Binsbergen, W. M. J. (1977) 'Law in the context of Nkoya society', in S. A. Roberts (ed.) *Law and the Family in Africa*, The Hague and Paris: Mouton.
—— (1985) 'From tribe to ethnicity in western Zambia: the unit of study as an ideological problem', in W. M. J. van Binsbergen and P. Geschiere (eds.) *Old Modes of Production and Capitalist Encroachment: Anthropological Explorations in Africa*, London: Kegan Paul International.
—— (1986) 'The postcolonial state, "state penetration" and the Nkoya experience in central western Zambia', in W. M. J. van Binsbergen, F. Reijntjens and G. Hesseling (eds.) *State and Local Community in Africa*, Brussels: Centre d'Etudes et de Documentation de l'Afrique (CEDAF).
—— (1987) 'Chiefs and the state in independent Zambia', *Journal of Legal Pluralism and Unofficial Law* 25-6: 139-201.
—— (ed.) (1988) *J. Shimunika's Likota lya Bankoya: Nkoya version* (Research report No. 31B), Leiden: African Studies Centre.
—— (1992a) *Tears of Rain: Ethnicity and History in Central Western Zambia*, London and Boston: Kegan Paul International.
—— (1992b) *Kazanga: Etniciteit in Afrika tussen staat en traditie*, inaugural lecture, Amsterdam: Free University; French version: (1993) '*Kazanga*: ethnicité en Afrique entre état et tradition', in W. M. J. van Binsbergen and C. Schilder (eds.) *Recent Dutch and Belgian Approaches to Ethnicity in Africa*, special issue, *Afrika Focus* (Gendt).
—— (1993) 'Making sense of urban space in Francistown, Botswana', in P. Nas (ed.) *Urban Symbolism*, Leiden: Brill.
—— (in press) 'African independent churches and the state in Botswana', in M. Bax (ed.) *Power and Prayer*, Amsterdam: Free University Press.

van Waarden, C. (1988) *The Oral History of the Balakanga of Botswana*, (Occasional Paper No. 2), Gaborone: Botswana Society.

von Sicard, H. (1954) 'Rhodesian sidelights on Bechuanaland history', *Native Affairs Department Annual (NADA)* 31: 67–94.

Weale, M. E. (1893) *Matabele and Makalaka Vocabulary: Intended for the Use of Prospectors and Farmers in Mashonaland*, Cape Town: Murray and St Leger Printers.

Wentzel, P. J. (1983) *Nau Dzaba Kalanga: a History of the Kalanga*, vol. i: *Text and Translations*; vol. ii: *Annotations*; vol. iii: *The relationship between Venda and Western Shona*, Pretoria: University of South Africa.

Werbner, R. P. (1970) 'Land and chiefship in the Tati concession', *Botswana Notes and Records* 2: 6–13.

—— (1971) 'Local adaptation and the transformation of an imperial concession in north-eastern Botswana', *Africa* 41, 1: 32–41.

—— (1975) 'Land, movement and status among Kalanga of Botswana', in M. Fortes and S. Patterson (eds.) *Essays in African Social Anthropology*, London: Academic Press.

—— (1989) *Ritual Passage, Sacred Journey: Form, Process and Organization of Religious Movement*, Washington and Manchester: Smithsonian Institution Press and Manchester University Press.

—— (1990) 'On cultural bias and the cosmos: home universes in Southern Africa', in M. Jackson and I. Karp (eds) *Personhood and Agency: the Experience of Self and Other in African Cultures*, Uppsala: Acta Universitatis Upsaliensis.

Wilmsen, E. N. (1988) 'The political economy of minorities and its bearing on current policy', paper read at the conference on Botswana, Edinburgh: Centre for African Studies.

—— (1989) *Land Filled with Flies: A Political Economy of the Kalahari*, Chicago and London: University of Chicago Press.

Wylie, D. (1991) *A Little God: the Twilight of Patriarchy in a Southern African Chiefdom*, Johannesburg: University of Witwatersrand Press, reprint of the original 1990 edition.

Yasutoshi Yukawa (1987) *A Classified Vocabulary of the Nkoya Language*, Tokyo: Institute for the Study of Languages and Cultures of Asia and Africa, Tokyo University of Foreign Studies.

Part III
East Africa

In addition to their regional concern with East Africa, the three papers in this Part share a focus on speakers' attitudes towards the languages that they speak, and more specifically on how attitudes towards a speaker's own language are inflected by the relationships held to prevail between that language and other languages of which the speaker is aware. These relational attitudes are elements of wide-ranging, and changing political and ideological, discourses about difference. In varied ways, each of the papers embeds its discussion of the evaluation of language difference in the broader contexts of ethnic, religious or political circumstance.

Schlee's paper valuably contrasts with the following pair, more centrally concerned with Swahili, insofar as one of the two languages he discusses, Rendille, has generally not been subjected to the politicization of language purity, although he notes that some missionary activity encourages such a development. Oromo, by contrast, a language with many times more speakers than Rendille, has become a political cause (albeit more so for Ethiopian Oromo than the Kenyan Oromo speakers among whom Schlee researched). Oromo and Rendille are perceived by their neighbours as non-Islamic languages (compare Parkin below on Swahili, Arabic and Kenyan vernaculars), yet both use some Islamic legal terms in order, Schlee suggests, to suggest an 'international' comparability between Muslim custom and their own. In the remainder of his paper he looks at loanwords exchanged between neighbouring languages (especially Rendille, Oromo and Samburu) by virtue of mutual political influence, as parts of youth cultures, or through the copying of ritual or customary practices. In conclusion he remarks upon the conventional character of different ways of classifying the languages in his area and, where sources allow, advocates the study of suppressed loanwords as a means of relating language change to past inter-ethnic relations.

Blommaert's account of discourse about Swahili in Tanzania goes some way towards meeting Schlee's strictures. He examines the metaphors of 'development' and 'modernization' applied to Kiswahili in the pursuit of language development to enable teaching and technical development in a national African language. These metaphors establish unattainable goals, so that, for instance, Kiswahili scholars find themselves continually forced to coin terms to replace English loanwords, thus ensuring that the language is always in need of further development. More generally, he argues that language development functions as part of development discourse, changing as development agendas also change. Such change occurs within the 'hybrid coherence' of policy in the post-colonial state. Discursive traditions about African languages in the post-colony have to deal with the relationship between African and colonial, or now globalized, languages. Changing attitudes towards the commensurability of languages, the borrowing or suppression of concepts and terms, and towards translatability more generally cannot be appreciated outside this context.

Blommaert's discussion of the interrelationship between global and local linguistic considerations in the context of secular development in Tanzania finds a religious counterpart in Parkin's extension of the idea of diglossia in Kenya. Parkin examines how, even within a 'single' language such as Kiswahili, the concept of ramifying diglossia illuminates the play on 'purity' and 'impurity' which arises pervasively: within the relations between a full knowledge of Arabic and the fragmentary knowledge of many Kenyan Muslims, between Arabic and Swahili as languages, between more and less Arabized forms of Kiswahili, and between Kiswahili and Kenyan vernaculars. In common with Blommaert, Parkin argues that the metaphor of 'purity' in Kenya (like that of 'modernization' in Tanzania) predicates a principled goal that is unattainable in practice by virtue of the inflationary potential for further desire generated relationally between languages and registers. Thus, Swahili can never become so Arabized or modernized that 'purity' and 'modernity' cease to remain desired goals.

These three papers share two focuses of recent anthropological research to which we drew attention in our Introduction: each of the authors uses fine-grained local research to discuss attitudes towards language and language change, but they do this with deconstructive unease concerning the identities of distinct languages and the metaphors of authenticity, modernity, or purity employed to evaluate or encourage their changing usages. Objectifications of language correlatively suppose relations between languages, and these are never solely linguistic in a narrow sense but cluster with other, strongly motivated, objectifications (that are religious, political, economic and ethnic).

12 Loanwords in Oromo and Rendille as a mirror of past inter-ethnic relations

Günther Schlee

Wherever people meet in an inter-ethnic or international context either they have to decide which language to use, or they find that the decision has been made for them by conventions established earlier. This conference, for instance, was held in English with some papers in French – a common pattern for such events. Such choices are evidently not determined by the sheer number of speakers a language has; were that so, Chinese would be the dominant world language, and Russian and German, the languages with the greatest number of speakers in Europe, would have a more marked presence on the European scene than they do. For a variety of reasons the history of language use has taken a different course.

Such questions – who speaks which language, where, and in what situations – have been emotionalized in Europe since the early nineteenth century when nationalist values were attached to language. According to Kummer, the inception of such processes has always involved the formation of an ethnic intelligentsia, whose members define themselves in contradistinction to an over-regional, supra-ethnic power, with another ethnicity at its nucleus. The definition of an oppressed group, the redescription of that group in cultural terms, and the perception of language as the most important element and most practical indicator of that culture then follow (Kummer 1990: 267; Schlee forthcoming). This politicization of language (which was one of the factors – albeit only a 'superstructural' one – in the disintegration of the Hapsburg and Ottoman empires) has started to look somewhat old fashioned to Western Europeans; but it can be be observed still in the backwaters of Europe, for instance, in the on-going process of the 'balkanization of the Balkans' (Schlee 1985a), or when the representatives of the three Baltic republics choose to hold their conferences through interpreters rather than speaking Russian, the language of the only one remaining of the four continental empires.

Lithuanian, Estonian and Latvian are small languages in the European context. From this perspective, the two languages about which I am going to speak are also small languages: Oromo has about twenty million speakers (more than all the Baltic and Finnish languages combined, but fewer than Dutch or Rumanian). However, in the African context, this many speakers makes Oromo one of the populous languages of the continent, as well as the largest of Ethiopia, but not the official 'national' language. In Kenya, where there are approximately a further 190,000 speakers, Oromo is one of the more important local languages. Rendille, the second language which concerns me, has no recognized national status. Even primary literacy, which according to official directives should be taught in every mother tongue, is hardly available in Rendille, for want of teaching materials, which are only now being produced. Rendille has about 20,000 speakers, which would be too few to survive in a network of communication of the European type. In Africa, however, there are hundreds of languages of similar size or smaller, and many of these, like Rendille, are not threatened by imminent disappearance. Nonetheless, a single change in external factors – a new road, or a mineral resource discovered in the area – can affect the fate of such a small language drastically.

From the European perspective which I adopt throughout as a heuristic and contrastive device, one would expect that by virtue of their small size and/or weak status (cf. Baxter 1978:288f) both Oromo and Rendille to be fiercely defended by romantic ethnic élites. In the case of Oromo, the OLF (Oromo Liberation Front) in Ethiopia does provide the ideological home for such an ethnic intelligentsia striving for emancipation on the grounds of cultural identity and linguistic unity. In Kenya, nothing of this sort exists. Abdullahi Shongolo, a Moyale school-teacher, and myself are working on a collection of Boran-Oromo tales and proverbs. Although this is a typical task of ethnic intelligentsias during periods of romantic, linguistic self-assertion (for instance, the Grimm brothers for German, F. Mistral for Provençal, J. Dobrovsky, J. Jungmann, F. Palacký and P. J. Šafařik for Czech and so on), we seem to have the field to ourselves. Most Kenyan Oromo whom I know have a relaxed attitude towards their language and are not engaged in any sort of cultural struggle.

The Rendille, similarly, are not defensive about their language. There exists a high degree of bilingualism (involving Boran-Oromo in the north and Samburu (Maa) in the south, as well as Swahili and English in the contexts of formal education and migrant labour). Rendille is itself found as a second language, learnt by traders who do not wish to impose either Somali (which is closely related to Rendille) or Swahili (unrelated) on their customers. The area inhabited primarily by Rendille mother tongue speakers has been stable during the seventeen-year period of my own observation. Heine's prediction (1976: 182–6; 1980: 73ff) of a northward shift of the southern border of the Rendille-speaking area has not come to pass. He extrapolated this retreat of Rendille from the observation that the older generation in the little southern town of Laisamis was predominantly Rendille-speaking while the younger generation tended to speak Samburu. But this situation seems to be in fluid equilibrium. Rendille become Samburu speakers, but as they do so new Rendille speakers come in. The area around Laisamis constitutes the southern gate of the Rendille-speaking area. The gate does not move; rather the people move through it, leaving this southern boundary more or less stable.

The lack of defensiveness about language implies a lack of concern with linguistic purity, another contrast with Europe and with Swahili discussed by Parkin. The example of German is again instructive. Since the Napoleonic wars German has been 'cleansed' of many French loanwords. It is less remarkable that there has been such a policy than that it has been partly successful, because language drift is typically resistant to policy initiatives. Language changes usually occur in directions which are unplanned and not desired by purists. But there are many French loanwords which I heard used by the elderly when I was a child for which one nowadays hears only 'German' replacements: for instance, *trottoir* – 'pedestrian pathway', now *Bürgersteig*; or, *perron* – (in real French *quai*) 'railway platform', now, *Bahnsteig*. The majority of remaining French loanwords (some of which are rendered here in their German spellings) have morally dubious or derogatory overtones: *kokett, kokott, Filou, Intrige, Bastard, Affäre, Kretin, Idiot, Separée, Negligé, Maitresse*.

Because German has been cleansed of many traces of former French domination, at least of those which reflect positive aspects of French influence, it would be hardly possible to write a cultural history of German and the Germans on the basis of the language as presently spoken; too many traces of earlier conditions have been replaced by faked 'German' words, which look old in spite of their recent invention. But why should one attempt to write about the history of German culture on the basis of contemporary German language alone? For German, unlike Rendille and Oromo, there is an abundance of documentation on the basis of which history can be written, including the history of covering the traces of French. For Oromo and Rendille, however, we are heavily reliant on the present languages as a basis from which to deduce the history of their speakers, since texts in earlier stages of these languages have not been preserved. Rendille and Oromo have adopted loanwords from different sources and from each other, and, so far, they have not been subjected to purists cleansing them of these. Our reliance upon present-day language as a source of historical reconstruction is both higher, because alternative sources are scarcer, and also more rewarding, because Oromo and Rendille languages are richer depositories of past influences than, say, German in its cleansed state.

Lately, missionaries from the Summer Institute of Linguistics have started to teach their charges that they should use the 'original' Rendille word whenever there are two words for the same thing. In their dictionaries these missionaries transcribe Rendille words in the most archaic, 'original' form they can find. Their reasons for doing this are beyond the scope of the present paper; why people should go half-way around the world to spread an ideology which is completely foreign to local people and potentially destructive to their forms of organization, and why they should do so in a form of the local language which is as 'pure' as their foreign mandibles are able to pronounce, are problems of Anglo-Saxon, rather than, Rendille ethnography. Missionary language cleansing has so far shown few effects; Rendille and Oromo continue to incorporate loanwords into their languages, reshape them to fit their phonemic systems, and so enrich their arsenal of wordshapes and are able to differentiate more concepts. Discovering which words have been borrowed from what languages, and to which semantic domains these belong, can tell much about the past inter-ethnic attitudes, relative levels of advancement in different fields of culture, fashions and power relations.

Although one could deduce much of the history of the speakers of these languages from their loanwords, I am not going to do this. I have already reconstructed a deal of Oromo, Somali and Rendille history from other sources (oral traditions, written sources, the comparison of cultural elements like forms of livestock management, food avoidances, calendrical systems and so on) and published the results elsewhere (Schlee 1989). Part of what I have to say about loanwords supports my previous findings about ethnogenetic processes and past forms of inter-ethnic relations; what does not directly support my earlier analyses at least does not contradict them. Much of the history I have reconstructed from other source materials could also have been reconstructed from analysis of the loanwords. It would have been nice to pretend to know less about the history of the area in order to reconstruct it anew from another set of data, but I cannot pretend to this sort of innocence and, therefore, present this analysis of loanwords in the light of earlier findings.

The actors of this presentation, however, are new. I am going to discuss the interactions between languages, while the actors of my book

(Schlee 1989) were clans. There, I described how clans split, and how parts of the products of such splits merged again, and how gradually during this process contemporary ethnicities emerged so that the products of a clan fission could belong to different ethnic groups, as clan brothers in different 'tribes'. Many clans in this part of the world are older than some of the ethnic groups. This implies that earlier forms of a given language were not necessarily spoken exclusively by the ancestors of their present-day speakers; they might have been spoken by some groups whose descendants now speak different languages, and some of those who speak a particular language now may not have done so for long. Organizational and linguistic units change their composition; individuals, clans and clan fragments reaffiliate themselves. Some Oromo groups, like the Gabbra and Sakuye, once spoke earlier varieties of Rendille or a similar language, fragments of which are preserved as archaisms in prayers (Schlee 1989: 71, 144). Because I am going to discuss ordinary language, my unit of study will be 'a language' and not 'a group'. To discuss who spoke a language and when, would complicate the analysis beyond the scope of a single essay (for such a discussion cf. Schlee 1987, 1989); however, because the point is germane to the broader topic of this book, the distinction between the language and its speakers at any moment needs to be kept in mind.

As in any play, the *dramatis personae* are introduced first. I list the names of the interacting languages with some conventional names of their respective sub-families and families, but without discussing the relative linguistic distances between them. It is enough to say that they are sufficiently different from one other not to be mutually intelligible to monolingual speakers; we are dealing here with languages, at a rather high level of difference, and not with dialects.

Oromo	Lowland-East-Cushitic	Afroasiatic
Rendille	Lowland-East-Cushitic	Afroasiatic
Arabic	Semitic	Afroasiatic
Swahili	Bantu	Niger-Congo
English	Germanic	Indo-European
Samburu (Maa)	Nilotic	Nilo-Saharan

ARABIC LOANWORDS IN OROMO AND RENDILLE

Jural terms

It requires some historical notes about the relationship of the two linguistic communities with the Islamic world to appreciate why the number of Arabic loanwords in Oromo and Rendille is remarkable. The Oromo expansion of the sixteenth century took place at the expense of both Christianity and Islam, which had already been weakened by wars with each other. The most famous of these wars are associated with the name of Ahmad Grany. The effects of Oromo expansion in the north, which caused the decline of Muslim sultanates at the southern fringe of the Christian Empire, are well known. However, there are grounds for assuming that Oromo expansion from their nuclear areas in what now is southern Ethiopia took place in all directions at roughly the same time. Because of the absence of written sources, we must rely heavily on oral traditions as far as forms and consequences of the Oromo expansion into what is now Kenya are concerned. Some traditions, told by Muslim Somali who are possibly extrapolating their present-day values into the past, claim that their ancestors had to flee the Boran, the most important Oromo group in the south, because living together with them was made impossible by their conflicting legal systems. The Muslims, of course, claim that their ancestors abided by the *shari'a*, while the Boran imposed their own laws on them in cases of inter-ethnic disagreement. (In internal matters, of course, each group could follow its own rules and apply its own conciliatory mechanisms. The idea of imposing a universal law upon all the inhabitants of a given territory was to develop much later and in a different part of the world (Schlee 1989: 97).)

Some sources, however, claim that the Boran tried to convert the local Somali, and Somali-like, populations under their domination to 'paganism' (*hín-kufaar*, Oromo, ex Arabic, 'to become non-believers') (Schlee 1989: 100). The Boran and Oromo culture and language in general are, therefore, perceived by their Muslim neighbours as non-Islamic or even anti-Islamic forms of identity and expression. I have even heard Somali refer to the Oromo language as the 'language of the Devil'. Boran (and Rendille) until recently conformed to this stereotype of them by ridiculing Muslim practices (on 'Galla' who rejected the message of Islam, see Huntingford 1955: 11, 20; on the identification of 'Galla' with 'pagans' by outsiders, see Haberland 1963: 258).

Despite the fact that some Somali and Somaloid groups (namely certain parts of the Garreh and Ajuran) which had earlier undergone a degree of Islamization have adopted Oromo language, and that some Boran (the Waso Boran) and other Oromo (e.g. the ones on the Tana) have converted to Islam in recent decades, being Boran stands for a non-Islamic social identity. The core of this identity is to be found in those domains of law which regulate marriage, inheritance, and compensation for torts, and thereby obstruct intermarriage between Muslim and non-Muslim communities and influence other forms of inter-ethnic relations. The legal system is an element of the 'surface' of a culture – part of its observable interface with other cultures. And, somewhat paradoxically, in terms of social identity the surface is also the core: the outer, visible, symbolically and interactionally relevant part is the most important part of an identity. In order to study these matters adequately, we have to be as superficial as we can, relegating apparently 'deeper', existential or essential issues to a less important position.

Having located Boran customary law at the surface, which is also the core, of a non-Islamic culture, we may be surprised to learn that the name of that institution derives from Arabic, Islamic legal terminology. It is called *aada Borana*, from Ar. *adat^un*, which refers to local customs and legal practices which are tolerated in Muslim communities as long as they are not in contradiction with the *shari'a*. Often *adat^un* is of pre-Islamic origin. It makes perfect sense that Muslims should use this term to refer to the Boran customary law, but why should the prototypical, non-Islamic, traditionalists of the area themselves refer to the core of their culture by a term of Arabo-Islamic derivation? And they do so constantly; in apologetic speeches in a legal contest, when somebody tries to legitimize his actions or claims, constant appeal is made to *aada*, a word used in a solemn way, with an undertone of reverence and a definitely moral ring.

The solution to the conundrum of an Arabic loanword which denotes a core element of a non-Islamic culture is possibly to be found in our earlier generalization – because the core is the surface. The *aada Borana* was an ethnic institution that applied to *nam Orma*, Oromo people, but it competed and coexisted in the wider inter-ethnic context with other legal systems. The meta-level or, so to speak, international level at which these systems met and interacted was pervaded by the influence of Islamic civilization. By using a term of wider acceptance for their customary law (one which, in fact, is understood from the Atlantic to Indonesia, although the Oromo might normally have been unaware of these geographical extremes), rather than a term derived from a Cushitic root of more restricted currency, the Oromo implicitly acknowledged that their law, however holy and God-given it might appear to them, was only one of a plurality of systems of law used to regulate human affairs in different places. They located their own customary law, *aada Borana*, inside the wider framework of the general category of *aada*, or *adat^un* as such, the common denominator of systems of *aada* in different societies and places.

Haberland points out that the roughly synonymous term *sera* is also of Semitic origin: *sar'at* is the word for 'law' in Ge'ez (1963: 226). By talking about *aada-sera*, a common compound expression, the Boran appear to ensure that they will be understood by all their Semitic neighbours.

As for the Rendille, I have shown (Schlee 1989: 40, 91, 112–14, 225–8) that, in spite of some Somali claims to the contrary, they are not a recent offshoot from the modern Muslim Somali, but derive from an early, pre-Islamic, Somali-like culture. As a collectivity, they have not been Muslims at any time in their history. Their ritual calendar, customary law, and camel management systems can all be shown to be of non-Islamic origin, and even today Islam has spread only among an urbanized minority of Rendille. Islam has not affected Rendille society so much as it has those Rendille who have left their society (Schlee 1982). The Rendille word for 'customary law' is *huggum*, a derivate of Arabic *ḥaqq^{un}*, and we may explain this usage in the same way as the case of *aada Borana*, that is to say as an international idiom used for an aspect of the interface between one culture and other cultures.

Another legal term common to Oromo and Rendille is *alál*, which is mainly used for 'full property' as distinct from shared rights in livestock, the various forms of which constitute a complex legal and economic system (Spencer 1973: 37–40; Schlee 1989: 56–9). It is further used for a 'rightful' wife, one's legal offspring as opposed to the hazards of biology, etc.; its Arabic etymon, *ḥalal*, has a similar range of meanings. *Alál* stands for everything which is proper and allowed – from marriageable kin categories to meat from animals which have been properly slaughtered (the Islamic equivalent of *kosher*) – as opposed to *ḥarām^{un}*, 'forbidden' things.

The customary law of the Rendille is incompatible with the *shari'a*. Without going into the details of marriage laws and inheritance rules, what must be stressed here is that what is *alál* for a Rendille would not be *ḥalal* for a Muslim Arab, nor vice versa. To transform one system of law into the other, one would have to take away wives from their husbands and to disown inheritors, because the rules concerning divorce, remarriage and so forth, which determine who is married to whom and who inherits from whom, differ in the two systems. However, the general categories used for discussing right or wrong are part of an international code. In a way one is reminded of Leach's argument in *Political Systems of Highland Burma* which stresses the existence in those ethnically fragmented highlands of an inter-ethnic metasystem in which all the cultural differences become meaningful at a higher level as boundary markers and guidelines for specialization and interaction.[1] In the case of the Rendille and Oromo, who lived on the fringe of the Islamic world, it was Arabic that provided some sort of common denominator for shared categories.

Calendrical units and their names

The cultures derived from the PRS stratum (Proto-Rendille-Somali, cf. Schlee 1989: 31–5, 54–92) which comprise the Rendille and various groups which have adopted Oromo speech since the sixteenth century, share a calendar which has a solar year and a cycle of twelve, named, empirical, lunar months. Unlike most other calendars, there is no attempt to adjust one of these reckonings to the other. They also share a seven-day week and a cycle of seven solar years, the units of which are identically named. The seven-year period is also an important unit of measurement of time in the various generation-set (*gada*) systems. Several units of the calendar, including those resulting from a combination of features (a given day of the week in a certain phase of the moon, etc.), are ascribed propitious or unpropitious meanings, especially for activities involving camels, which are the focal point of the cultures in question.

It is not difficult to recognize the names of the days of the week (and of the years in the cycle of seven) as Arabic:

Rendille	*Oromo*	*Arabic*	*English*
Alasmin	Alsinin	Yawm-ul Ithnayni	Monday
Talaa'da	Talasa	Yawm-uth Thalatha'i	Tuesday
Arbah	Arba	Yawm-ul Arba'a'i	Wednesday
Khamiis	Kamis	Yawm-ul Khamiisi	Thursday
Guma'd	Gumat	Yawm-ul Jum'ati[2]	Friday
Sab'di	Sabdi	Yawm-us Sabti	Saturday
Ahad	Ahad	Yawm-ul Ahadi	Sunday

To decide whether this is a case of mere loanwords or of 'loan things' (the borrowing of calendrical units along with the names for them), we have to determine the origin of these cycles of seven.

The origin of the cycles of seven

We know that the seven-day week is of ancient oriental, specifically Sumerian, origin. It has been diffused from there to Europe, where its units were renamed according to the pantheons of the different branches of the Indo-Europeans. In the absence of evidence for an alternative origin, it is plausible that this same system of time reckoning was also diffused into north-eastern Africa and became a cultural possession of the PRS peoples. The question is when. In trying to answer this, we cannot pin down particular centuries, but we can discuss two alternative gross hypotheses:

200   East Africa

Hypothesis 1   The cycles of seven represent an Arabo-Islamic influence; therefore, the units of time reckoning derive from the same source as the names used for them.

Hypothesis 2   The cycles of seven were already part of north-eastern African cultures before Islam made its influence felt; therefore, the units of time reckoning have been in the area longer than the current names for them.

The following arguments support hypothesis 1.

a) The seven-day week is neither common Cushitic nor the only way of classifying days in the area. The Boran recognise an additional cycle of twenty-seven named days (*ayaana*) which is quite different from the seven-day week and not even a multiple of it. If the seven-day week was established anciently in the area, one would expect it to have been more generally accepted.

b) The names of the days, which are of Arabo-Islamic derivation, are associated among one Oromo-speaking group, the Gabbra, with the custom of giving children gender specific names, also of Arabic origin, which correspond to their day of birth.

day of the week	boy's name	girl's name
Alsinin (Monday)	Mammo (Maḥmud, Muḥammad)	Midín
Talasa (Tuesday)	Isaako (Is'ḥaq)	Talaso
Arba (Wednesday)	Ali ('Ali)	Arbe
Kamis (Thursday)	Umuro ('Umar)	Kamme
Gumat (Friday)	Adan (Adam)	Gumato
Sabdi (Saturday)	Abudo ('Abd . . .)	Sabdio
Ahad (Sunday)	Ibrai (Ibrahim)	Aad

The names for boys obviously correspond to the Arabic names given in brackets, and the names for girls are derived from the Arabic words, mostly numerals, which also form the names of the days of the week.[3] These names are by no means the only personal names in use among the Gabbra. There are others, of Boran origin, which, as is usual in many African societies, refer to the circumstances of birth: like Diramo for a girl born in the morning, or Tura (Latecomer) or Dullac (The Old One) for a boy who kept his mother waiting a long time, perhaps following a series of miscarriages or other reproductive mishaps. The association of Arabic names for the days of the week with Muslim boys' names may strengthen the hypothesis of an Arabo-Islamic origin for the time-reckoning system itself, although no similar link between personal names and the names of weekdays is known to me from elsewhere in the Muslim world outside north-east Africa.[4]

Other arguments support hypothesis 2.

a) One might argue that the cycle of seven days is an older feature of PRS culture than the Arabic names given to the days because of the alternative names and associated myths mentioned above cursorily. Tablino (1980: 79f) gives an almost full set of these names which now have widely fallen into disuse. The only gap in his list is Thursday.[5]

ayaan ree	'the day of the smallstock'	Monday
ayaan worabesa	'the day of the hyena'[6]	Tuesday
ayaan arba[7]	'the day of the elephant'	Wednesday
ayaan dabela	'the day of the *dabela* elders', or,	
ayaan dikira	'the day of the *dikir* chants'	Friday
ayaan loon	'the day of the cattle'	Saturday
ayaan gaala	'the day of the camel'	Sunday

While the association of Friday with ritual activities reminds one of Islam, the remainder of this list is not only un-Islamic, but may even sound slightly heterodox and blasphemous to Muslim ears.

b) The cycle of seven days is linked, as we have seen, to a cycle of homonymous years which, being solar, have nothing to do with the Muslim calendar which ignores the solar year and applies the name 'year' ($sanna^{tun}$) to the cycle of twelve lunar months instead. One author derives the solar year and the associated custom of *dab shid*, as the Somali call it, from Iranian origins and assumes that they were established on African soil during the Persian occupation of Zeila in the fifth century (Hunt 1951: 9; Lewis 1955: 62). Two things we know for certain about this element of the calendrical system is that it is non-Islamic, and that it is of some antiquity among the Somali; Cerulli (1926: 6) quotes an inscription on a Mogadishu tombstone which allows the conclusion that the 22 August 1365 fell into a Saturday year. If we extrapolate the present-day Rendille solar calendar, which is based on seasons, backwards, we come to the conclusion that the year from the autumn rains 1364 to the autumn rains 1365 should have been a Sunday year. Possibly the old Somali have counted the year from some other point of the solar cycle, or they just have counted 365 days without adjustments for astronomical or metereological events, as the Gabbra do. In this latter case, the difference between any given day of this cycle and any given date of the Gregorian calendar, which reckons with intercalary days, would grow at a rate of twenty-five days per century. This would result in dates which are 150 days later in the Gregorian year six centuries ago. A third possible explanation of this discrepancy would be that somebody, whether the stonecutter or the PRS or Cerulli or myself, has made an error of one year. Whatever the case, the system seems to have been in use in Mogadishu in 1365, and to have been expressed in an inscription side by side on the same tombstone with the date of a lunar Hijra year which gave the chronological clue to Cerulli.

The reader may have noticed that I incline towards hypothesis 2, a pre-Islamic origin for the cycles of seven, but I admit that the supporting evidence is not sufficiently conclusive to reject entirely the alternative hypothesis of an Islamic origin.

Other Arabic loanwords in Rendille

Rendille is a Somaloid language. It would have been classified as a Somali dialect had it been recorded in Somalia rather than in Kenya (Lamberti 1983: 458–63); and the Rendille would have been regarded as a kind of fringe-Somali if they had been Muslims at the beginning of the colonial period, when such identities were relatively hardened by becoming administrative categories. Not being Muslims, Rendille cannot be Somali, because Islam is an integral part of Somali identity. Historically, however, Rendille is a Somaloid language of the older and more 'original' kind; it reflects the stage of the language before the massive incorporation of Arabic loanwords which are characteristic of Somali. There are, however, a number of Arabic loanwords some of which may have penetrated into Rendille via Somali in recent times (although the contiguous Rendille/Somali settlement area has been fissured by a wedge of Oromo speakers since the sixteenth century). Other Arabic loanwords look older than this.

In Arabic, for example, *'ajuz* means 'old woman'. The Somali form *ħajuus* (more examples for ' → ħ can be found) has the same meaning and is used with a great deal of reverence. In Rendille, however, *hajuus* means 'slut'; it has undergone a change of meaning by acquiring a negative connotation. Changes of meaning (if the basic meaning remains the same and there is no doubt about the identity of the word) and changes of shape (if corresponding to regular sound shifts) are indicators that a word has had sufficient time to change and develop in a language. In the above example, the fact that, unlike many recent loans in the speech of Islamized Rendille, the word does not belong to the religious sphere, reinforces the impression of antiquity. Today, Somali is no longer important as a source of Arabic loanwords in Rendille; most recent Arabic loans get into Rendille via Swahili and have a distinctly Swahili touch: *siasa, adabu, (ku)dharau.* I give a few more examples of Arabic loans in Rendille which look old to me, and leave it to my readers to judge whether they share my impression.

Rendille		Arabic
(h)araam	'mean, greedy'	harām^{un}, 'forbidden, unclean'
a-soom-a	'I fast, spend the day hungry (especially about animals which cannot go to pasture)	ṣāma yaṣūmu, 'to fast'
fara'd	'horse'	faras^{un}, 'horse'

THE LINGUISTIC ASSIMILATION OF SOMALOID GROUPS BY THE OROMO AND OROMO LOANWORDS IN RENDILLE

Before the Oromo expansion of the sixteenth century, the PRS complex of cultural features was associated with a Somali-like (Somaloid) language or a cluster of related languages (dialects?) of Somaloid affiliation. The Gabbra and Sakuye, now Oromo speakers, recall traditions of once having a language of their own, and some sources specify that this language was shared with the ancestral Rendille (for a more detailed account of this history cf. Schlee 1989). Certain Ajuran and Garre also changed from different varieties of Somali to the Oromo language. People became Oromo speakers after political affiliation, the establishment of a relationship (called *tiriso*) at the clan level with the dominant Oromo group of the area, the Boran. Certain Boran influences, however, extended even beyond this network of political and ritual relationships to affect the Rendille, who successfully remained independent of the Boran, and paid a high blood-toll for their independence by being constantly exposed to Boran raids. Until now, the fact that some Somaloid groups have become linguistically assimilated to the Oromo, leads to confused classifications by outsiders with some strange administrative consequences. It has been mainly on the grounds of language that administrators, anthropologists and historians have always divided the peoples of the lowlands of the Horn into the two broad categories 'Galla' and 'Somali'. Language has barred the view from other subsystems of culture whose comparison would have led to quite different categorizations.

Nevertheless we should not forget that linguistic links are strong and that language, apart from being a means of communication, is the major tool of the human mind. The tool of an artisan, although made by hand, may make the hand in turn by training the grip and shaping the palm. In a similar way language, our major tool of thought, may have an intricate Humboldtian relationship of mutual stimulation with other aspects of the human mind. Language is something very close to us.

Even more than the political links, which vary in strength and are sometimes absent, it may be the community of the language that links Oromo speakers together and makes them *nam Orma*, 'Oromo people'. The rich oral literature, the treasure of proverbs and the sophisticated poetry are inexhaustible sources of intellectual inspiration and pleasure to anyone who is lucky enough to be a speaker of this language.

The second sphere in which Oromo – in our case mainly Boran – culture transcends the framework of the original Oromo is in political organization. One can acquire features of a political organization in two ways: by participating in it, or by copying it. The Alganna phratry of the Gabbra, the Sakuye and the Ajuran (in certain phases) may been seen as an extension of the Boran polity.[8] Their *jallaba*s, or age-set spokesmen, are installed either directly by the *qallu* of one or the other Boran moiety, or derive their authority from him by the fur ring of a sacrificial animal which he sends to them as a sign of installation, even though the actual choice of a spokesman may be made by others. The other Gabbra, who independently install their age-set officials, copy Boran terminology and many aspects of their political institutions. Their *hayyu*s have the *boku*, or sceptre, and the whip (*licho*) as symbols of power in the same way as the Boran *abba gada* and *hayyu*s. Their *jallaba*s are also installed in office in a similar fashion to those of the Boran.

The division between *eebiftu* (praying) or *qallu* lineages and lineages which are not *eebiftu*, and therefore eligible as *hayyu*, is also shared by the Boran (who oppose *worr qallu* to *worr boku*); however, this division is probably not derived from the Boran culture but represents instead the common original possession of both the PRS and the Boran cultures. The Rendille, who show few Boran influences, also have this division; and even Muslim Somali claim lineage-specific powers to heal, pray for, curse and miraculously harm or kill others – although such powers are hardly compatible with orthodox Islam.

Even among the Rendille, who have kept their original Somaloid language, the Boran influence – although significantly weaker – should not be underestimated. The Rendille use the Oromo term *jaldab*[9] but, given that their political system is quite distinct, with a different meaning. It does not denote a specific office but a senior elder, an 'old gentleman' in general.[10] Like the Gabbra, the Rendille use certain Boran-type milk vessels along with the Boran names for these. *Madal* (*madala* in Boran) and *jijo* (*cico* in Boran) are milk containers made of plant fibres which are plaited, or better sewn with a needle. This is by no means a marginal feature because of the ritual functions of these vessels in the *sorio* and *almado* ceremonies and their association with elderhood.[11]

SAMBURU (MAA) WORDS AND ITEMS IN RENDILLE CULTURE AND LANGUAGE

Muslim traditions[12] claim that the early Rendille were Muslims and were forced by the Samburu to pierce their earlobes and to abandon Islam. While there is no evidence to confirm that Islam was ever a core element of Rendille culture, the second part of this tradition may contain some truth. While other Cushites either pierce their earlobes (or, like the Gabbra, just the right earlobe) enough to pass an earring through them, or like the Muslim Somali do not pierce their ears at all, many Nilotes (e.g. the Samburu, the Maasai, the Nandi and traditionally also their Bantu neighbours, such as Kikuyu) broaden their earlobes with successively larger plugs until, in elderhood, when these plugs have been replaced by small metal earrings, their earlobes dangle down almost to the shoulders.[13] The name for the perforated ivory discs worn as ear plugs by circumcised warriors, *il-kaba*, is Maa and probably borrowed from the Samburu (*il-kamba*).[14]

Another feature shared with Nilotes and probably derived from them is the removal of the two lower middle incisor teeth. These two features – pierced and enlarged earlobes and the removal of two, and only two, lower incisors[15] – are shared with the Rendille not only by the Samburu but by the whole Maasai/Nandi cluster.[16] Apart from the Rendille, to my knowledge, no Cushites share these features. This strengthens the hypothesis of a Nilotic origin. The piercing of the earlobes and the extraction (more precisely levering out) of the lower incisors are delayed until puberty in the case of twins and breech-born children. Ear-piercing in these cases is done with a 'bleeding arrow', made and blessed by a blacksmith, instead of acacia thorns which are normally used for the purpose. This custom applies to Rendille, Samburu and possibly others.

This is not to say that all manipulations on the body are common to the Rendille and Samburu and borrowed from the latter. Some very conspicuous features, like the incisions around the navel which make the skin contract over it and leave a very small hole[17] and the three pairs of circular ornamental scars on the belly,[18] are typical for Rendille men and exclusive to them. Circumcision, socially the most important form of ritual surgery, was probably an original Rendille custom, but many of the details associated with it have been borrowed from the Samburu. The institution as such seems to be of Cushitic origin and borrowed by some Nilotes, while later elaborations on this theme may have been borrowed back from the Nilotic Samburu by the Cushitic Rendille.

Proceeding outwards from the surface of the body to its cover – the attire and hairdress – we can note that many items of warrior fashion, the expression of the culminating phase of male vanity among the Rendille,[19] are of Samburu origin and have Samburu names. The word for 'red ochre' *il-karia* (from *ol-karia*, pl. *il-karian*[20]) which, mixed with fat, is so liberally applied to hair and shoulders, is of Maa origin, and so are the names for the various types of beads, e.g. *in-gorowo* which are worn as a necklace, *in-geri*[21] for the long chain of beads worn across the chest, *il-katar*[22] for beads worn as a bracelet, *in-kantarre* which are worn around the ankles, and *im-bageti* for small red beads in general. The long plaited hair, *halhal*, is referred to by a Rendille word (the Samburu would say *il-maasi*), but is, nonetheless, an original feature of Samburu warriors, which according to Spencer (1973: 144) has been copied by the Rendille as recently as the 1940s.

Just as the Samburu warriors for a while adopted the blue coiffure of the Turkana and later abandoned it (Spencer 1973: 152), so the Rendille warriors, no less receptive to foreign influences than European youth cultures, are presently at the height of a Samburu fad. To what extent elements of this fashion will become stable elements of Rendille culture is difficult to guess. Samburu youth culture, apart from bodily ornaments, has affected the institution of premarital concubinage. *Targén*, the name for a ram slaughtered by a warrior at the parental home of his girlfriend, is a Samburu institution which was adopted at the same time as their hairdress. This custom has replaced *labardús*, the milk which was formerly given to the mother of the girl. The word and the object, *labardús* (probably Samburu *il-bardús*) were also of Maa origin. Here we have a case of Rendille replacing one Samburu custom with another.

Apart from the terminology of the youth culture, a number of other words are common to Maa and Rendille. It is unclear in every case who has borrowed these from whom, because early Nilotes borrowed terms from Cushites, probably Somaloids (Fleming 1964: 90f), a process which gave rise to the similarities which later were used to justify the name 'Nilo-Hamites' (Schlee 1989: 34f). Later borrowing from the Samburu is obvious in the case of certain words which retain the Maa prefixes, *en-* and *ol-*, as *in-* and *il-* in Rendille. Examples of Swahili words which seem to have reached the Rendille via Samburu include:

il-banga	(Sw. *panga*)	'matchet'
il-dawa	(Sw. *dawa*)	'medicine'
il-kasi	(Sw. *kazi*)	'work'
il-tuba	(Sw. *chupa*)	'bottle'
il-tukan	(Sw. *duka* ex Ar. *dakkān^{un}*)	'shop'

Other examples include the key ideological concept, 'respect' (towards one's elders, towards those whom one avoids sexually) which is expressed by a Samburu word, *in-kanyit*. *En-aisugi*[23] snuff, Rendille *neysugi*, is an important item of youth culture, and it is plausible on these grounds that Rendille have borrowed it from Samburu.

The following similarities, some of which may be coincidental, are not so easy to explain. The question whether all of them are cognates and, if so, what was the direction of borrowing could be ascertained only by closer linguistic comparison, also involving the distribution of these words in other Nilotic and Cushitic languages. Somebody more familiar with Maa than I may notice further similarities with Rendille.

Maa	Rendille	English
pa-supen[24]	*subén*	'young ewe'
ol-turrur	*urur*	'gathering, crowd'
a-ipiri	*bir-nan*	'to whisk, to kindle (fire)'
ol-koroi	*karraw*	'colobus monkey'
a-sik	*sig-nán*	'to rub'
suuji	*suuj*	'ugly'
o-sina	*sina*	'grief, sorrow'

While I find the above similarities difficult to explain, in the case of Maa and Rendille kinship terminologies it seems obvious that the Rendille have combined two terminologies – a Cushitic one, largely shared with the Somali and Boran speakers, and the Nilotic Maa terminology – to form a complex new terminology with a larger number of terms that allow more semantic distinctions between relatives to be distinguished than in either of the two source systems. In this process of combining two terminologies, they must have changed their type of cousin terminology. In the Cushitic languages most closely related to Rendille, kinship terminologies have 'descriptive' and 'Sudanese' features. Rendille now closely approximates the 'Omaha' type. Although nobody would claim that there is an exact correspondence between Omaha terminologies and patrilineal clan systems, this form of terminology and type of social organization harmonize well, and Rendille kinship terminology is pervaded by the logic of patrilineal clan organization. Similar 'Omaha' systems can be found among the Nilotes. One can, therefore, assume that the borrowing of Nilotic kinship terms went along with influence of Nilotic ideas about social organization, and that the remaining Somaloid terms changed their range of meaning to adjust to the new categories (Schlee 1985b). Among the bilingual Ariaal, a transitional group between Rendille and Samburu, much more Samburu culture is found. Some Ariaal can be said to be not only bi-lingual but also bi-cultural.

Bearing in mind the numerous resemblances to the Samburu, not only of the Ariaal but also of the 'white' Rendille, the inter-ethnic, Nilotic, perspective adopted by Spencer in his 1973 book appears fully justified. Spencer deals with 'symbiosis', exchange and integration between Rendille and Samburu. The perspective I took (Schlee 1989) is neither better nor worse than Spencer's but simply different; I looked in the opposite direction, north and north-east, and, therefore, discovered similarities with other Cushites (rather than Nilotes), with whom Spencer hardly deals at all. According to one set of criteria, we would group the Rendille with other cultures deriving from the ancestral PRS stratum, a relatively early stratum (pre-1500); an emphasis on more recent mutual borrowings and on the fluidity of transition between them, would make the Rendille/Ariaal/Samburu/Maasai as a whole appear to form a loose unit. Different criteria thus lead to different classifications.

CONCLUDING REMARKS

It goes without saying that the material presented here is by no means exhaustive. Far from covering all recorded loanwords in even one of the languages discussed, I have not even discussed all types of loanword relationships. For instance, Oromo loans in Somaloid languages have been mentioned but not Somali loans in certain Oromo dialects and so on. A major source language in recent times has been English. While many English loanwords in Rendille are still a generational phenomenon and limited to the slang of schoolchildren ('Anglo-Rendille'), other loanwords, particularly those associated with the military, are longer standing. An example for the first type would be, *gruuba kombleyn khabo feranda sooromate* – 'the group which has a complaint has come to sit on the verandah', in which all lexemes apart from frequent verbs are (phonemically reinterpreted) English, while the grammatical morphemes and the syntactic structures are Rendille. Rendille examples for the second type would include, *koblo* 'corporal', and *ambús* 'ambush'.

I have demonstrated that loanwords tell us much about history and about past and present inter-ethnic relations, especially where linguistic purity and language cleansing have not historically been a concern for those we study. From the historical and anthropological points of view it would be as interesting to study the process of elimination of loanwords from a language and other forms of loss of vocabulary as it is to study lexical growth and the incorporation of new words. We do not have old linguistic documents for Oromo and Rendille in which we might find words that are no longer used; the only linguistic witnesses of the past are the words which exist now. Historians who work in archives have the same problem, they have to base their reconstructions and interpretations on sources which exist, knowing well that those which no longer exist (especially those which have been actively suppressed but also those which have been destroyed by selective neglect) might have been much more interesting. So much about obliterated sources, defunct words and the secrets of silence.

NOTES

1 This may not be quite the way Leach put it. I am using my own terms which, however, are inspired by Leach (1954), Barth (1969) and many others; cf. also Schlee (forthcoming).
2 That the 'jim' of this word reached Rendille and Oromo as 'gim', suggests a route of diffusion via Egypt and the Sudan rather than from the Arabic Peninsula via the Swahili coast. I do not have, however, any independent historical evidence for such contacts.
3 In his, otherwise laudable, effort to analyse Gabbra personal names Tablino (1980–1) fails to point out that this set of seven boys' names is of Arabo-Islamic derivation. In his view 'l'esame morfologico-semantico delle singole forme resta da compiere' (77).
4 The closest parallel which has been pointed out to me (by Gillian Hansford, personal communication) is the Hausa custom of naming girls according to the Arabic numerals denoting the days of the week on which they were born. (Outside the Muslim world, examples for days of the week lending their names to human beings can be found, for instance, among Asante and Chumburung speakers, Hansford personal communication.) Robinson Crusoe, who calls his companion Friday, also fits this pattern.

A set of names which is *not* etymologically related to the names of the week but is, nevertheless, conventionally given in accordance with the day of the week on which a child is born seems, however, to be rare. The Gabbra practice is the only case of which I know. While both sets of elements (the names of the boys and those of the days) are of Arabo-Islamic origin (a fact which would support hypothesis 1), the association between them may be specific to the Gabbra.
5 I have departed from Tablino's transcription in order to reflect my ideas about vowel length.
6 Tablino here translates in the plural 'il giorno delle iene' for reasons unknown to me.
7 Note the homonymity with the corresponding name based on an Arabic numeral. Could 'elephant' here be a popular etymology of the Arabic numeral 'four'? This would let the name appear to be older than its association with

an animal species, because something needs to be there before it can be interpreted. Mere coincidence of sound cannot be excluded in this case.

8 The term 'Boran' has also been used in this wider sense by Goto (1972: 1, 4) who includes the Gabbra, Sakuye and Waat ('Watta') under this label.

9 Probably derived from some earlier stage of Boran, since in modern speech the word has been phonetically simplified to *jallab*.

10 The situation seems to be similar in the case of Mursi. They also use the term *jalaba* but, not having formalized offices like the Boran, they do so with reference to men with the skill to make significant contributions to a debate by summing up arguments and speeding up decisions (Turton 1975: 174).

11 Cf. Schlee 1979: 102, 113, 115f, 120, 123, 296f, 445.

12 Cf. Schlee 1989: chapter 4b.

13 For a graphic illustration see Schlee 1979: 165.

14 Nowadays some warriors fashion pieces of plastic into ear plugs which are indistinguishable to the eye from ivory ones. Uncircumcised boys are allowed to wear only wooden plugs.

15 Other Nilotes may remove more teeth.

16 Cf. Huntingford 1969, on Nandi (37), on Kipsigis (52), on Dorobo of the North Tinderet Forest (62), on Elgeyo (73), on Maasai (15). The Suk (15, 89), who belong to the Maasai/Nandi cluster linguistically, are culturally more similar to the Karamojong.

17 Cf. Spencer 1973: 43f.

18 For a pictorial illustration cf. Schlee 1979: 154.

19 In the mid-1970s, when mirrors were still rare among the Rendille, it often happened that warriors admired themselves for hours in the rear-view mirror of my motorcycle, applying minor corrections to their hairdress or red ochre make-up.

20 Cf. Mol's (1978) Maa dictionary.

21 This is the Rendille pronounciation. Mol (1978) gives *en-keri*, pl. *in-kerin*, as the Maa form.

22 Mol (1978) gives the Maa equivalent, *ol-kataar*, pl. *il-kataari*.

23 This and the following Maa terms are rendered in Mol's (1978) spellings.

24 Ehret (1971: 166; 1974: 90) reconstructs *-supeni for Proto-Maasai (cf. Vossen 1982: 98). Rottland (1982: 432, 464) reconstructs *supein* for Proto-Kalenjin: Omotic. This does not necessarily mean that the word is ultimately of Nilotic origin since it is *sabéen-tii* (Abrahams 1964: 213) in Somali. Ehret lists this word as an Eastern Cushitic loan in Southern Nilotic (1971: 110).

REFERENCES

Abrahams, R. C. (1964) *Somali-English Dictionary*, London: University of London Press.

Barth, F. (ed.) (1969) *Ethnic Groups and Boundaries*, London: G. Allen & Unwin.

Baxter, P. T. W. (1978) 'Ethiopia's unacknowledged problem: the Oromo', *African Affairs* 77, No. 308: 283–96.

Cerulli, E. (1926) 'Iscrizioni e documenti Arabi per la storia della Somalia', *Rivista degli Studi Orientali* II: 1–24.

Ehret, C. (1971) *Southern Nilotic History*, Evanston: Northwestern University Press.

—— (1974) *Ethiopians and East Africans: the Problem of Contacts*, Nairobi: East African Publishing House (Historical Studies 3).

Fleming, H. C. (1964) 'Baiso and Rendille: Somali outliers', *Rassegna di Studi Etiopici* 20: 35–96.

Goto, S. G. (1972) 'The Boran of Northern Kenya: origin, migrations and settlements in the nineteenth century', unpublished BA thesis, University of Nairobi.

Haberland, E. (1963) *Galla Süd-Äthiopiens*, Stuttgart: Kohlhammer.

Heine, B. (1976) 'Notes on the Rendille language (Kenya)', *Afrika und Übersee*, 59(3): 176–223.

Heine, B. (1980) (with W. J. G. Möhlig) *Language and Dialect Atlas of Kenya*, vol. I *Geographical and Historical Introduction*, Berlin: Reimer.

Hunt, J. A. (1951) *A General Survey of the Somaliland Protectorate 1944–50*, Colonial Development and Welfare Scheme, D. 484, London: Crown Agents for the Colonies.

Huntingford, G. W. B. (1955) *The Galla of Ethiopia*, Ethnographic Survey of Africa, North Eastern Africa, Part 2, London: International African Institute.

—— (1969) *The Southern Nilo-Hamites*, Ethnographic Survey of Africa, East Central Africa, Part 8, London: International African Institute.

Kummer, W. (1990) 'Sprache und Kulturelle Identität' in E. J. Dittrich and F. O. Radtke (eds.) *Ethnizität: Wissenschaften und Minderheiten*, Opladen: Westdeutscher Verlag.

Lamberti, M. (1983) 'Die Somali-Dialekte: eine vergleichende Untersuchung', unpublished Ph.D. thesis, University of Cologne.

Leach, E. R. (1954) *Political Systems of Highland Burma*, London: Athlone.

Lewis, I. M. (1955) *Peoples of the Horn of Africa: Somali, Afar and Saho*, Ethnographic Survey of Africa, North-Eastern Africa, Part 1, London: International African Institute.

Mol, F. (1978) *Maa: a Dictionary of the Maasai Language and Folklore*, Nairobi: Marketing and Publishing Ltd.

Rottland, F. (1982) *Die südnilotischen Sprachen*, Berlin: Reimer.

Schlee, G. (1979) *Das Glaubens- und Sozialsystem der Rendille: Kamelnomaden Nordkenias*, Berlin: Reimer.

—— (1982) 'Annahme und Ablehnung von Christentum und Islam bei den Rendille in Nord-Kenia', in *Ostafrikanische Völker zwischen Mission und Regierung*, Erlangen: Lehrstuhl für Missionswissenschaften.

—— (1985a) 'Les nomades et l'État au nord du Kénia', paper presented at the Colloque Européen, *Perspectives anthropologiques sur l'histoire africaine: pouvoirs et État*, Paris (also, Sociology of Development Research Centre, Bielefeld: Working Paper No. 149).

—— (1985b) 'Sprache als Vermittler, Ausdruck und Inhalt kultureller Identität: eine vergleichende semantische Untersuchung dreier kuschitischer Sprachen', SFB 214, *Identität in Afrika*, Berichtsband 1984/84, Universität Bayreuth.

—— (1987) 'Somaloid history: oral tradition, *Kulturgeschichte* and historical linguistics in an area of Oromo/Somaloid interaction', in H. Jungraithmayr and W. W. Müller (eds), *Proceedings of the Fourth International Hamito-Semitic Congress*, Marburg, September 1983, Amsterdam and Philadelphia: John Benjamins.

—— (1989) *Identities on the Move: Clanship and Pastoralism in Northern Kenya*, Manchester: Manchester University Press and New York: St Martin's Press.

—— (forthcoming) 'Ethnicity emblems, diacritical features, identity markers: some East African examples', in D. Brokensha (ed.) *Oromo Studies and Other Essays in Honour of Paul Baxter*, Syracuse, NY: Foreign and Comparative Studies/African Series 43.

Spencer, P. (1973) *Nomads in Alliance: Symbiosis and Growth among the Rendille and Samburu of Kenya*, London: Oxford University Press.

Tablino, P. (1980) *I Gabbra del Kenya*, Bologna: EMI.

—— (1980–1) 'Nomi personali usati dai Gabbra del Kenya', *Rassegna di Studi Etiopici* 28: 77–91.

Turton, D. (1975) 'The relationship between oratory and the exercise of influence among the Mursi', in M. Bloch (ed.) *Political Language and Oratory in Traditional Society*, London: Cambridge University Press.

Vossen, R. (1982) *The Eastern Nilotes*, Berlin: Reimer.

13 The metaphors of development and modernization in Tanzanian language policy and research

Jan Blommaert

INTRODUCTION

This paper aims to analyse the conceptual background against which an African tradition of thinking about language, and working on language, has emerged.[1] After Independence the Tanzanian Government introduced, stimulated and promoted research by Tanzanians on the new national language Kiswahili (Kihore 1976; Abdulaziz Mkilifi 1972). Gradually, the structures of Kiswahili research and language planning, initiated by the German and British colonial administrations (Wright 1965; Snoxall 1985), were adopted by Tanzanians, and a new discourse on Kiswahili was developed.

I will concentrate on features of this new discourse, more precisely, on two key metaphors consistently used since Independence to denote the intention of the Tanzanian Government and parastatal research institutes with regard to Kiswahili: 'development' and 'modernization'. For this purpose, I shall use the journal *Kiswahili* (formerly *Swahili*), published by the Institute of Kiswahili Research (TUKI: *Taasisi ya Uchunguzi wa Kiswahili*) of the University of Dar es Salaam as primary textual evidence. TUKI is the official Kiswahili research centre, where priorities and requests formulated by the Tanzanian authorities are implemented. It has an advisory function, and all its proposals have to be sanctioned by the Government body BAKITA (*Baraza la Kiswahili la Taifa*, 'National Kiswahili Council'). Proposed terminology, coined by TUKI researchers, thus has to be approved by BAKITA officers before it can be disseminated. The journal *Kiswahili* provides us with a picture of:

1 the types of research done on Kiswahili within the official Tanzanian linguistic circles;
2 the way in which this research is being done, viz. by whom, with what theoretical and methodological instruments, in what domains, and for what purpose;
3 the general attitudes and ideology underlying linguistic research.

When combined with some other papers published by TUKI researchers elsewhere (thereby offering the advantage of explicitness), a fairly precise (but, of course, not an exhaustive) picture can be drawn of the way in which an 'official' tradition of linguistics emerges in the context of a 'young', third world state.

Underlying this paper is my conviction that linguistic or sociolinguistic research on languages such as Kiswahili is part of third world studies, and should thus be capable of offering a contribution to the study of crucial development problems. Considering the tremendous sociolinguistic complexity of African states, and the communication problems following from it, this point should be abundantly clear.

THEORETICAL PRELIMINARIES

The type of research I am proposing aims, in general, to yield insights into the emergence of new, local socio-cultural traditions by means of a discourse-analytic approach. It should therefore be situated at the disciplinary crossroads of anthropology, philology and history, where scholars such as Foucault, Bakhtin and Ginzburg have been active. My own approach is a kind of 'historiography of text', in the sense that I try to uncover features of texts which indicate larger scale historical processes of social genesis and change (see also Fabian 1990). I assume that decolonization has been a critical historical moment for African societies, in which a process of tremendous socio-cultural transformation was started. This socio-cultural transformation also implied far-reaching conceptual changes, in which ideas and attitudes about things such as the political system, the state, and the role of the individual citizen therein, drastically changed.

These processes of change were and are expressed in language, in structured and coherent discursive patterns. With respect to the discourse on Kiswahili, these patterns can be found in the journal *Kiswahili*. Moreover, these patterns of talking about Kiswahili have a metalevel. Apart from the way in which one talks about Kiswahili, the discourse will reveal ideas, attitudes and assumptions about how Kiswahili should function as a medium of social interaction in general. In other words, this is a way of speaking about ways of speaking.

Concretely, my research will be guided by three assumptions:

1. The metaphors of 'development' and 'modernization' must be seen against the background of an emerging tradition of Kiswahili science in Tanzania. They are embedded in

    a) a set of legitimate ways of speaking about Kiswahili;

Metaphors of development and modernization 215

b) a set of correspondences between reality and theory which creates the basis for assessments of scientific 'truth' and knowledgeability;
c) a series of action procedures (specific forms of research) considered to be in line with the emerging tradition.

2 This new tradition requires a model or archetype of Kiswahili linguistics to provide the sources for constructing the tradition. Concretely, a specific model of linguistic research must be reflected in the emergence of a local linguistic tradition.

3 This new linguistic tradition has a larger scale dimension: that of the emergence of a post-colonial African society in which new layers of society, social structures, forms of knowledge and power and forms of social action are generated.

THE CONTEXTUAL SEMANTICS OF DEVELOPMENT AND MODERNIZATION

We can start this analysis with a definition of 'language development' given by David Massamba (1987a: 180):[2]

> We might say that language development is a deliberate move by a social group (e.g. a nation) to adopt, choose from available dialects or languages, or even invent a language for the sole purpose of equipping it with the capability of being used as a medium of either instruction or communication. In order for this end to be realized a number of factors have to be considered seriously. These are factors such as Language Policy, Language Planning and Language Modernization.

In the elaboration of this definition,[3] Massamba sketches the following procedural model. Language development is the overall term denoting a three-step programme consisting of:

1 language policy, i.e. an elaborate statement of priorities formulated by the nation;
2 language planning, i.e. the scientific translation of language policy into a plan for scientific research;
3 language modernization, i.e. concrete steps undertaken by scholars within the frame of language planning (cf. Massamba 1987a: 181ff.)

Massamba strongly emphasizes the technocratic nature of language development work, and complains about political interference in the process. He then spells out three exemplary domains in which language planning could and should be elaborated (1987a: 183–4):

1 language planning for pedagogic purposes, i.e. the production of adequate textbooks and didactic materials for formal education in the target language Kiswahili;
2 language planning for normative purposes, aimed at producing descriptive/prescriptive grammars, dictionaries and orthography;
3 language planning for modernization, i.e. designed to 'enable the language to cope with modern technological advancement'.

The latter domain is further defined in these terms:

> Language modernization may be defined as the development of a language in a way that will enable it to express both new and technological concepts. The most crucial aspect of language modernization is the development of scientific and/or technical neologisms. With new scientific and technological innovations and inventions new concepts are bound to emerge. Hence the need for terminology.
> (Massamba 1987a: 184)

From these extracts, we can deduce that 'language development' is directed at three target areas: teaching materials, language standardization, and 'lexicological updating'. Moreover, all this is a technocratic and self-conscious undertaking, done by trained linguists in line with political directives. 'Modernization' is a specific part of this programme, defined as the creation of new Kiswahili terms for innovations in the field of science and technology.

These recent definitions reflect a long history of thinking about and working on Kiswahili. Massamba himself (1989: 61ff.) refers to the first white missionaries in the Tanganyika region, who in the second half of the nineteenth century began to use Kiswahili 'for their purposes'. Next, he cites the 1925 British Education Commission for East Africa, which recommended the 'promotion' of Kiswahili as a medium of primary education throughout the British East African territories. These recommendations gave rise to the Inter-Territorial Language Committee (founded in 1930, later the East African Swahili Committee), whose activities were continued by the TUKI in post-colonial Tanzania. So, there seems to be a *single historical thread (started by the British and continued by the Tanzanians) leading to the 'development' of Kiswahili*. All activities past and present that resulted in a larger spread, an increase of grammatical description or standardization, or literary production, are captured under the term 'development'. A close look at the agenda set for the Inter-Territorial Language Committee (reviewed by Massamba 1989: 62) reveals that, already by 1930, basically the same target areas for language development were selected as the ones mentioned above.

The tasks formulated by the ITLC revolved around (1) the production of Swahili teaching materials and (2) language standardization in general (grammar, lexicography, orthography). The modernization bias proposed by Massamba in 1987 is, however, absent.[4] This 'modernization' aspect must have evolved *de facto*, as an additional problem for another domain, and chronologically much later in the history of Kiswahili language development.

To find a reason for the prominence of 'modernization', we must look into the debate on Tanzanian education and the role of Kiswahili therein (see Mulokozi 1986 and 1991 for excellent surveys). From the early days of independence onwards, education became a high priority for the government led by Nyerere, a former schoolteacher himself. Problems at all levels of education led him to propose a completely new education policy in 1967. In line with the Arusha Declaration, in which the *Ujamaa* policy was presented, Tanzanian education should be *Elimu ya Kujitegemea* ('Education for self-reliance'), i.e. a form of education adapted to the local circumstances and the needs of the country. Education had to be 'Tanzanian', that is, based upon *Ujamaa* principles and open to all Tanzanian citizens (Morrison 1976: 255ff). Evidently, completely Swahilized education was foreseen, since Kiswahili was the only medium of instruction that could guarantee a democratic distribution of knowledge and an Africanization of thought.

Already by the early 1970s, it was realised that in order to be able to teach in Kiswahili at a high level of scientific sophistication, adequate equivalent Kiswahili terminology would be required. Optimism was great in that period, and researchers at TUKI started to coin terms in domains such as politics, social sciences, engineering, medicine, mathematics, biology, physics, etc. Various procedures and techniques were used (see Temu 1972 and 1984; MacWilliam 1985; Mutahi 1986; Mdee 1986; Berwouts 1989), ranging from borrowings (from Arabic and English), to phonological adaptation of internationally standardized terms, and outright 'assemblage' on the basis of existing terminology.

Word-coining is, however, a very problematic activity, especially when it is associated with a concept such as 'modernization'. Basically, word-coining involves *translating* already existing (mainly English) terminology. Thus, 'modernization', in its word-coining reality, carries a clear implication of backwardness, since 'inventions' are situated outside the Swahili speech community. If Kiswahili, in Massamba's terms, is to be equipped with a capacity to function as a medium of scientific communication, then in order to do so it has to rely on the translation of previously introduced English or international terms. Thus, Kiswahili will obviously never be equivalent to English, since English will always be the source language from which new terms are to be introduced. It will always seem superior, and the modernization of Kiswahili will seem never-ending. This eternal backlog of Kiswahili vis-à-vis the source language English has in fact been used by the Tanzanian Government as an argument to delay the introduction of Kiswahili as a medium of higher education.

Similarly, the idea of 'developing' Kiswahili – which is consistently defined as a 'developing' language by contrast to 'developed' languages such as English, French or German (see Massamba 1987a and 1989, passim) – must be frustrating in the long run. The reason for this is the assumption of a model or a target inherent in the metaphor of development (see Blommaert 1990a). Apart from the relative absurdity of a distinction such as 'developed–underdeveloped' for natural, widespread languages, there is the simple observation that a developed language is not a steady state object, but something dynamic. An underdeveloped language can, therefore, never become 'developed', since the 'developed' languages themselves develop further. Kiswahili will, on the basis of this metaphorical scheme, never be able to close the gap between its state of underdevelopment and the state of development of languages such as English.

THE ALLEGORICAL ASPECTS OF LANGUAGE DEVELOPMENT AND MODERNIZATION

The view of Kiswahili as an underdeveloped language in need of modernization is an allegory of more general development attitudes in Tanzania. The gradual shift from optimism to pessimism among Tanzanian linguists (witnessed amongst others by Massamba 1989; Mulokozi 1991) runs parallel to the evolution of the country's economic and social problems (see Blommaert & Gysels 1987: 12ff).

The optimism of the early Ujamaa period is reflected in euphoric papers by Tanzanian scholars and politicians.[5] Kiswahili had become more and more 'Africanized' as a scientific object. African authors largely outnumbered westerners in the post-Arusha volumes of *Kiswahili*; an increase of papers on Kiswahili in education was triggered by Nyerere's *Elimu ya Kujitegemea* ('Education for self-reliance') paper; language planning as a general topic was the most prominent feature of *Kiswahili* between 1969 and 1973. Around the same time, literary criticism of Kiswahili literature had taken off, and the first papers began to appear in *Kiswahili*.

From 1975 onwards, when the failure of Ujamaa began to dawn upon the people, and when the Oil Crisis had severely struck the Tanzanian economy, the tone and type of papers in *Kiswahili* drastically changed. First, the volume of published material decreased. Far fewer papers were published. Second, language planning papers virtually disappeared, except for strongly apologetic papers on the education problem. Papers on less ideologically biased subjects such as (descriptive) ethnolinguistics, hardcore linguistics and literary analysis figured more prominently.

When in 1982, at the height of the economic crisis in Tanzania, Nyerere declared that Swahilization of higher education would be postponed indefinitely, researchers reacted as might have been expected. 'Neutral' papers on linguistics, literature and lexicography and apologetic papers on the education problem continued to dominate the tables of contents of *Kiswahili*. *Isimujamii* ('sociolinguistics') disappeared altogether as a separate section of the journal. The only sociolinguistic papers were assessments *post hoc* of language planning measures undertaken earlier (e.g. Ohly 1982; Massamba 1987b).

Whereas, in the early days of Independence and after the Arusha Declaration of 1967, Kiswahili was conceived as a motor of national development and as the language of liberation and Africanhood, from 1974/1975 onwards attitudes towards its fiercest enemy, English, changed. In line with the increased need for foreign economic support, English regained respectability in the eyes of Tanzanian policy makers. Even Nyerere, a champion of Kiswahili, declared in 1974 that 'Tanzanians would be foolish to reject English' (quoted in Kihore 1976: 50).

The association between economic developments and attitudes towards Kiswahili is not only a matter of the historical facts. The linguistic ideology governing Tanzanian linguistics after 1967 dictated a close connection between language and socio-economic structures. The growing impact of radical socialists on the University of Dar es Salaam since 1966/1967 certainly contributed to the growth and elaboration of this trend. This is most prominently articulated in Rajmund Ohly's works (especially 1978, but see also 1982). Ohly views language as a material thing which can be manipulated, influenced and planned very much like other material sectors of society (e.g. industrial production or agriculture). Linguistics, to Ohly, seems to be a matter of assessing market demand, then producing and marketing the product. Traces of this attitude can still be found in Massamba's ideas quoted above.

The pervasiveness of this linguistic materialism is sufficient to give the impression that Kiswahili is the psychological correlate of general socioeconomic development. The same model is used in both instances; especially since the end of the Nyerere era, the west (the English-speaking world in particular) has become the model for development, just as English is the model for Kiswahili language development. The refutation of western recipes for development, contained in the Arusha Declaration, caused a strong commitment to Kiswahili as a medium of education and boosted Kiswahili research. The decline of this self-reliance ideology during the second half of the 1970s triggered a decline in Kiswahili research and an accentuation of the role of English as a model for language development. The turn to the west in the early 1980s was reflected in a radicalization of the Kiswahili-in-education debate (see e.g. Mulokozi 1986 and 1991; Massamba 1989) and a continuing decline of (especially socio-) linguistic research.

Thus, attitudes towards Kiswahili seem to be governed by more general attitudes concerning the way out of underdevelopment. In the aftermath of Ujamaa, papers expressing linguistic and cultural self-confidence were abundant (e.g. Abdulaziz 1971; Abdulaziz Lodhi 1974; Akida 1974; Ansre 1977; Besha 1972; Kombo 1972; Mhina 1972 and 1977; Burhan Mkelle 1971; Mwangomango 1970). Papers such as Mwangomango (1970) emphatically stressed the relationship between the teaching and correct usage of Kiswahili, and the development of a truly independent unified nation in which the vestiges of (British) colonialism would be eradicated. Papers by western scholars who pointed out some difficulties in Tanzanian language planning (e.g. Harries 1968) were severely attacked by local scholars. This euphoria and radicalism vanishes from 1974 onwards, to be replaced by more conservative and neutral papers. The second half of the 1980s (when the Swahilization project faded together with the Ujamaa policy) generated papers such as Mulokozi's (1986; 1991) and Massamba's (1987a; 1989), in which disappointment about the development of language policy was expressed. It also generated an increased importance for lexicography, the type of linguistic work in which the frustrating 'modernization' metaphor and the role of English as a model are most prominent.

SOURCES OF LINGUISTIC DISCOURSE

The discourse on Kiswahili, observable in the journal *Kiswahili*, is somewhat hybrid. One substantial genre of papers has a curiously non-linguistic tone from a linguist's point of view. The authors of these papers, who mostly deal with sociolinguistics (language planning) and literary criticism, blend linguistic and ethnographic observations with strongly ideological statements. Language planning measures are motivated by means of ideological principles, as in this typical statement:

> Therefore, in teaching Kiswahili, we should realize that we are waging war against the colonial ideas. It is necessary that we teach Kiswahili

in order to 'build' [*kuwajenga*] young people who adhere to the ideas of Ujamaa.

(Mwangomango 1970: 33, translation mine)

To Mwangomango and to many others, the rationale for introducing Kiswahili in education is its nationalistic character, which contrasts with the connotations of colonial oppression attached to English. Another argument in favour of the introduction of Kiswahili in education is the fact that it is a truly African language – a point which many authors have hammered home repeatedly. Papers on Kiswahili literature very often adopt a kind of *Négritude* attitude. Literature is seen as evidence of the cultural and intellectual equivalence of Africans with Europeans – a point the authors of many papers apparently feel to be in need of demonstration (see e.g. Balisidya 1987).

A second genre of papers in *Kiswahili* concerns core-grammatical or phonological issues, mostly applications of existing grammatical/phonological theories to Kiswahili or other Tanzanian languages (e.g. Batibo 1987; Mukama 1978; Mazrui 1983). Theories such as systemic grammar, lexicase and transformational grammar are adopted in their standard versions, aspects of which are then applied to fragments of Kiswahili grammar. Lexicography, a prominent interest, is characterized by a pragmatic approach which keeps in touch with recent developments in the field of lexicography and dictionary-making (e.g. MacWilliam 1984). But here again, an ideological undercurrent can be distinguished (e.g. Temu 1984).

On the whole, *Kiswahili* oscillates between two extremes. On the one hand, there is politically totally committed science, in which scientific research is granted the status of political action. On the other hand, there is politically totally uncommitted science, in which theoretical elegance, detachment and, ultimately, a low degree of applicability seem to figure. So at the one end of the spectrum there seems to be a scientific credo which dictates that Kiswahili research is part of politics, while at the other end is one which denies this connection and places high hopes on empiricism, objectivism, and the most central approaches of western linguistic science. Whereas the committed end of the spectrum could be seen as maximally socioculturally embedded, the uncommitted end aspires to a totally decontextualized nature (although, as I shall show, such decontextualization is itself socio-culturally symptomatic). There is nothing between the extremes: peripheral linguistic subjects such as ethnography of speaking, interactional sociolinguistics, psycholinguistics, pragmatics or discourse analysis, are virtually absent.

Two outside discourses can be connected to these features of Tanzanian linguistic discourse:

1. on the one hand, Kiswahili linguistic discourse is linked to political discourse, particularly to Ujamaa discourse (see Blommaert 1990b);
2. on the other hand, it is linked to positivistic, formalist linguistic discourse in the structuralist-generativist tradition.

Again, we can recognize an allegory of the overall ideology of development and modernization. Kiswahili linguistics is part of a general development strategy outlined by Ujamaa policy, and closely follows its historical track (first discourse). This development strategy is geared to modernization, *vide* technologization. In this context, 'high-tech' is intuitively associated with 'modern' linguistic theories within the formal paradigm, provided these theories have demonstrated their usefulness (second discourse). Hence the interest in successful widespread theoretical models such as transformational grammar, and the absence of more peripheral types of linguistics. Just as would be predicted by the contextual semantics of 'modernization', Kiswahili linguists scrupulously adopt successful western methods, since these methods represent 'progress' or 'development' in linguistics and thereby fit into the 'development' ideology governing linguistic research. Hardly any local solutions are tried or tested; Kiswahili and the other local languages are plied into existing, borrowed frameworks of western origin. The sources of Kiswahili linguistic discourse prevent innovation in more than one way, because the idea of development implies a foreign model, to be copied as accurately as possible.

THE EMERGING TRADITION

The observations made above are symptoms of the emergence of a new subcultural tradition of linguistic research in a post-colonial society. This post-colonial society is, as Ali A. Mazrui (1967) noted, a weird, incoherent construction in which concepts and definitions derived from the political culture of the former colonial powers are blended with local African socio-cultural structures. Concretely, the western concept of a nation state was imposed upon societies which, in most instances, were historically unprepared for it. There was a degree of incommensurability between the new structure and the old reality. The consequences – extremely multi-ethnic societies, state boundaries cutting across ethnic territories, etc. – are well known.

This historical moment must have caused far-reaching conceptual and attitudinal shifts. I will speculate on four points, which I think are crucial for a clearer understanding of emerging traditions in Africa:

1 Independent states had to be organized on the basis of western parliamentary democratic structures. As a consequence, political parties became a new power basis, superior to more traditional ones (tribes, clans, etc.). Politics, in the newly independent African states, became a totally new domain of thinking, discourse and action.
2 The system adopted by the newly independent states had always been a negative system for Africans. The direct experience they had of the western type of political and administrative organization derived from a century of oppression by the colonial powers. Almost overnight, that very same system had to be adopted as a positive thing: as the recipe for development, modernization, freedom and prosperity.
3 Within the independent societies, identities changed drastically. In general, yesterday's oppressed became today's rulers. More concretely, social statuses hitherto precluded to Africans (bourgeoisie, intelligentsia, senior civil servants, senior military personnel . . .) became accessible to Africans. The distribution of forms of power and hegemony among groups of the population changed radically.
4 The struggle for independence had boosted African nationalism and self-esteem. As a consequence, the newly acquired structures and identities necessarily had to be 'Africanized'. So states which were typologically and structurally completely westernized still maintained or even cultivated an African decorum.

These four points together constitute the conditions for a formidable field of tension, conceptually as well as behaviourally. As a consequence, we see the emergence of a number of hybrid cultural products bearing the genetic traces of western structures and African customs, yet irreducible to either, or indeed both. Obvious domains in which these new traditions have emerged are African literature and African politics.[6] I have tried to demonstrate that the linguistic tradition which emerged in Tanzania after Independence is a similar case of hybrid coherence. We notice the same field of tension: on the one hand there is an attempt to make linguistics more Tanzanian in nature and ideology, on the other hand there is the identification of 'progress' and 'modernization' with the scrupulous adoption of western canons, rules and methods.

As soon as linguistic research and language planning became accessible to Tanzanians, the dilemma of Tanzanian linguists became that of a trade-off between the need to become or remain 'good linguists' (i.e. being capable of using state of the art linguistic theories and methods) and the need to be so in a Tanzanian way, by making linguistics part of a broader development strategy; more precisely, by making the ideological basis of this general development strategy also part of their theoretical linguistic apparatus. This resulted in a focus on applied linguistic work: dictionary-making, writing teaching materials, etc. Therefore, Kiswahili linguistics became strongly redefining in purpose: redefining the history, structure, function and social significance of Kiswahili, thus adapting it to the new reality of an independent state.

NOTES

1 Fieldwork on this topic was done at the Institute of Kiswahili Research of the University of Dar es Salaam, 1989. I am indebted to Mugyabuso Mulokozi, Yohani Msanjila, David Massamba and Shaaban Mlacha for stimulating discussions on the subject. The opinions expressed in this paper are, however, not all endorsed by the above-mentioned; I am solely responsible for them. Part of the research for this paper was sponsored by the Belgian National Fund for Collective Fundamental Research.
2 The papers by David Massamba quoted here (1987a, 1987b, 1989) were all written during his directorship of TUKI; he was also the editor of *Kiswahili*. His papers, therefore, have a strongly apologetic or programmatic character.
3 It is interesting to note that the first part of the definition is quite odd from a sociolinguistic or pragmatic point of view. First there is the 'either/or' construction: either a language serves as a medium of instruction (meaning, presumably, that it is used in formal education) or it is used as a medium of communication (which would entail that 'instruction' is not communication, and that there are languages which do not serve as means of communication). Second there is the 'equipping it with the capability . . .' phrase, which begs the question of how a language could *not* be equipped with the capability to be used as a medium of communication, and if so, how such a language could consciously be equipped with that capability.
4 The 'modernization' bias is also absent from the original agendas of TUKI and BAKITA (see Massamba 1989: 63–4). There is, however, a close link between the activities of TUKI and 'current and long-term development plans' in other areas. Most of the tasks given to both institutions are mainly conservative (the correct usage of the language; descriptive studies) and logistical (support in publications; encouragement to public usage of Kiswahili). The continuity between present research and research undertaken by the former colonial authorities is a recurrent feature in many contemporary papers by Tanzanian linguists.
5 The data in this section were partly collected by An Stans. I am indebted to her for letting me use this material.
6 With regard to African politics, the amazing amount of creative ideological writings could be interpreted as a feature of the emergence of such a new tradition. We have, to name just a few, N'Krumah's 'African Socialism', Nyerere's 'Ujamaa', Senghor's 'Négritude', Biya's 'libéralisme communautaire', Kenyatta's 'Harambee', Moi's 'Nyayoism' and Mobutu's 'authenticité'.

REFERENCES

Abdulaziz, M. H. (1971) 'Tanzania's national language policy and the rise of Swahili political culture', in W. H. Whiteley (ed.) *Language Use and Social Change*, London: Oxford University Press.

Abdulaziz Lodhi (1974) 'Language and cultural unity in Tanzania', *Kiswahili* 44, 2: 10–13.

Abdulaziz Mkilifi (1972) 'Triglossia and Swahili-English bilingualism in Tanzania', *Language in Society* 1: 197–213.

Akida, H. (1974) 'Language for the coming generation of the scientific age in Tanzania', *Kiswahili* 44, 2: 1–6.

Ansre, G. (1977) 'Four rationalizations for maintaining the European languages in education in Africa', *Kiswahili* 47, 2: 55–61.

Balisidya, M. L. N. (1987) 'Adopted or adapted to? Neo Swahili literature in Tanzania', *Kiswahili* 54, 1–2: 14–33.

Batibo, H. (1987) 'Le statut morphosyntaxique du referent sujet en langues bantou', *Kiswahili* 54, 1–2: 135–41.

Berwouts, K. (1989) 'Language and modernization: Kiswahili lexical expansion in the domain of the organisation of the modern nation/state', *Working Papers in Kiswahili* 5.

Besha, R. (1972) 'Lugha ya Kiswahili hivi leo; hasa katika siasa', *Kiswahili* 42, 1: 22–38.

Blommaert, J. (1990a) 'Ontwikkeling en integratie: een pleidooi voor Whorf', *Tijdschrift voor Sociale Wetenschappen* 35, 1: 66–73.

—— (1990b) 'Modern African political style: strategies and genre in Swahili political discourse', *Discourse and Society* 1, 2: 115–31.

Blommaert, J. & M. Gysels (1987) 'Campus Kiswahili', *Working Papers in Kiswahili* 1.

Burhan Mkelle (1971) 'Kiswahili in the age of full commitment', *Kiswahili* 41, 2: 72–83.

Fabian, J. (1990) *History from Below*, Amsterdam: John Benjamins.

Harries, L. (1968) 'Swahili in modern East Africa', in J. Fishman, C. Ferguson & J. Das Gupta (eds.) *Language Problems of Developing Nations*, New York: Wiley & Sons.

Kihore, Y. (1976) 'Tanzania's language policy and Kiswahili's historical background', *Kiswahili* 46, 2: 47–69.

Kombo, S. (1972) 'The role of Swahili language in Tanzania as both national and working language', *Kiswahili* 42, 1: 39–42.

MacWilliam, A. (1984) 'Research work in dictionary-making', *Kiswahili* 51, 1–2: 102–11.

—— (1985) 'Some thoughts on translation of scientific terminology in Kiswahili', *Kiswahili* 52, 1–2: 114–28.

Massamba, D. (1987a) 'The impact of politics in language development in Tanzania', *Kiswahili* 54, 1–2: 180–91.

—— (1987b) 'The effect of language modernization on the phonological system of the Kiswahili language', *Kiswahili* 54, 1–2: 142–51.

—— (1989) 'An assessment of the development and modernization of the Kiswahili language in Tanzania', in F. Coulmas (ed.) *Language Adaptation*, Cambridge: Cambridge University Press.

Mazrui, Al-Amin (1983) 'The passive transformation in Swahili', *Kiswahili* 50, 1: 19-28.
Mazrui, Ali A. (1967) *Towards a Pax Africana*, Chicago: University of Chicago Press.
Mdee, J. S. (1986) 'Matatizo ya kuunda istilahi kama yanavyojitokeza katika Kiswahili', *Kiswahili* 53, 1-2: 115-27.
Mhina, G. A. (1972) 'Problems being faced in the process of developing African languages with special reference to Kiswahili', *Kiswahili* 42, 1: 43-57.
—— (1977) 'The Tanzanian experience in the use of Kiswahili in education', *Kiswahili* 47, 2: 62-9.
Morrison, D. R. (1976) *Education and Politics in Africa: the Tanzanian Case*, London: Hurst & Co.
Mukama, R. G. (1978) 'On prepositionality and causativity in Swahili', *Kiswahili* 48, 1: 26-41.
Mulokozi, M. M. (1986) 'Kiswahili as a medium of education in Tanzania: some observations on recent policy shifts', paper given at the International Symposium on Language Standardization, Mainz.
—— (1991) 'English versus Kiswahili in Tanzanian secondary education', in J. Blommaert (ed.) *Swahili Studies*, Ghent: Academia Press.
Mutahi, K. (1986) 'Swahili lexical expansion – prospects and problems', *Kiswahili*, 53, 1-2: 104-14.
Mwangomango, J. (1970) 'Kiswahili katika kujenga Utanzania', *Kiswahili* 40, 2: 30-4.
Ohly, R. (1978) *Language + Revolution = Swahili*, Dar es Salaam: Dar es Salaam University Press.
—— (1982) 'Report on the state of modern Swahili in urban Bukoba', *Kiswahili* 49, 2: 81-92.
Snoxall, R. A. (1985) 'The East African Interterritorial Language (Swahili) Committee', in J. Maw & D. Parkin (eds.) *Swahili Language and Society*, Wien: Afro-Pub.
Temu, C. (1972) 'Swahili vocabulary expansion: a preliminary observation', *Kiswahili* 42, 1: 1-3.
—— (1984) 'Kiswahili terminology: principles adopted for the enrichment of the Kiswahili language', *Kiswahili* 51, 1-2: 112-27.
Wright, M. (1965) 'Swahili language policies 1890-1940', *Swahili* 35, 1: 40-8.

14 Language, government and the play on purity and impurity
Arabic, Swahili and the vernaculars in Kenya

David Parkin

THE THEORETICAL BASIS

Among current tensions in anthropological theory (see Ulin 1991), there is one that appears to be acting as a prolegomenon to a new synthesis. On the one hand, there is the now rapidly fading postmodernist position, dating especially from Lyotard (1984), that technological specialization and compartmentalization in the modern world have shattered the universalist illusions of grand theory and have broken it up into an infinitely expanding number of relativized discourses. On the other hand, there is the continuing influence of political economy, emanating from Taussig (1980), Habermas (1981), Wolf (1982) and Mintz (1985), with its insistence on global interconnectedness as the overall determining context of human action, development and history. With regard to the synthesis, it might be argued that the current experimentation with such conceptual metaphors as global 'creolization' and 'post-pluralism' (meaning, in effect, old-type oppositional pluralism, but with the constituent elements now in communication with each other) is a blending of the postmodernist concern with fragmentation and the universalist premise of political economists that social formations are grounded historically in the irreducible reality of human labour and the exchange of its products. In this new synthesis, the products are, of course, seen as commodities, whose principal feature is not that they have become alienated from their producers in the classical Marxist sense (which is taken for granted), but that they have become embedded in endless chains of consumerism, whose proliferation is stimulated by the promise that they will return to satisfy the equally endless desires of the producers-turned-consumers (cf. Baudrillard 1972).

Language has also nowadays become commoditized to the extent that it is commonly held up as the property of an ethnic or national group, class and even caste, often regardless of how many members of the group speak it and whether they do so fluently. Thus, to take obvious examples from Europe, there are many Basques, Bretons, Welsh and Poles of German extraction whose identification with their purported ethnic languages is more in their promise to speak it than in their current proficiency but who are imperceptibly merged with those for whom these are indeed first languages. There is, then, here an overall premise of identification with the object, language, which is ontologically central to some persons but only peripheral to others, even if desired by them. The distinction between linguistic haves and have-nots reproduces the motivating force in consumerism as all-pervasive or global and yet highlights the fragmentary and fragmenting reality of uneven linguistic distribution.

The point here is that language proficiency is only ever partial and never evenly distributed. Among a close community of, say, native English or Swahili speakers, there is always at some moment or other a recognition that someone speaks the language more 'fluently' (or 'elegantly', 'expressively', 'correctly', or whatever is chosen as the relevant criterion) than someone else. In direct comparison with other purported speakers of the same language from another community, however, the differences are dissolved in favour of an unambiguous distinction between the different characteristics of each speech community: 'they speak a purer/less pure form than us'. Further comparisons move from those of mutually intelligible dialects to allegedly unintelligible 'foreign' languages, sometimes acknowledged as related and sometimes as totally unconnected historically.

This segmentary feature of comparison underlines one of the problems in a concept like 'creolization' which, by presupposing the continuing interchangeability and recombination of new and old elements within a growing synthesis, imposes a panchrony or globalization over and above the fragmentary aspects of language use. Language is commoditized but, like commodities in capitalist consumerism, is held out at one level as potentially available to all who desire it but at another level is in practice accessible in different forms to separate and often specialized and privileged sectors of a community.

Government policies on language diffusion and development commonly presuppose an egalitarian distribution of the desired language. We could hardly expect otherwise. Yet we are never surprised that purported proficiency is in fact unevenly spread, as a result of unequal educational opportunites, regional remoteness from the sources of diffusion, and differential access incurred through differences of status, gender, age and ethnic origin. This is one side of the problem of linguistic engineering that confronts any government, particularly one in Africa and Asia.

The other side is that which stems from the fact that, like a commodity, a language can be believed to develop a life of its own. In other words, there are processes of language dispersion which may exist independently of government policy and even in defiance of it.

THE ARGUMENT WITH REFERENCE TO KENYA

I describe such a case on the Kenya coast with reference to the role of Arabic both as a religious register and as having practical significance for those who seek work in the Middle East. My aim is to show that language viewed as a commodity may be 'produced' in schools according to formal government programmes and yet may also flourish independently of such factors, as if self-determining. I suggest that this is the same tension implicit in the metaphor of global socio-cultural 'creolization', which blends the idea of fragments of supposedly autonomous or specialized knowledge with that of a universal interconnectedness of knowledge. I further suggest that this obliges us to reconsider the linguistic concept of diglossia as concerned not with discrete diatypes but as resting on the idea of unattainable linguistic desire.

First, by way of general introduction, I describe the formal distribution of languages in Kenya and the government's broad policy with regard to them. English is Kenya's official language, while Swahili is its national one. The official language, English, is prescribed as the medium of instruction in schools, the state central bureaucracy and in parliament. Although Swahili is much used informally in these contexts, and sometimes formally, there is considerable use of English, reflecting more generally the high competence in the language nationally compared with the neighbouring countries of Tanzania, Uganda (where more English is spoken than in Tanzania) and Ethiopia. Swahili is a compulsory taught subject in schools but not a medium of instruction. There are Swahili and English radio stations and newspapers. Swahili radio is listened to much more than English, while English newspapers sell more than Swahili ones. Television is mainly broadcast in English. Most people use more Swahili for everyday issues in towns and in ethnically mixed contexts than English. The ethnic vernaculars are not taught in schools and are not used in any governmental context. They are exclusively ethnic and domestic languages whose significance for expressions of regional and local identity remain strong. They are 'mother tongues' while, for the vast majority of people, Swahili and English are acquired second languages.

On the Kenya coast are people for whom Swahili is their first or 'mother tongue'. Although now a numerical minority, the Swahili-speaking peoples and their rich, textualized culture have shaped coastal society indelibly. Among these Swahili-speaking peoples are some who regard themselves and are regarded by others as 'Arabs', and who can to various degrees trace ancestry from the Middle East, principally either the Hadhramaut (the so-called Hadhrami) or Oman (the Omani). Since these 'Arabs' have migrated to East Africa in different waves over many centuries, the concept of 'Arab' is a contestable one, shaped nevertheless by the recognition that the most recent arrivals are likely to be the most 'Arab'.

Coastal East Africa up to a depth of ten miles inland was in fact a British Protectorate ruled by the Sultan of Zanzibar, an Omani Arab, from 1895 to 1963. The hinterland of Kenya, but not its coastal strip, was a British colony. In 1963 the coastal strip of Kenya and the hinterland, that is to say the Kenya part of the Protectorate and the colony, became the single, unitary republic of Kenya. Before 1963, Arabs and some non-Arab Kenya coastal Muslims had campaigned for the political autonomy and even independence of the coastal strip. They failed in their attempt and, under the new African Government, became politically less active, especially after the Zanzibar revolution in 1964 in which large numbers of alleged 'Arab' landowners were massacred.

Their demands for regional autonomy were echoed by other so-called minority peoples, and resulted, before 1963, in the formation of a political party, the Kenya African Democratic Union (KADU), which wanted a federal Kenya in which all regions would be represented. The opposition party, the Kenya African National Union (KANU), in fact came to power. It was dominated by the two large ethnic groups, the Kikuyu and the Luo, and was opposed to federation. KADU disbanded itself shortly afterwards, allegedly in the interests of national unity. Still later, in 1969, another opposition party, the Kenya Peoples Union (KPU), was banned and some years later, Kenya was declared a one-party state.

Under the Kenya Government of KANU and Jomo Kenyatta from 1963 until 1978, the small minority of Arabs and Muslims received no special privileges and, nowadays, will often claim that their coastal area, religious institutions and schools suffered privations.

In 1978 Daniel arap Moi became president. Although chosen as head of the KANU Government, he had previously been a prominent member of the now disbanded federalist party, KADU. He was himself a member of the minority group, the Kalenjin. He survived an abortive coup d'état in 1982, and it was widely reported that he and his government had been saved by the commander of the Kenya armed forces, a Somali and

Muslim, both minority categories. Whether Moi had already embarked on a policy of covert federalism, or at least of appointing members of minority groups to key positions, is speculative. After 1982, however, a rapidly increasing number of such appointments were made. By 1990, Moi was resisting calls for multi-party democracy on the grounds that this would simply make it possible for the two large groups, the Kikuyu and Luo, to regain control of the state and usher in 'tribal' (*sic*) conflict. Coupled with his dispersal of political, fiscal, administrative and military appointments, this was almost a formal acknowledgement that a kind of federalism through adequate minority representation was being practised.

As a result of this quiet policy under Moi, Muslims saw themselves as benefitting from a more equitable distribution of school places at all levels of the system and of resources for the coast. Whereas under Kenyatta, Muslims had felt insecure regarding their religion, they did not do so under Moi. Money for mosques, *madrasa*, and bursaries to study at mosque colleges in Kenya or the Middle East flowed in freely from individuals resident in or linked to Saudi Arabia, Kuwait and the Gulf Emirates, and Iran and Pakistan. Under Kenyatta, these inflows of money had been questioned while under Moi there was little interference, despite his own Christian beliefs. The general verdict both of Muslims and the Arabs among them was that Moi valued them, as members of a minority group like himself, for their political support, an assumption that has been borne out by later events, including most recently a change in the Kenya inheritance law which respects and takes full account of the Islamic *sharia*.

During the late 1980s, an increasing number of Kenya coastal Muslims returned from courses at Middle East theological, or heavily theological, universities and mosque colleges. Schooled in a profound knowledge of Islamic *sharia*, texts and the Arabic language, but uninstructed in the secular subjects taught in Kenyan schools, such returnees had little alternative but to teach in the proliferating rural and urban *madrasa* (Islamic schools) which were being sponsored by benefactors, many from or connected with the Middle East, Iran and Pakistan. A consequence was not only an acceleration in the number of young persons able to receive Islamic instruction, but also a revitalization of the Arabic language. Previously in the *madrasas*, pupils had only ever learned to recite the Koran, without understanding the language itself. The recent revival changed all that, and Arabic became a language usable for religious but also non-religious purposes. Accompanying this development was the propensity of many young men of Hadhrami origin to seek work in Saudi Arabia and other Gulf countries, many of whom also returned with a spoken, if not literary, knowledge of Arabic.

Traditionally, a notion of 'Arabization' had always been regarded as a desirable feature of high Muslim status in coastal Kenya and other parts of the former Protectorate. But few people could do more than recite memorized passages from the Koran. From the early and, especially, the mid-1980s onwards, 'Arabization' took on new meaning as enabling creative communication in the language and not merely a phatic religious communication.

Although still confined to a minority of Muslims, this new Arab articulateness has accentuated the phatic and religious value of the language among the mass of other Muslims. These latter aspire to competence, however limited, in a language which, for them, has sacred value as the 'true' language of Islam. There has always been this reverence for Arabic among Muslims who could not speak it. Now, however, their reverence is reinforced by the value placed on it by the increasing number of young Muslims learning it as a full language.

In this development, Arabic has taken on the ambivalent qualities of a commodity as I have described it. At the level of the new teachers of the *madrasa* it is purveyed as a universal good which can be deployed in a fuller understanding of Islamic texts and in communication with other Islamic scholars, as well as for practical work purposes. At the continuing level of the mass of Muslims, it exists in the fragments of memorized Koran and in the desire on the part of individuals to know more of the language and Islamic texts as sacred sources.

Arabic is thus developing a kind of internal diglossia which is not however that of a formal versus informal kind, but rather that of universalizing assumptions and productive efficacy, on the one hand, and of individual, relativized, and incomplete linguistic knowledge on the other hand. The difference is indeed reminiscent of that distinguishing political economy and postmodernism.

Arabic is, however, inscribed in the values and uses of other elements that make up its linguistic environment, principally Swahili. For, just as the two sides of Arabic have a distinctive relationship to each other, so do Arabic as a whole and Swahili. Arabic and Swahili are thus also diglossic in the sense of the former being set apart as a diatype from the latter. In addition, however, Swahili is also seen as at the beginning of a desirable route to competence in Arabic: one desires in Swahili the sacredness and 'civilizing' qualities ascribed to a full knowledge of Arabic.

However, and this is where the logic of commodity consumerism shows its falsity, while a full, proper and perfect command of Arabic is the desired goal of Muslims, this is in practice never attainable. There is always a better version, phrase or speaker, an unattainability which reinforces the sacred status of the language. Moreover, Swahili becomes regarded in the same light: there is always a more 'Arabized' and therefore more desirable form of Swahili one can speak. Diglossia is, then, not concerned only with the delineation of linguistic diatypes on the basis of formal communication contexts and status, as was Ferguson's original suggestion (1964) and as has become an accepted basis of the concept. It arises out of a pursuit of linguistic forms which, as in the desire for the endless proliferation of commodities in modern capitalist consumerism, can never be satisfied.

ARABIC AND SACREDNESS

In embarking on this argument, let me take as my starting point the relation between the Koran and the Arabic language. I begin with the early and bold assertion by Guillaume that the Koran has a different holy status from the Christian and Jewish Bibles. He claims that 'textual criticism and modern study have made it impossible for modern scholars', apart from a minority of fundamentalists, to hold the belief that God inspired every word contained in the Bible. By contrast, he says:

> in Islam the doctrine of the infallible word of God is an article of faith, and the few who have questioned it have for the most part expressed their doubts in enigmatic language, so as to leave themselves a way of retreat from a dangerous position.
>
> (Guillaume 1956: 55)

For Guillaume, these believed qualities of the Koran can only truly be appreciated in its Arabic form or version. Since Guillaume wrote, fundamentalism may have become a more marked feature of both Christianity and Judaism, as it has also of Islam. Nevertheless, the difference is one with which most researchers working in Islamic communities will be familiar. The Koran in its Arabic form is held to be unquestionably sacred or holy, and exegetical disagreements about it among Muslim scholars appear to be relatively few.

Guillaume also mentions that the Koran must never rest beneath other books, but always on top of them, that, when it is being read aloud, listeners must never drink or smoke and must remain silent, and that it is used to counter disease and disaster (Guillaume 1956: 74). It is admired by many Arabic speakers not only for its religious import, but also as a literary work of poetry and prose and a source of wisdom through parables as well as through assertion and command.

This is the Koran basking in the idealism surrounding it. By contrast, Gilsenan also emphasizes the authoritative element in the designation in Islam of the Koran as the holiest of holy texts. Produced as it was during a period when the masses were illiterate, any exegeses of the Holy Book were the sole preserve of the few who could read it. As time went on, more and more textual specialists would add their own, distinctive commentaries on the Koran, piling sub-text upon sub-text and so making it ever more difficult for the religious non-specialist, even if literate, to dare to assume the right to a personal interpretation of the original version. At the same time, as Gilsenan notes, any Muslim can in theory be accepted into religious training and so, in due course, join the ranks of those deemed qualified to comment on the Koran and on the texts it has spawned (1982: 31). The process of exclusion from, and of achieving the right to be included among the scholarly ranks serves to perpetuate the hierarchy of and respect for learning.

For those who do not reach this position of being able to offer such textual commentary, particularly the illiterate, the holiness of the Koran as text is metonymically re-cast as the sacredness of its Arabic script and of the Arabic language, especially for those who don't know it. Set down by the Prophet himself as the proper language of the Koran and of Islam (Chapter 12, verse 2; Chapter 41, verse 3, see Akinnaso and Ogunbiyi 1990: 1), the sanctity of Arabic is of course a view shared by many Muslims. It may become the basis of a political protest movement, as when the Salafiya movement in Algeria based itself in the Arabic language of the Koran, itself regarded as a miraculous creation, and fought French cultural and linguistic hegemony (Gilsenan 1982: 153).

In many parts of Africa today, the sacred status of Arabic may be unquestioned, and its associated administrative and judicial functions much valued, but this by itself does not always qualify it for inclusion in school language education. As in Akinnaso and Ogunbiyi's study of language planning in Nigeria (1990), the secular educational position of Arabic may be under constant threat despite its high religious standing.

ARABIC AND KISWAHILI IN EAST AFRICA: A STORY OF HEGEMONY, ABSORPTION AND ALTERNATING FORTUNES

In the Kenya coast area, where I have worked, as elsewhere in African and other Muslim communities, we meet some of the same general characteristics, although, at the same time, there are also locally distinctive aspects.

The East African coast, from Mogadishu to northern Mozambique and mainly comprising the Kenya and Tanzania shorelines, has experienced extensive Arab settlement over a period of centuries, mainly from the Hadhramaut (now south Yemen) and Oman. Arab influence on the language of the Swahili-speaking peoples of the east African coast primarily takes the form of religious and legal idioms, those concerned with courtly etiquette and behaviour and with evaluations of personal morality, and with medical therapy allegedly derived from the Koran. Amazingly, however, the Swahili language has remained resolutely Bantu in most of its vocabulary, and in all its syntax and grammar. Wave after wave of new Hadhrami and Omani Arab visitors settled at the coast. The most recent tended to assume overall power. These new arrivals would, for a generation or so, speak Arabic as their first tongue. However, after some few generations, sometimes through intermarriage with Swahili women, these Arabs would speak Swahili as their first language, gradually forgetting their Arabic. Thus, the Arabic language remained the preserve of whatever Arab élite was in power, while other, earlier groups would call themselves Arab and recall Arab genealogies, sometimes recruiting a wife from the Hadhramaut or Oman, but would themselves become Swahili-speaking.

It is for this reason that I. A. Salim prefers to refer to such peoples of the coast, of both Arab and African descent, as Swahili-speaking (1973). At any point in time, there would always be a small minority of East African coastal people who spoke Arabic, but they and their descendants were parties to a more general process of assimilation into Swahili language and culture.

Indeed, two inverse processes of assimilation occurred and continue to occur. One is the absorption into Swahili language and culture of peoples of Arab origins; and the other is the assimilation of coastal peoples of African and mixed descent into the various versions of Islam. These varieties of Islam were, and still are, carried and propagated by Muslim arrivals, who come, not just from the Hadhramaut and Oman but from other areas of the Middle East, and also from Pakistan and India. Despite such variations, most by far of East Africa's Muslims are Sunni.

Islamic and Arabic identities have had oscillating fortunes in recent generations. As mentioned above, in 1895 the British agreed with the Omani Sultan of Zanzibar to recognise his sovereignty over the whole East African coast up to a distance of sixteen kilometres inland (ten miles). This ensured Muslim dominance over the coastal area with respect to *sharia* law and land and property holdings. At about the same time, the British curtailment of the slave trade ruined the productivity of Arab plantations in the area, as agricultural labour became scarce. Tensions between so-called 'Arab' landlords and 'African' plantation workers (including ex-slaves) became severe, especially when the latter preferred no longer to work for the landlords and simply to use the land as their own, and were joined by new African migrants doing the same. Many of the ex-workers had themselves adopted Islam, and so the Arab-African division cut into the wider Islamic community.

If I may focus now on Kenya, Afro-Arab Muslim solidarity was regained for a while in the years immediately preceding Kenya's independence in 1963. The various political movements seeking coastal autonomy, principally that called *Mwambao*, emphasized coastal interests over and above internal differences. They sought to counter the growing influence of non-Muslim migrants from up-country Kenya. In census and other population returns, the numbers of respondents prepared to call themselves Arab and Swahili was considerable. They were seemingly prepared to announce such ethnic and Muslim identies unambiguously and with confidence.

Coastal autonomy was never achieved, however, and the area fell under the political control of the new, independent non-Muslim Government of President Jomo Kenyatta. Thereafter, the numbers of people referring to themselves in official censuses as either Arab or Swahili dropped markedly. Arabs might call themselves Swahili, and Swahili who could trace non-Swahili African descent, e.g. Digo, would refer to themselves as being of that African ethnic group.

Fortunes were, from the local viewpoint, reversed yet again from 1973 onwards, the year of the Arab-Israeli war. The war prompted a huge increase in the price of Arab-produced oil. Large amounts of money from the Middle East were poured into East African Islamic communities, as part of the more general Arab attempt to proselytize and expand Arab Muslim infuence. The money was for new or refurbished mosques, scholarships for studying religious and other subjects in Saudi Arabia, Kuwait, or elsewhere in the Middle East, and for building schools in which Islamic as well as secular subjects would be taught.

In one area in which I worked, the southern coastal area of Kilifi district, several new mosques were built. They were rapidly followed by new Pentecostal churches constructed with North American funds. Visiting Arab Muslim scholars and American Christian missionaries and teachers proselytized in open competition with each other. Swahili, the language common to all communities, whether Muslim, Christian or drawn from traditional African pantheistic religion, became the medium of such proselytization.

At the same time, the new Arab money has encouraged young men of Sunni persuasion to study in Saudi Arabia, Kuwait, or, if they have Shi'ite links or are prepared to convert, in Iran. Paralleling this is the new desire on the part of men of Hadhrami Arab origin to try to seek work in Saudi Arabia and to go there as migrant workers. Both influences have led to an increased knowledge of the Arabic language among people who, as second and even first generation Kenyan residents, had largely forgotten it.

Take, as an example, a Hadhrami family known to me (called Bawazir) who live in Mombasa. They consist of three brothers, two sisters, various cousins, and an aged father and mother. Two brothers run their own businesses independently of each other. They are ship chandlers, with one of them also trading to and from Uganda, where his wife lives nearly all the time and where he also spends long periods. Their father arrived in Mombasa from the Hadhramaut in the 1920s, where he immediately began work as a water carrier. He built up a small business of water-selling from this humble base, employing local people. He married a woman from a local Hadhrami family, whose children, including the man's wife, now spoke only Swahili. As the couple produced children, these latter, too, learned Swahili rather than Arabic, which their father himself had less and less occasion to use. But the wheel has come full circle. While the sons and daughter in the 1980s had Swahili as their mother tongue, the sons had taken a renewed interest in converting their rudimentary knowledge of Arabic into fluency. They saw this as another possible benefit of working in Saudi Arabia. They also listened to Egyptian-produced videos of Arabic-speaking stars of song and dance. They saw themselves as becoming re-Arabized. An entailed part of this process was to attend the mosque and pray five times a day, and to observe all other ritual demands. They were conscious of themselves becoming integrated within the strengthening stream of Islamic fundamentalism.

On the face of it, then, this recent process of re-Arabization among Hadhrami families of recent origin, has a religious dimension. It entails greater commitment to Islam. But what about those other Muslims, the vast majority, who will not be going to Saudi Arabia, and for whom Swahili continues to be the language with which they will continue for the rest of their lives? How are they affected by the processes of re-Arabization and Islamic fundamentalism?

We can begin to answer this question by tracing the ties of the same Hadhrami family, the Bawazir, to their locus among these other, non-Arab, Swahili-speaking Muslims. Thus, the Bawazir Arabs, while having their main residence and businesses in Mombasa, also run shops in rural, or semi-urban, areas outside Mombasa. They run them through other members of the family, namely a brother or cousin. The brother, whom I first knew well, not only ran a shop in a rural centre (called Majengo), he also attended the local Friday mosque, which had itself been set up with funds donated by a prominent Muslim of South Asian origin, who had been to Mecca and was versed in Islamic learning.

This man, let us call him Mohammed, did not himself claim to be an Islamic scholar nor yet to know much Arabic, but he was commonly spoken of by local people as closer to God through his rudimentary knowledge of Arabic and his intention to go to Saudi Arabia, both to visit Mecca and to seek work. At local *maulidi* celebrations in honour of the Prophet's birth, he could explain to those who didn't know them, the meanings of portions of holy Arabic script taken from verses of the Koran and imprinted on the large cloths used to create an enclosure, or *riyadha*, round the men participating in the ceremony and between the men inside and the women outside.

The same veneration is accorded to those *maalims* and Muslim healers who take paper containing verses of the Koran written in Arabic and use it for both preventive and curative medicine. A piece of paper containing the requisite verse may be wrapped securely in a piece of cloth or leather and worn as an amulet. Or, Arabic verse may be written on, say, a slate or piece of glass, and then washed off with water, which is then drunk by the client seeking cure, good fortune, or an end to illness or misfortune. This use of the Koran to make talismans is well known throughout the Muslim world.

Here, in the coastal area of Kenya in which I worked, southern Kilifi district, these practices serve as a device to illustrate the extraordinary value given both to the utility and grandeur of a speaking knowledge of Arabic, and to the language's mystical powers. The people in the area do not on the whole themselves speak Arabic, although certain of their *maalims* may have anything from a smattering to a good command. Let us call them the Swahili, an appellation which is a crude, but useful, shorthand label. To repeat, the number of permanent residents in Kenya who speak Arabic is very small, but they represent the possibilities that are available to any pious Muslim scholar, Arab or Swahili, to study Islam and the Arabic language.

There are many other ways in which I could show the local people's view of the sacredness both of the Koran and of the Arabic script, especially when taken from the Koran. This veneration of the Holy Book and its script percolates down and takes the form also of a preeminence accorded to Arabic itself, as a whole language. It further serves to denote the life-style of high-status Muslims, including Arabs originating from or having spent time in the Middle East. There is in fact a Swahili verb, *ku-staarabu* or *ku-staarabika*, which means to acquire understanding, wisdom and civilization, and which is sometimes taken to be derived etymologically from the idea of becoming Arabized.

None of this is to say that, as individuals, persons designated as Arabs are unconditionally accorded respect. They, like anyone else, must demonstrate good manners (*adabu*), humility and piety, in order to earn respect. It is rather that such people are potential carriers of a line that reaches back to the heart and origins of Islam. This is an idea most explicit in the designation of certain Hadhrami agnatic lines as containing Sharifs, or Sayyids, who claim descent from the Prophet. The idea of Arabness, as fused with the sanctity of the Arabic language, thus provides a model to be aimed at. Some Swahili aim to marry their daughters to men regarded as 'Arab', while the high-status form of Swahili marriage is itself said to be of Arabic origin.

Institutions and roles may also be characterized by local people as either 'Arabic' or 'Swahili'. Thus, people distinguish between Arabic and Swahili *maulidi*, diviners, marriages, and life-styles. For example, an Arabic *maulidi* opens up with Arabic prayers. Its verses, also called *maulidi* (i.e. as well as the overall ceremony) are long-established ones originally composed in Arabic, and in at least one case still untranslated into Swahili. In some cases they are verses on the life of the Prophet taken from the Koran. Such *maulidi* are relatively formal. By contrast, the so-called Swahili *maulidi* begin with prayers said in Swahili, while Arabic may not be used at all in the proceedings. The sung *maulidi* verses are not only in Swahili but are commonly made up specially for the occasion, and even created spontaneously on the spot, rather than being of ancient origin. Moreover, the Arabic *maulidi* ceremonies are said also to be larger than the Swahili ones, an observation that is broadly correct, as far as I can judge.

The larger and more important *maulidi* sermons contain a much higher proportion of Swahili words of Arabic origin than the smaller ones. On one occasion, at the prominent *maulidi* ceremony held at Takaungu in 1978, not only I but also some of the Swahili speakers who accompanied me, were baffled by certain highly Arabized passages as presented by the sermon giver, namely the then Chief Kadhi of Kenya, Sheikh A. S. Al-Farsy. Ironically, it was Al-Farsy who had produced one of the best Swahili translations of the Koran. The irony to which I refer is that Al-Farsy could, on the one hand, provide the non-Arabic speaking masses with a Swahili version of the Koran which they could read, and yet could also present a sermon before thousands of the same people which not all could fully understand. An authoritative Muslim response, which I heard once or twice from *maalims*, was that this was a deliberate and wise ploy on his part to underline how necessary it was to have children and adults learn to read, write and understand Arabic, for then they would have direct and full access to the wisdom and purity of Islam. Did not the Prophet describe the Koran as 'A book whereof the verses are explained in detail – a Qur'an in Arabic for a people who understand' (chapter 41, verse 3 of the Koran. Cited from Akinnaso and Ogunbiyi 1990: 1)?

The linking of wisdom and understanding with purity, and of these with piety, is, of course, common in Islamic pronouncements. To be pious is to achieve understanding, and this is to achieve purity. But how widespread in Kenya is the view that this is in practice only fully possible through a knowledge of the Koran in Arabic, and that those who do not possess this knowledge suffer a definite handicap? Is in fact the purity that leads to Godly understanding linguistic as well as based on prayer and righteous observances?

Justo Lacunza (1991) considers this question in comparing the pronouncements of three religious writers, one of whom is Sheikh Al-Farsy mentioned above. The earliest writer, Sheikh Al-Amin bin Aly Al-Mazrui, 1875–1949, takes a hard, pro-Arabic line. Writing in 1939, he claims that 'Arabic is the language of the Qur'an, Almighty God has commanded us that we think about the meaning of the Qur'an every time we read it, and how will we know its meaning if we do not know the Arabic language?' (cited by Justo Lacunza, 1991, from Sh. Al-Amin b. Aly (1939) *Uwongozi*, Mombasa: EAMWS, 21). Much later, in 1976, Sheikh Al-Farsy (1912–82), the *maulidi* preacher referred to above, sees an insistence on the knowledge of Arabic as tantamount to the colonization of religion. He does not dispute the supreme importance of the language among the Muslim scholarly élite of the East African coast, but, in the words of Lacunza, he 'realised that Kiswahili had become de facto the language of Islam in the context of East Africa . . . (and wished) to harmonize, from the point of view of Islam, the coast and the interior, the Arab and the non-Arab, the Swahili and the non-Swahili' (Lacunza 1991 in which he cites Sh. A. S. Al-Farsy (1976) *Tunda la Qur'an*, Mombasa: Adam Traders, 4–5). In 1987 the most recent of the three writers, Sheikh Saidi Musa (born 1944), expresses unambiguously his support for the Islamic revolution of Iran and Khomeini's leadership, seeing it as a model which East Africa should emulate, and finds no need at all to tie Islam to the Arabic language, since, in East Africa, Kiswahili is for him now the indispensable medium for teaching and propagating the religion and organizing Muslim society.

It may well be, as these examples intimate, that among the East African literati and scholars, the Swahili language is beginning to take precedence over Arabic as the medium by which Islam should be communicated and discussed. There is no doubting the impact of Al-Farsy's Swahili translation of the Koran, which, heavily subsidized by Middle East benefactors, is available to all Muslims at a low price. But how far has this relative dismissal of Arabic percolated down to the vast majority of ordinary Muslims? I would argue that, among such people, little has changed with regard to the sacred and purificatory healing potentialities offered by the Arabic Koran and its scriptural text, as I have outlined above. I would also suggest that, as a result of the proliferation of new *madrasas* headed by Islamic teachers trained in the Middle East or local mosque college in Arabic and in the religion, the sanctity of Arabic has been further boosted.

Indeed, as we move down the social hierarchy, we see that the notion of purity takes on even greater significance as a route to understanding and self-improvement. Here, too, this purity is given linguistic essence.

A MUSLIM FISHING COMMUNITY IN MTWAPA, COASTAL KENYA

More microscopically, let me move at this point to consider a small community of Muslim fishermen inhabiting the shoreland of an area north of Mombasa, called Mtwapa. These are poor Muslims. They use Swahili as their first language in conversation with each other, both publicly and privately, but the older ones among them can understand surrounding dialects of peoples related to the Swahili but, until recently, non-Muslim, from whom the community of fishermen derives. These dialects are in fact the vernacular varieties of a people called the Mijikenda. Thus, we may call the fishermen intermediary Swahili, for they no longer speak the Mijikenda language, but instead speak Swahili, and have the appearance of being transitional between their non-Muslim Mijikenda origins and the full Swahili status to which they aspire. Most other Mijikenda both continue to speak their Mijikenda dialects and remain non-Muslim.

Taking a broad view, then, people will speak of there being three language groups, each associated with one of three, roughly defined, groups of people standing at different distances from Islam: Arabs, Swahili, and the non-Muslim Mijikenda. Those fishermen I am calling intermediary Swahili thus stand between the latter two groups.

Kiswahili comprises the vocabulary both of Arabic and the Mijikenda vernacular. It is often itself seen as intermediary in religious terms between Arabic, which has high diglossic status, and the non-Muslim Mijikenda vernacular which has low status in the eyes of Muslims.

But these Swahili-speaking fishermen see themselves, also, as intermediary in a cultural and ethnic sense. This is a theme that comes out often in sermons, divinations, and conversation. A *maalim* speaking at a *maulidi* ceremony will denounce palm-wine tapping and, of course, drinking, and will link such activities to neglect of Islamic prayer, ritual and attendance at mosques. He will also link the origin of such behaviour to the origin of the people themselves, namely their non-Muslim Mijikenda 'cousins' (*wenzetu*). He argues that such misconduct is sin or negligence bordering on sinfulness.

Outside of the context of ceremonies and sermons, *maalims* combine ideas about proper religious conduct with those of proper social behaviour. The use of language commonly features in such ideas. From an early age, children are scolded if they reciprocate the non-Muslim forms of greeting. Such training is easy in a totally Muslim home. It also occurs, though with greater difficulty, in homes of mixed religion. For example, a non-Muslim Giriama friend and I entered a Giriama homestead, in which one of the women had converted to Islam as a result of spirit possession. My friend greeted the woman's six-year-old daughter in Giriama, but the child did not answer. This is normally unheard of, but was explained as necessary, since both mother and child would suffer severe sickness if they were not to obey the dictates of their possessory Islamic spirit, which is in fact called an 'Arab' spirit (*pepo* or *nyama ya kiarabu*) and which refuses to be addressed by a non-Muslim and in an 'impure' (*chafu*) language. The mother and her daughter would only speak to and answer members of her homestead in Swahili. Moreover, this was neither opposed nor discouraged by the homestead members, who well recognized the power of Islamic spirits to determine people's destinies in this way.

Among the fishermen I have been describing, not only is Swahili the only acceptable language of communication, but also its members will not normally respond to any of the non-Muslim Mijikenda dialects, despite the fact that in a few cases at least they must have a passive knowledge of them. They explain this by claiming that to speak and respond to such non-Muslim dialects is to lay oneself open to the contaminating practices associated with the non-Muslim speakers, namely their production and drinking of alcohol, their heavy reliance on non-Koranic divination and therapy, their lengthy funerals involving dance and drink, and the fact that their diets may include pork and other foodstuffs forbidden to Muslims. To speak and know a non-Muslim language is to become consubstantial with the character and practices of its speakers.

The Swahili word that is used most succinctly to define these non-Islamic practices is *ushirikina*, which, deriving from the Arabic, *shirk*, refers to the worship of many gods, or polytheism. Certainly, the traditional religion of the non-Muslim peoples can reasonably be called pantheism or animism, but its sophistication is lost in the translation as *shirk* or *ushirikina*. It is, moreover, described by Muslim *maalims* and their followers as the root cause of impurity, for they see it as opposed to the idea of a single God and as therefore liable to re-contaminate those whose conversion to Islam is historically only recent. They say that speaking the language of those who practise *ushirikina* is like communicating with, and in the tongues of, the Devil, who manifests himself in the form of countless possessory spirits or demons, which, unlike the jinns identified in the Koran, have no legitimate religious status.

At the other end of the diglossic spectrum, children and adults in this fishing community are encouraged by their local *maalim* to incorporate as many Arabic words as possible into their Swahili vocabulary, and children are urged to emulate the few African *maalims* in the district who have studied Arabic at one of the prominent mosque colleges in either Lamu, Kenya, or the Middle East. The Arabic terms denote concepts of a religious and legal nature, but also prescribe and evaluate so-called 'civilized' behaviour. The effect is that people become aware not only of their distinctive Muslim status but of a putatively Arabized life-style and manner of speaking. Religious, linguistic and behavioural socialization here go together. The purity of Arabic language and conduct becomes an inseparable part of the unquestioned purity of Islam.

Thus, the non-Muslim dialects are shunned as contaminating, while Arabic vocabulary, language, text and script are embraced as providing the purest communicative access to Islam.

Lacking the possibility of almost any of them ever learning Arabic, we might at this point imagine that the members of this fishing community would be happy, therefore, to settle on Swahili, albeit as Arabized as possible, as the language most appropriate to the social and religious demands made of them by their *maalim*.

Incredibly, however, the process of differentiation and of proliferation does not end here. The *maalim* not only specifies the use of Swahili over and against the Mijikenda dialects, he also insists on a distinctive form of Swahili pronunciation, which we may gloss as Ki-Mvita or, as some put it more specifically, Ki-Jomvu, which is broadly associated with the long-established élite of Mombasa Old Town. He rebukes children and young people who use the standard Swahili forms as heard, for instance, on the radio and as spoken by non-Muslim Mijikenda or up-country people as a second language.

For example, the standard Swahili form, *njoo* (come!) is rendered as *ndo-oo*. As one young girl put it, 'If any of us were to say *njoo*, *maalim*

Hassan would get very angry and ask, "Who ever taught you to speak like that? That is modern Swahili (*ya siku hizi*), but it is not of any importance (*si ya maana*) and is not polite (*si ya adabu*).'" According to *maalim* Hassan, one should also say *mwiche*, 'call him', and not the standard form, *mwite*, and so on. For him, such standard forms are not sources of impurity, as is the use of the non-Muslim Mijikenda vernaculars, but they are debased or fallen forms. This is an ironic judgement, in that standard Swahili is in fact founded on an older form of Zanzibari Swahili (*Ki-Unguja*). Even when one thinks one has mastered the distinctive consonantal changes and nasal sounds, one may then be told by the *maalim* to use an Arabic word rather than a Bantu one. 'Say, "taib", not "nzuri", and say "ku-arifu" and not "ku-ambia" whenever possible', he will declare.

Some contrasts between standard and Kimvita Swahili are as follows:

	Kimvita	Standard Kiswahili
(to) take	*tukua*	*chukua*
play	*teza*	*cheza*
slaughter	*tinda*	*chinja*
throw	*tupa* (explosive, tongue forward)	*tupa*
bottle	*tupa* (implosive, tongue back a little)	*chupa*
uncooked rice	*mtele*	*mchele*
leave!	*ata*	*acha*
hunger	*ndaa*	*njaa*
outside	*nde*	*nje*

CONCLUSION

At issue in this drive by this and other *maalims* are two contradictory tendencies. On the one hand, the *maalim* attempts to differentiate ever more finely the Islamic distinctiveness of his group of Muslim fishermen. In seeking increasingly refined concepts of religious purity, he focusses on language and, in doing so, identifies people with these language differences. Alleged speech differences are the most salient identity tag and come to summarize other differences, some desired as in the case of Arabic and high forms of Swahili, and some unacceptable and impure as in the case of the non-Muslim Mijikenda dialects. On the other hand, the *maalim* evidently believes in some kind of core Islamic purity, an ideal that can be attained through both speech and behaviour. But in seeking this ideal, he sets up one line of differentiation after another:

speak Arabic and not Mijikenda; speak this Swahili and not that; incorporate Arabic words rather than Bantu words in Swahili vocabulary. Neither he nor those he admonishes can ever reach this core. All he can ever do is to attempt always to move away from what he regards as the contaminating effects of non-Muslim life and language. But this constant escape, so vividly captured in *maulidi* sermons given by himself and others (see Parkin 1985), does not in fact evidently bring him closer to the core of Islamic purity that he advocates. Like Zeno's arrow which, in distancing itself further and further from its point of origin, nevertheless has to move through an infinity of mid-points, this and other *maalims* seem never to reach the destination. The play on language is, after all, a play on the endlessness of signification. Diglossia comprising high and low diatypes is one such play, which, having a life of its own, may fall through the net of government policy.

REFERENCES

Akinnaso, F. N. and Ogunbiyi, I. A. (1990) 'The place of Arabic in language planning in Nigeria', *Language Problems and Language Planning* 14, 1: 1–20.

Baudrillard, J. (1972) *Pour une critique de l'économie politique du signe*, Paris: Gallimard.

Ferguson, C. (1964) 'Diglossia', in D. Hymes (ed.) *Language in Culture and Society*, New York, Evanston and London: Harper and Row.

Gilsenan, M. (1982) *Recognizing Islam: an Anthropologist's Introduction*, London and Sydney: Croom Helm.

Guillaume, A. (1954) *Islam*, Harmondsworth, Middlesex: Penguin.

Habermas, J. (1983) [1981] 'Modernity – an incomplete project', in H. Foster (ed.) *Postmodern Culture*, London and Sydney: Pluto Press.

Lacunza Balda, J. (1991) 'Tendances de la littérature islamique swahili', in Françoise Le Guennec-Coppens and Pat Caplan (eds.) *Les Swahili entre Afrique et Arabie*, Paris and Nairobi: Credu-Karthala.

Lyotard, J. F. (1984) [1979] *The Postmodern Condition: a Report on Knowledge*, Manchester: Manchester University Press.

Mintz, S. (1985) *Sweetness and Power*, London and New York: Penguin.

Parkin, D. (1985) 'Being and selfhood among intermediary Swahili', in J. Maw and D. Parkin (eds.) *Swahili Language and Society*, Vienna: Institut für Afrikanistik und Ägyptologie der Universität Wien.

Salim, A. I. (1973) *The Swahili-Speaking Peoples of the Kenya Coast 1895–1965*, Nairobi: East African Publishing House.

Taussig, M. (1980) *The Devil and Commodity Fetishism in South America*, Chapel Hill: University of North Carolina Press.

Ulin, R. C. (1991) 'Critical anthropology twenty years later', *Critique of Anthropology* 11, 1: 63–90.

Wolf, E. (1982) *Europe and the People without History*, Berkeley: University of California Press.

Name index

Abdulaziz, Lodhi 220
Abdulaziz, M. H. 220
Abdulaziz, Mkilifi 213
Akida, H. 220
Akinnaso, F. N. 234
Alexander, N. 102, 104
Alexandre, P. 56, 143
Allardt, E. 37
Amayo, A. 64
Ansre, G. 40, 220
Appadurai, A. 15
Asad, T. 6–9, 16, 76

Badejo, R. 25 (n.9)
Balisidya, M. L. N. 221
Bamgbose, A. 4, 36, 76, 102, 103
Banks, A. 37
Bataille, L. 40
Batibo, H.221
Baudrillard, J. 227
Baxter, P. T. W. 192
Baylies, C. 151
Bendor Samuel, J. 62
Berwouts, K. 217
Besha, R. 220
Bhebe, N. M. B. 155
Bigirumwami, A. 129
Bledsoe, C. 133
Blench, R. 62, 71
Blommaert, J. 6, 9, 218, 222
Bourdieu, P. 14
Bourhis, R. Y. 102
Brown, D. 99, 101, 102, 104
Bunting, B. 103
Burnham, P. 23

Campbell, D. J. 139 (n.16)
Caplan, G. 162
Carpez, A. 129, 139 (n.8, 9, 12)
Cerulli, E. 201
Chen, A. 104
Chinweizu, 20
Cluver, A. B. de V. 100, 101, 104
Connor, W. 38
Croll, E. 4
Crozier, D. 62

Dalby, D. 62
Davids, A. 100
Derive, J. 26 (n.11)
Derive, M. J. 26 (n.11)
d'Hertefelt, M. 129, 139 (n.8, 9, 12)
Diki-Kidiri, M. 26 (n.13)
Dirven, R. 105
Du Plessis, L. T. 100
Duggal, N. K. 36
Dumont, B. 41
Duran, R. 104

Ekeh, P. B. 5
Elugbe, B. O. 70, 71, 76, 81–3
Emenanjo, E. N. 5, 74
Epstein, A. L. 143, 181 (n.2)

Fabian, J. 168, 214
Fairhead, J. 25 (n.6), 125, 131, 136
Fardon, R. 76–7, 83, 168
Ferguson, C. 233
Fishman, J. 34, 35, 37, 38, 42
Fleming, H. C. 206
Ford. C. C. 154

Name index

Fortune, G. 182 (n.18), 183 (n.29, 34)
Foucault, M. 8, 26 (n.11), 131
Furniss, G. 76-7, 83, 168
Fyfe, C. 44
Fyle, C. M. 9, 44, 53
Fyle, C. N. 44, 45, 46

Gadibolae, M. 153
Gbedemah, F. F. K. 77, 81, 82
Geertz, C. 155
Gellner, E. 6-8
Giles, H. 102
Gillett, S. 154
Gilsenan, M. 234
Gluckman, M. 144
Good, K. 166
Gottlieb, A. 139 (n.11)
Goubaud, M. 133
Guillaume, A. 233
Gysels, M. 218

Haberland, E. 196, 197
Habermas, J. 227
Hakuta, K. 104
Hansford, K. J. 9, 62
Harries, L. 220
Heine, B. 91, 193
Hirson, B. 103
Hobart, M. 20
Holm, J. 156
Horton, R. M. F. 52
Hountondji, P. 20
Hunt, J. A. 201
Huntingford, G. W. B. 196

Igué, M. A. 55-8, 76
Ikara, B. 64
Isayev, M. I. 35

Jacob, I. 138 (n.3, 15)
Jenewari, E. C. 65
Jibril, M. 26 (n.15)
Jones, E. D. 45
Jordan, P. 106

Kashoki, M. 34, 36
Katuala, K. K. 136
Kelman, H. 35
Kenyatta, Jomo 230
Kihore, Y. 213, 219

Kombo, S. 220
Kummer, W. 191
Kwele, D. 155

Lacunza, J. 240
Laitin, D. 18-19, 25 (n.5)
Lambert, W. 104
Lamberti, M. 202
Le Page, R. B. 34, 35-6
Lee, J. D. 65
Lestrade, A. 127, 128, 135, 139 (n.8, 10, 13)
Lewis, I. M. 201
Lindholm, K. J. 104
Lithuli, A. 101
Louw-Potgieter, J. 100
Lyotard, J. F. 227

Mackey, W. F. 48
McLean, D. 99, 104, 105, 106
MacWilliam, A. 217, 221
Malikongwa, D. M. 154
Maripe, K. 155, 160, 166
Massamba, D. 215-17, 218, 219, 220
Matante, P. 155
Mautle, G. 153
Mazrui, A. A. 221, 222
Mdee, J. S. 217
Meebelo, H. S. 155
Meerkotter, D. 104
Meintjies, F. 99-100, 103
Mhina, G. A. 220
Mintz, S. 227
Mitchell, 143, 181 (n.2)
Mkelle, B. 220
Moi, Daniel arap 230-1
Molutsi, P. 156
Mongwa, T. 155
Morrison, D. R. 217
Mphahlele, E. 116
Mudimbe, V. Y. 20
Mukama, R. G. 221
Mulford, D. C. 162
Mulokozi, M. M. 217, 218, 220
Murray, A. 155
Mutahi, K. 217
Mwangomango, J. 220, 221
Mytton, G. 16

N'Ouéni, R. 58-60, 76

Ndebele, N. 105
Nengwekhulu, H. R. 155
Ngalasso, M. M. 26 (n.14)
Nhlapo, J. 102
Nkomo, J. 155
Nyerere, Julius 39–40, 219

Ogieriaixi, E. 71
Ogunbiyi, I. A. 234
Ohly, R. 219
Okpewho, I. 20
Omamor, O. P. 73–4

Padilla, A. M. 104
Papstein, R. 181 (n.2)
Parkin, D. 4, 5, 6, 8, 9, 20, 170, 171, 245
Pelzer, A. N. 115, 117
Picard, L. A. 153, 156
Pool, J. 38
Pottier, J. P. J. 20, 125

Ramsay, J. 155
Reagan, T. N. 100, 101, 103
Richards, P. 20, 25 (n.7)
Riddell, J. C. 139 (n.16)
Robin, J. 48

Said, E. 8
Salim, I. A. 235
Schapera, I. 154, 156
Schlee, G. 5, 191, 194, 195, 196, 198, 206, 208
Schoffeleers, J. M. 130
Schramm, W. 41
Schumacher, E. F. 39
Schwarz Jr, F. A. O. 34
Seruraho, N. 137
Sesay, K. 47
Silitshena, R. M. K. 154
Sitoe, A. 94
Skutnabb-Kangas, T. 17

Smith, P. 140 (n.8)
Snoxall, R. A. 213
Sofunke, B. 25 (n.9)
Soyinka, W. 20, 36
Sparks, A. 117
Spencer, P. 198, 206
Stanford, R. 62
Steyn, J. C. 100
Szeftel, M. 151

Tablino, P. 209 (n.3, 6, 7)
Tambo, Oliver 106
Taussig, M. 227
Taylor, C. 128, 131, 139 (n.7, 9)
Taylor, D. M. 102
Temu, C. 217, 221
Textor, R. B. 37
Treffgarne, C. 11
Troup, F. 103
Trudgill, P. 100, 103
Tshibasu, M. 136
Tucker, A. N. 102
Tucker, G. R. 104

Ulin, R. C. 227

Vail, L. 181 (n.2)
Van Binsbergen, W. 19, 26 (n.12) 147, 151, 166, 170
Van Diepen, M. 106
Van Waarden, C. 154
Vischer, H. 21

wa Thiong'o, N. 20, 89
Webb, V. 98
Weiner, M. 41
Whitehead, A. 135
Willemse, H. 102–3, 104, 105
Williamson, K. 65, 67-8, 74
Wolf, E. 227
Wright, M. 213
Wyse, A. J. G. 46, 53

Subject index

Aboh 70
Abua 66
Adja-fon 59
Adja-mina 59
African National Congress: and Bantu Education 101–3; and English as lingua franca 104; language policy 108
Afrikaans 97; official status 98–9, 101, 113–14; and power relations 100–1; withdrawal from black schools 100
Akan 34
Akassa 66
Akwapim 77
anthropological research 3–6
Arabization: Kenya 232–3; Muslim communities 9; Sudan 26 (n.13)
Asante 77–8, 80, 81
Atẹ (Atte)-Okpela-North Ibie 70
authenticity 20–1, 26 (n.14)

Bachama 23
Bantu: Mozambique 90–3; South Africa 99, 101–4, 114–16
Banyabwisha *see* Bwisha community
Barotseland 145, 147
Bemba 145, 147
Bénin 55–61; economic growth 59–60; education 55–8, 60; French language 56–8, 59–60; independence 55–6; language policy 55–8; literacy programme 57–8; multilingualism 58
Benue-Congo languages 69, 65–6, 70–1

Biseni 66
Boran 196–8, 203–5
Botswana: Botswana People's Party 155–6, 160; challenge to Tswana hegemony 156–7; constitution 182 (n.13); economic boom 156; education 154–5; ethnic groups 152–3; Kalanga *see* Kalanga; Khoi-San (Sarwa) 143; language policy 165–6; Ngwato administration 153–4; non-Tswana-speaking groups 153; percentage of Kalanga speakers 161–2; Society for the Propagation of the Ikalanga Language 158–9; Tswana domination 153–4
Bwisha community 122–41; Belgian rule 134; crop health 124–6; *ikizungu/ikinyabwisha* distinction 133–7; *ivitamin* 124, 130–3, 135; land ownership 134–6; linguistic pluralism 137–8; medical care 123–4; *Mwami* 123, 126, 129; procreation/production/politics /putrefaction 126–30; state institutions 136

Cameroon 23
Chamba 23
chi-Chewa (chi-Manganja) 90
chi-Chopi 90
chi-Makonde (chi-Maviha) 90
chi-Manyika 90
chi-Ndau 90
chi-Nsenga 90

chi-Nyanja 90, 91
chi-Nyungwe 90
chi-Sena (chi-Ruwe, chi-Podzo) 90
chi-Shona 91
chi-Tewe 90
chi-Yao 90
Chokwe 146
Chopi 90
Chumburung: case study 77–8; literacy projects 78–80
communication: and development 38–42; indigenous languages 41–2
Cross River languages 65, 66
cultural translation *see* translation

Dahomey *see* Bénin
Defaka (Afakani) 65–6
Degema 67
Dendi 59, 60
development 19–21; language heterogeneity 37–8; multilingualism 33, 37–42; role of language 38–42

Ebira (Igbirra) 69, 71
Ebiroid languages 69, 71
Echie 67
e-Chuwabo 90
economic development *see* development
Edo (Bini) 70; orthography 71–2
Edoid languages 65, 67, 69, 70
Efik 34
Egbema 66
Ehueun (Ekpenmi, Epenmi) 70
Ekpeye 66
Eleme 66
e-Lomwe 90
e-Makhuwa 90
Engenni (Egene) 67
English language in South Africa: elitism 105–6; as lingua franca 104–6; offical status 98–9, 113–14, 120; thought control 105
e-Ngulu 90
Epie-Atisa 67
Eruwa (Erohwa, Arohwa) 70
Esan (Ishan) 70, 72
Ethiopia 192
Etuno 69, 71

Ewe 77

Fante 34, 77
Fon-aizo 59
Fongbé 60
Fon-goun 59
Fon-mina 59
Fulani 22
Fulfulde 22; Cameroon 23

Ga 77
Ghana 76–84; Chumburung language *see* Chumburung; Chumburung people 77–8; church as educator 80; English as language of education 78, 82; Ghana Institute of Linguistics, Literacy and Bible Translation (GILLBT) 77–83; language development 76–7, 80–3; languages 34; minority languages 77; mother tongue education 80–3; official languages 79; teacher training 78, 82
Ghotuọ (OtuF34017%-50/o, Otwa) 70; development 72, 74
gi-Tonga 90
globalization 15–16
Gokana 66
Gwari 23

Hausa language: diversity 34; as lingua franca 21–3, 34; as mother tongue 21–3; as national language, Nigeria 62, 64–5, 73; orthography 21
hegemony 17–19

Ịbani 66
Ibibio 34
Igala dialects 71
Igbo 22
Igbo/Ibo (Aniocha) 20, 67, 69, 70, 72; as national language, Nigeria 62, 64–5, 73
Igbo-Igbani 66
Igboid languages 65, 66–7, 69, 70
Ijọ 65–6, 69
Ijoid languages 65–6, 69, 71
Ịka 69, 70, 72

Subject index

Ikpeshi 70
Ikwere 66, 67
Işękiri (Itsekiri, Shekiri, Jekri) 71; development 72, 73–4
Isoko 70, 72
Ivbiadaobi 70
Ivbimion 70
Izon (Ijaw) 66, 67, 69, 71, 72

Kalabari 66, 67
Kalanga 152–61; Bible Translation Project 158, 167–8; language policy 172–3, 180; linguistic objectification 168–9; minority status 161–2, 162–3; and Nkoya, compared 174–9; proletarianization 169–72; Shona 152–61; Society for the Propagation of the Ikalanga Language 158–9; traditional rulers 164–5
Kana (Khana) 66, 67
Kanuri 22
Kaonde 145
Kenya: Arabic 229–45; Arabization 232–3; broadcast media 229; English as official language 229; Hadhrami Arabs 230, 235; Kikuyu 230–1; language distribution 229–30; Luo 230–1; Muslim fishing community 241–4; Muslims 230–3, 236; Omani Arabs 230, 235; Oromo *see* Oromo; re-Arabization 236–9; Rendille *see* Rendille; Swahili as national language 229; Swahili-speakers 230
ki-Mwaani 90
Kinyabwisha 122, 137–8
Kinyarwanda 123
Kiswahili: as African national language 36; and Arabic in East Africa 234–41; BAKITA (National Kiswahili Council) 213; English as source language 217–18; grammar/lexicography 221; Islamic medium 240–1; Kenyan Muslim fishing community 241–4; as Kenyan national language 229; Kenyan speakers 230; Kimvita 243–4; language development 215–20; linguistic discourse 220–2; modernization 216–18; Mozambique 90, 94; research parameters 214–15; research tradition 222–4; Tanzania 213–27; TUKI (Institute of Kiswahili Research) 213; word-coining 217–18; Zaïre 138
Koma 23
Koran 233–4, 238–9
Krio language: attitude of Krio people 48–9; current situation 47–8, 82; drama 47–8, 53; education 47, 48; English elements 45–6; Freetown Krio 49–50, 50–1; as lingua franca 47–8, 53; migration from Freetown 49; non-Krio Sierra Leoneans 49–51; official recognition 51–3; origins 46–7; politics 47; up-line Krio 49, 50–1; Yoruba elements 46–7
Krio society, development 44–7
Kugbo 66

language: artifical 36; commoditization 227–9; development 215–16; indigenous 41–2; languages of wider communication (LWCs) 41–2; and national integration 33–6; objectification 9–15, 168–9; patterns of discourse 14–15; planning 5–6; politics 3–4, 6–10, 191–2; purity 193–4, 227–9; rationalization 17–19; rights 16–17, 104; sectoral uses 13–14; sponsorship 17–19, 24; as subject of discourse 10
Lilima 152, 158; orthography 167
Limba 51–2
Lingala 34
lingua francas: Arabization in Muslim communities 9; emerging 34; and modernization 9; multilingualism as 4; problems for Government 4–5
literacy: and development 38–42;

252 *African languages, development and the state*

indigenous languages 41–2;
languages of wider
  communication 41–2
Lozi 144–9, 162, 163
Luchazi 146
Lukolwe 144
Lunda 145
Lushange 144
Luvale 145, 146

Makua 90
maps 10–13; refashioning 15–17
Mashasha 144
Mbundu 146, 147
Mbwela 144
Mende 47, 51–2
Mina 60
Mini 66
Mozambique 89–96; Bantu 90–3;
  bilingualism 92–3, 94–5;
  education system 92, 94–5;
  FRELIMO 91; Kiswahili 90, 94;
  language policy 91–4; language
  situation 90–1; news media 93;
  Portuguese language 91–4; Shona
  90; *swi-ngondo* 94; Tsonga 90, 94
multilingualism: and development
  33, 37–42; as lingua franca 4;
  linguistic skills 5–6; and
  nation-building 24–5, 35; and
  national integration 33–6

national development *see*
  development
national language, discussion 5
Ndebele 112, 120, 152–5
Ndoki/Asa 66
Ndoni 66
négritude movement 20, 221
Nembe 66
Niger 21
Nigeria: 6–3–3–4 programme 26
  (n.13); Adamawa State 22, 23, 27
  (n.16); Akwa-Ibom State 34;
  Bendel State 62, 69–74; Borno
  State 22; Chamba people 23;
  discrimination 34–5; Edo people
  34; education 63–4; English
  language 64–5; Hausa as national
  language 62, 64–5, 73;

Independence 64–5; language
  policy 63–5; language
  rationalization 19, 26 (n. 13,
  n.15); languages 22–3, 34; lingua
  francas 22–3, 24; linguistic
  diversity 65–9; literacy campaign
  64; minority languages 26–7
  (n.15), 62–75, 83; national
  language 22; national unity 64;
  news media 67, 69; official
  language 64–5; oral policy 73;
  Pidgin 64–5, 67, 72; Rivers
  Readers Project 67–9; Rivers
  State 62, 65–9; Taraba State 22,
  23, 27 (n.16)
Nkoro 66
Nkoya 144–52; and Kalanga,
  compared 174–9; language policy
  172–3, 180; linguistic
  objectification 168–9; minority
  status 161–2; traditional rulers
  164–5
Northern Sotho 112, 119, 120
Nsenga-Sena 90
Nyanja 90, 145

Obolo (Andoni) 66
Obulom (Abuloma) 66
Oḍual 66
Ogbah 66
Ogbia 66
Ogbogolo 66
Ogbronuagum 66
Ogoi 66
Okọdja 66
Okpamheri 70, 72
Okpẹ 70; development 74
Okpẹ-Idesa 70
Okrika 66
Oloma 70
Opobo 66
Ora-Emai-Iuleha 70, 72
Oromo: adopted by Somalis 196;
  Arabic loanwords 195–8,
  199–202; linguistic assimilation of
  Somaloid groups 203–5;
  loanwords 193–202; numbers of
  speakers 192
orthographies, standardized: Edo
  71–2; Hausa 21; Nigerian

minority languages 83
Ọsọsọ 70

politics of language 3–4, 6–10, 191–2

Rendille: Arabic loanwords 198–203; Boran influences 203–5; loanwords 193–4; numbers of speakers 192; Oromo loanwords 203–5; purification by missionaries 194; Samburu (Maa) words/cultural items 205–8
rights attached to languages 16–17, 104

Sahwè-fon 59
Sahwè-mina 59
Samburu 193; words/cultural items in Rendille 205–8
Sango 26 (n.13)
Sasaru-Enwa-Igwe 70
Senegal 34
shi-Changana 90
shi-Ronga 90
shi-Tsonga 91
shi-Tswa 90
Shona: Kalanga 152–61; Mozambique 90
Shuwa 22
Sierra Leone 44–54; education 47, 48, 51–2; English-derived language 45–6; indigenous language teaching 51–2; Liberated Africans (resettlers) 45; news media 51; non-Krio people 49–51; official language policy 51–3; post-colonial politics 50; Settlers 44–5; wardship system 49; Yoruba (Krio) people 46–7
South Africa 97–110, 111–21; African languages 101–3, 111–21; Afrikaans *see* Afrikaans; apartheid language policy 97–8, 99, 104; Asian languages 120; Bantu Education 99, 101–4, 114–16; control over African languages 116–18; economic development 119–21; English language *see* English language in South Africa; homeland policy 113; Language Boards 117; language distribution 111–14; language diversity 106; language policies 114–16; language and power relations 99–100; language used to divide and rule 99, 104; mother tongue education 103–4, 107–8; multilingualism 103, 118–19; new language dispensation 106–7; official languages 120; Separatist Churches 118–19; South African Broadcasting Corporation 117; trade unions 119–20; Tsonga 112, 120
Southern Sotho 112, 119, 120
strong and weak languages 7–10, 76–7
Sudan 26 (n.13)
Swahili *see* Kiswahili
Swazi 112

Tanzania 213–27; Arab settlement 234–5; education 217, 221; Kiswahili *see* Kiswahili; linguistic ideology 218–20, 221
technology 15–16, 42
Temne 47, 51–2
Tiv 23
Tonga 145
translation: context and 6–7; and relations between languages 10; strong and weak languages 7–10
Tsonga: Mozambique 90, 94; South Africa 112, 120
Tswana 112, 152–3; as language of discourse 165–6; as national/regional language 163–4; sub-groups 182 (n.14); *see also* Botswana
Tuareg 22
Twi 34

Uhami-Iyayu 70
Ukaan (Kakumo) languages 69, 71
Ukue (Ukpe) 70
Ukwuanị (Kwale) 69, 70, 72
Unẹmẹ 70, 72
Urhobo (Sobo) 70, 72
Uvwiẹ (Effurun, Evhron) 70

Venda 112, 120
Vomni 23

Wazobia languages 22, 27 (n.15); *see also* Hausa; Igbo; Yoruba
Wolof 34

Xhosa 107, 112, 118, 120

Yao 90
Yẹkhee (Etsako, Afenmai, Kukuruku) 70, 72
Yoruba: elements in Krio 46–7; as national language, Nigeria 22, 62, 64–5, 73; Sierra Leone 46–7
Yoruba-fon 59
Yoruba-goun 59
Yoruboid languages 69, 71

Zaïre: Bwisha community (Banyabwisha) *see* Bwisha community; Kiswahili 138; languages 26 (n.13), 34
Zambia: Lozi 144–9, 162, 163; Nkoya *see* Nkoya
Zulu 112, 118, 119, 120

Printed in Great Britain
by Amazon